WINDOWS™ 3.1
Quick Start

MARLY BERGERUD
Dean, Business Science Division
Saddleback College

DON BUSCHÉ, Ed. D.
Dean, Vocational Education and
   Academic Support Services
Saddleback College

● SOUTH-WESTERN PUBLISHING CO. ●

Editor-In-Chief:	Robert E. First
Acquisitions Editor:	Randy R. Sims
Developmental Editor:	Diana Trabel
Senior Production Editor:	Mary Todd
Production Editor:	Lois Boggs-Leavens
Coordinating Editor:	Lisa McClary
Marketing Manager:	Brian Taylor
Consulting Editor:	Margaret Cheatham

2 3 4 5 6 7 8 K 00 99 98 97 96 95 94 93

Printed in the United States of America

Bergerud, Marly
      Windows 3.1/Marly Bergerud, Don Busche.
          p.   cm.--(Quick start)
      Includes index.
      ISBN 0-538-71086-1
      1. Windows (Computer programs) 2. Microsoft Windows (Computer
file)   I. Busche, Don.   II. Title.   III. Series
QA76.76.W56B45   1994
005.4 ' 3--dc20   92-46644
                                                                CIP

CONTENTS

INTRODUCTION: WHAT IS WINDOWS?

Perhaps you are wondering about the name **Windows**—a very simple and familiar name. It is certainly not a "technical" or difficult name. Yet Windows is, as you will see, an accurate name for this software program.

As you use Windows, each view lets you communicate with your computer by simply pointing at images you see. Each image, called an **icon**, is a little picture or symbol that identifies a closed window which you can open and use for a specific purpose. Together, the icons and the windows they represent make up the desktop. These desktop elements offer choices that, when selected, will let you tell the computer what you want in the easiest way. Just as you choose from icons, you also choose from menus that give you lists of options. With Windows, all you do to make a choice is point at an icon, a menu, or an option.

Your pointer is a mouse, a small device that fits in the palm of your hand. Because the mouse sits on a ball, you can roll the mouse on your tabletop. As you roll the mouse, you move the pointer across the screen. The mouse is a quick way of letting you point to icons, menus, and options without using the keyboard.

If you are familiar with computers, you know that in the past you had to memorize, remember, and finally key a variety of difficult system (DOS, or disk operating system) commands in order to direct the computer to perform various actions. With Windows, you will not encounter difficult commands, yet you will be able to perform the same kinds of tasks, use a variety of familiar software programs, organize your hard disk, and more.

In place of difficult commands, Windows offers you a selection of easy-to-understand icons (in color, if you have a color monitor). And Windows menus offer you a few somple words. The result: Using your computer is easier because you understand what you must do, and at the same time you have fun and receive satisfaction. Perhaps best of all, you use menus and menu software, so you do not have to learn different commands for each new program! You can play games, send messages, set an alarm clock, draw pictures, schedule your day, create a calendar, and even customize Windows to make each window appear the way you want it to appear just by choosing from icons and menus.

Perhaps you now understand that Windows creates a visual relationship between you and your computer called a *graphical environment.* From this visual setting, you choose familiar images that represent office applications, instead of memorizing diffucult commands. This new, easier way to work with computers is called a *graphical user interface* (for short, *GUI*, pronounced "gooey").

Why is the GUI environment important? Because it provides one consistent way of using and switching between many different programs. For example, in this GUI environment you can use programs that come with Windows, such as Write, Paintbrush, and Cardfile. Plus, you can use hundreds of other popular programs, such as WordPerfect and Lotus 1-2-3.

Naming Conventions

You will find this book easier to read and understand if you know how it treats special terms. In this book:

- The word **Windows** refers to the software program Windows 3.1 (created by Microsoft Corporation). The capitalized word **Window** refers to a menu of that name, that is, the *Window menu.* The lowercase word **window** means, broadly, *screen;* thus you will read about **window elements** as well as specifically titled windows, such as the Directory Tree window, the Color window, and yes, the Window window—the screen that opens when you select the Window menu.

- Capital letters and brackets identify function keys and other labeled keys, for example:

  [F3]   **[F9]**   **[Backspace]**

  [Enter]   **[Spacebar]**

- When you must press two (or more) keys at the same time, the keys will be shown in brackets with a plus sign, for example: **[Alt]+[T]**.

- The names of menus and menu options, of commands, of dialog boxes, and of specific windows are capitalized, for example:

  the Help menu
  the Print option
  the Save As ... command
  the Save As ... dialog box
  the Write window

- *Italics* identify characters that you must key (for example, "key *Word Processing* in the Description text box").

Menu Conventions

One of the nice things about using Windows is that the standard user interface menus look pretty much the same, regardless of the application being used. Of course, Windows has a few conventions of its own for using the menus.

- Menu commands that are unavailable to you at the current time may appear dimmed, grayed, or not visible. (You may need to select another item from the menu before you are allowed to use this command.)

- An ellipsis (...) following a command indicates that a dialog box will appear after you choose the command. You will need to select items in the dialog box before the command can be carried out.

- A check mark (✓) next to a command indicates that command is in effect. Selecting a checked command will remove the check mark; then the command will no longer be in effect.

- A triangle (▶) next to a command informs you that when this command is selected, a cascading menu will appear, listing additional commands.

- A keystroke combination next to a menu command tells you that you can use this combination of keys (instead of using the mouse) to select the command.

Computer System Requirements

The suggested *minimum* computer hardware requirements for Windows 3.1 are:

- An IBM or IBM-compatible PC.

- Either and 80386 processor or higher (386-*Enhanced Mode*), 640 kilobytes (K) of conventional memory or an 80286 processor or higher (*Standard Mode*), 640K of conventional memory, plus 256K of extended memory.

MS-DOS operating system (DOS version 3.1 or higher). To check your version, key *ver* at the MS-DOS prompt and press [Enter].

- One hard disk with a minimum of 6 to 8 megabytes (Mb) of free disk space. For better performance, 8 to 10 Mb of free disk space are recommended (depending on the processor being used). Minimum disk space requirements are based on having no optional components, not running on a network, and having no printer. Recommended requirements assume that some optional components are installed, including a printer, and that the system may be running on a network.

- At least one 3 1/2- or 5 1/4-inch disk drive.

- A display adapter supported by Windows.

- An enhanced keyboard.

- A mouse or pen pointer.

- A printer that is supported by Windows, if you want to print with Windows.

Again, these are the suggested minimum requirements. If your system has an 8088 or 8086 microprocessor, Windows 3.1 will not work. Having less than 4 Mb of RAM is not recommended because of the large amount of memory required when running a number of programs at one time.

While a mouse is not "essential" (every menu lists keyboard commands), a mouse supported by Windows is highly recommended to take full advantage of the easy-to-use Windows graphical interface and greatly increases efficiency and productivity. A color monitor (VGA) and a laser printer are nice to have but also not essential.

If you want to use Terminal, the Windows communications application, a Hayes, Multi-Tech, Trail Blazer, or compatible modem is required.

Ready, Set, ...

Windows 3.1 Quick Start is a friendly, step-by-step book. Each Session is divided into Views. Each View discusses new concepts in the Preview section and provides activities in the Exercise section.

When you should be using your computer to complete an exercise, you will see this icon in the margin. Otherwise, you should be reading text (as in the Preview, for example).

Before you begin with Session 1, make sure that Windows has been installed on your hard drive (usually drive C). Further, make sure that you have received specific instructions for saving your complete work, and that you have a high-density disk available for storage.

...Go!

● ● ● ● ● ● ● ● ● ● ● ● ●

OBJECTIVES

When you complete this session, you will be able to:

- Define basic terms such as *system prompt, desktop, window screens, icons, title bar, menu bar, mouse,* and *mouse pointer*.

- Use a mouse to pull down menus, select icons, and issue commands.

- Recognize on-screen pointers and explain their meaning.

- Practice using keyboard shortcuts.

- Work with menus, menu bars, dialog boxes, and messages.

- Open, close, and control the size and the location of windows.

- Utilize the Windows Help system.

- Start, close, and exit Windows.

SESSION 1 *EXPLORING WINDOWS*

1

EXPLORING WINDOWS

● ● ● ● ● ● ● ● ● ● ● ● ●

PREVIEW

Your computer may be set up so that Windows starts automatically when you power up. If not, then you must know where the Windows program resides in your computer. For most computers, Windows will be located on drive C. For some computers, the Windows program may be on drive D. Does Windows automatically start up when you power up your computer? If it does not, do you know where Windows is located on your computer system?

As you start to use Windows, remember what you have already learned about its graphical environment. As you work through each session in this text, you will be reinforcing *one consistent way* of performing common tasks for different programs within Windows.

Look at Figure 1.1, the opening screen of the Windows desktop. The **desktop**, the overall work area on the screen, is the Windows equivalent of the top surface of your desk. You put things on your desk, take things off your desk, and move things around on your desk. In the same way, you will place items on, remove items from, and move items around your desktop.

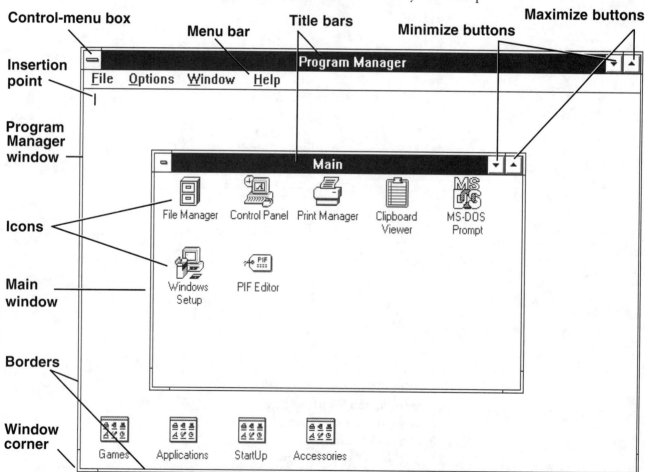

Figure 1.1 The Windows opening screen shows two windows: the Program Manager window and, within it, the Main window.

Now take a closer look at the Windows opening screen as shown in Figure 1.1.

VIEW 2

EXAMINING THE WINDOWS SCREEN

PREVIEW

At first sight, the Windows screen in Figure 1.1 may look rather complicated because it contains a variety of symbols and words that are now meaningless to you. A closer look will *un*complicate this screen and make the elements clear and understandable. Then, because all the other screens follow the same basic format and have the same parts, you will have no trouble using the many different options Windows has to offer.

To begin, just look at the opening screen as two windows: the Program Manager window and the Main window.

The Program Manager Window

The words *Program Manager* appear on the first line of the Program Manager window. As shown in Figure 1.1, this darkened part of the first line is called a **title bar**. The title bar contains the name of the application running in a window. Directly below the title bar is a **menu bar**. The menu bar is a list of choices, and the specific choices depend upon the application you are running. For instance, the Program Manager menu bar offers these four choices: File Options Window Help.

The Main Window

Within the Program Manager window sits the Main window. Look again at Figure 1.1. Find the word *Main* in the title bar at the top of the Main window. Then look at the small images or pictures in the Main window. These small images, called **icons**, appear often. The Main window, with its icons, is shown in Figure 1.1. Each icon represents a choice of a different window or a different application you can use. We will discuss icons and the choices they represent in greater detail later.

Other Elements of the Windows Screen

In addition to icons, title bars, and menu bars, you need to know about some other window elements. Again, look at Figure 1.1, noting the labels that show various elements of the Program Manager window. Then read the following explanations of those elements:

- The **Control-menu box** lies in the upper-left corner of the Program Manager window, on the same line as the title bar. In this box is a short line; it looks like a dash. This box opens the Control menu, which offers you options for "controlling" the size of the window displays or moving elements within the window displays.

- The **minimize and maximize buttons** are at the upper-right corner, also on the same line as the title bar. The minimize button reduces the window to an icon, and the maximize button enlarges the window to fill the screen.

- The **borders** are the four lines that define the limits of the window. Later you will see how to enlarge and reduce the size of a window by moving its borders.

As soon as you learn to move around the screen, you will better understand the above explanations.

VIEW 3
MOVING AROUND THE SCREEN

Question: How do you move around the Windows screen? Answer: With a mouse, or with a keyboard. The keyboard lets you crawl around, step by step. The mouse lets you race all over the screen—and if you want, carry materials with you as you move! The mouse and the keyboard are both used in Windows. You will see later in this text how some tasks are easier to perform with a mouse and some tasks are easier with the keyboard.

Using the Mouse

The mouse is an input device that allows you to find, move to, and grab any tools or files you need to place on the Windows desktop; you can also use the mouse to put those tools or files away. The mouse serves a number of other convenient uses, which will be discussed later. Your desktop is a visual work area, and the mouse is the key to that work area. As you use and feel more comfortable with the mouse, you'll know why Windows works more effectively when you use a mouse.

Mouse Starters. Next to the keyboard on your computer desk, clear an area (at least one square foot) for moving the mouse. This area must be clean and smooth because the mouse uses a rotating ball to sense movement: Any grease or dust on the desk surface can clog the ball and cause difficulty in operating the mouse. For best performance, use a specially designed mouse pad under your mouse.

Hold the mouse so that the cable extends forward from your hand and the body of the mouse rests under the palm of your hand. Your index finger should rest lightly on one of the buttons. Windows uses the left button to indicate most selections. You will learn later how to make the right button the selection button if you find it more convenient to operate the mouse with your left hand.

The Mouse Pointer. The mouse controls an on-screen pointer in the shape of an arrow (see Figure 1.2). To move the pointer up or down, to the left or right, just slide the mouse in that direction. When you get "cornered," that is, when you run out of room on your real desk, you can lift the mouse off your desk (or mouse pad), move the mouse, then set it back down—all without moving the on-screen pointer.

The on-screen pointer changes its appearance. Depending on where you are on the screen and what you are doing, the pointer will change to look like an hourglass, a pointing finger, or a crosshair as shown in Figure 1.3.

The Mouse Buttons. So, the mouse lets you move around the screen quickly, but what do you do when you "get there"? Besides moving the pointer around the screen, the mouse allows you to move windows and to choose various applications. How? By using mouse **buttons**.

Every mouse has one, two, or three buttons, depending on the particular brand (the left button is the one you will use most often). Pressing and then releasing

Figure 1.2

The mouse controls an on-screen
pointer.

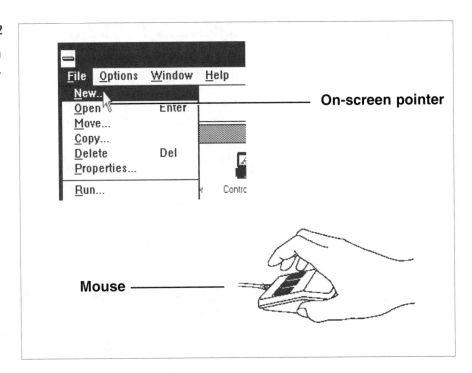

Figure 1.3
Each of these on-screen pointers
has its own unique message.

a mouse button is referred to as **clicking**; for some commands, you will need to **double-click**; that is, click twice quickly. As you practice using Windows, you will learn exactly what to do and when to do it. Figure 1.4 lists and explains four common mouse techniques.

In addition to moving the pointer, the mouse can also be used to move objects or icons around the screen. Moving objects with the mouse is known as **dragging**. You "drag" an object by placing the mouse pointer on the item to be moved, then pressing and *holding the mouse button* while moving the object. When the pointer is at the right location, release the mouse button. That is all there is to dragging.

Using the mouse requires a little practice; soon you will become comfortable—and proficient—in using it. Just be patient.

Figure 1.4

Mouse techniques

Mouse Techniques

To	Do this:
Drag	Press the mouse button and move the mouse in the desired direction.
Click	Press and release the mouse button.
Select	Point and click on the mouse button.
Double-click	Click twice in rapid succession on the mouse button.

EXERCISE 1 • 1   STARTING WINDOWS AND USING THE MOUSE

The text exercises assume that Windows is located on drive C on your computer system and that the system prompt (C:\>) will display when you power up your system. If those assumptions do not apply to your computer, ask your instructor or lab attendant for alternate instructions for accessing Windows.

1. Power up your computer system.

2. Start your Windows program by keying *WIN* [Enter] at the system prompt. (Remember: Brackets [ ] indicate the name of a specific key. Therefore, you should key the text *WIN* and press the [Enter] key.)

3. Compare your screen with the one illustrated in Figure 1.1. The appearance of your screen may differ sightly from the one illustrated, but the basic elements should be the same. Do you see a **title bar** or **menu bar** as shown in Figure 1.1? Spend a few minutes looking at the layout of the screen and the position of these elements—the boxes, the symbols, the words. Remember, there may be slight differences. If your screen does not display elements similar to those shown in Figure 1.1, ask for assistance.

4. Move the mouse around the desktop (or mouse pad, if you have one) and watch the screen to see how the pointer moves.

   a. Move the pointer to the far left of your screen by sliding the mouse to the left on the desktop or mouse pad. Do not lift the mouse.

   b. Move the pointer to the far right of your screen by sliding the mouse to the right.

   c. Move the pointer to the top of your screen by moving the mouse toward the top of your desktop.

   d. Move the pointer to the bottom of your screen by moving the mouse toward the bottom of your desktop or mouse pad.

5. Display and close the Control-menu box.

   a. Point to the Control-menu box in the upper-left corner of the Program Manager window.

   b. Click (press and release) the mouse button.

   c. Compare your screen with the one illustrated in Figure 1.5.

   d. Point on the Control-menu box and click the mouse button. The menu window should close.

6. Display and close each of the Program Manager menus.

   a. Display the File menu by pointing on the word *File* on the Program Manager menu bar and clicking the mouse button.

   b. Display the Options menu by pointing on the word *Options* on the Program Manager menu bar and clicking the mouse button. Did you notice that when you selected the new menu, the previously selected menu window was closed and the new window was displayed?

   c. Display each of the remaining Program Manager menus by pointing and clicking on them one at a time.

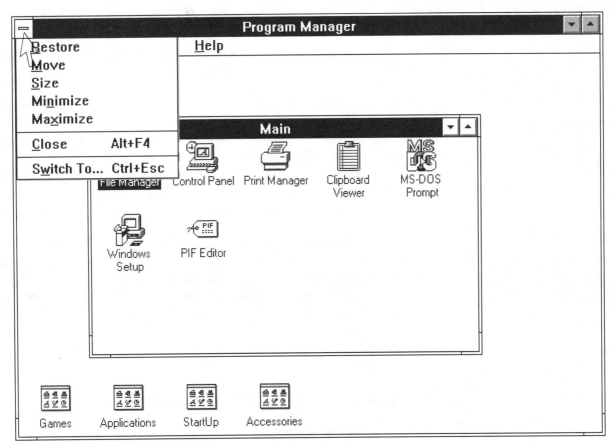

Figure 1.5 Control-menu box displayed over Program Manager and Windows

7. If icons are displayed at the bottom of the Program Manager window, display the menu of each of the icons. (If icons aren't displayed at the bottom of your screen, skip ahead to Step 8.)

   a. Point on the far-left icon and click the mouse button.

   b. Point on the icon to the right of the one you just clicked on. Notice that when you selected the new icon, the previously selected menu was closed and the new icon menu was displayed.

   c. Display each of the remaining icon menus by pointing and clicking on each icon one at a time.

   d. Click on any clear area on the screen to close the displayed menu.

8. Rearrange the order of the icons on the desktop.

   a. First, select an icon to move. For this example, point on the Print Manager icon. While holding the mouse button, drag the icon to the desired location and release the mouse button. Place the icon slightly above the current row of icons near the position you want it to appear.

   b. Point on another icon to be repositioned, and drag the icon to the desired location.

   c. Continue to drag the icons until they appear in the desired sequence.

Using the Keyboard

Whether you have a mouse or not, you can use the keyboard to perform most of the same functions that the mouse performs. In fact, many windows tell you which keystrokes to use as an alternate to using the mouse. These **keyboard shortcuts**, as they are called, often use a combination of keys (usually the [Alt] key or the [Ctrl] key with some other key).

For example, the keyboard shortcut to display the Program Manager File menu is [Alt]+[F]. Using the [F] for File makes this combination easy to remember. (Note: All other menu shortcuts are indicated by the underlined letter shown beneath a word on the various menu bars. They can be accessed by pressing and holding down [Alt] with the appropriate underlined letter shown on the menu bar.)

In the following exercises, the keyboard shortcuts will be indicated in their short form, that is, capitalized and enclosed in brackets. For example, you will see [F1], [F2], etc., for the function keys and [Tab], [Shift], etc., for the labeled keys. When you are to press two or more keys simultaneously, these keys are shown with a plus symbol between them; for example, [Alt] + [F]. When you must issue two keyboard shortcuts, one after the other, the word then will separate the shortcuts. For example, the keyboard shortcuts [Alt] key [F] key and [Control] key, [W] key are written [Alt] + [F] then [Control] + [W].

EXERCISE 1 • 2   USING KEYBOARD SHORTCUTS

1. Display each of the Program Manager menus using the keyboard shortcut.

   a. Display the File menu [Alt]+[F]. Release the keys once the menu is displayed.

   b. Display the Options menu [Alt]+[O]. Did you notice that in each case, the keyboard shortcut consisted of holding the [Alt] key and pressing the letter underscored on the menu bar?

   c. Display the Windows menu [Alt]+[W].

   d. Display the Help menu [Alt]+[H].

2. Close the displayed menu by pressing [Esc].

Clearly, Windows works best with a mouse; therefore, *all future instructions assume you are using a mouse.* Of course, whenever you want to use a keyboard shortcut, you will find it on the appropriate pull-down menu. They are also listed in the back of this book.

VIEW 4	
MENUS AND MENU BARS	

PREVIEW

Earlier, you learned that a **menu** is a list of options or choices. Now you will see and work with menus.

If all menus were on your desktop at the same time, then your work area would be too cluttered to be useful. Windows' menus are out of sight but within reach: You can easily pull down a menu and find what you want.

In the last exercise, when you displayed the various Program Manager menus, did you notice that each menu contained different options? That is how you will issue commands—by choosing from among menu options. To make your choice, select an option from the menu bar. Then look at the menu bar, point at the option you want, and click the mouse button. As you click, you will "pull down" another menu from the menu bar. A pull-down menu is shown in Figure 1.6.

When you see the pull-down menu, select one of the options listed. Again, look at the pull-down menu, point at the option you want, then click the mouse button. Your command will be executed.

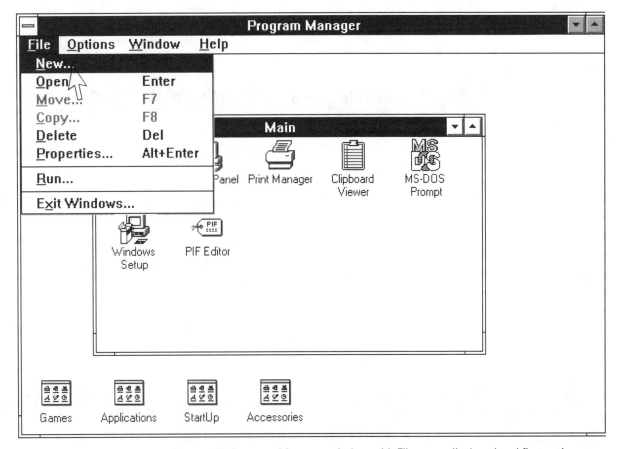

Figure 1.6 Program Manager window with File menu displayed and first option highlighted

Window Screen Elements

If you look closely at Figure 1.6, you will notice some differences in how options appear. Some are highlighted, some are in dark black print, some are followed by ellipsis points (...), but all have one letter underlined. All of these visual elements have special meanings, as explained below.

HIGHLIGHTING   The first menu option is highlighted. **Highlighting** means that the words appear in white letters within a black box and indicates that this option is currently "selected." If you wish to select a different option, point and click on the desired option. Use the [Up Arrow] and [Down Arrow] keys to move the black highlight box up and down the menu list. When you click the mouse button, the highlighted option becomes selected.

COLOR   Not all menu options are available to you. The dark or black print indicates options that are currently available. Light or grayish print indicates options that are not available. Look closely at the File menu in Figure 1.6. How many of its options are currently available? (Answer: six)

ELLIPSIS   A series of three periods (...) following a command, called an **ellipsis**, appears to the right of some menu options. An ellipsis tells you that if you choose this option, a second window or dialog box will be displayed, requesting more information from you. (You will learn more about dialog boxes later.)

KEYBOARD SHORTCUTS   Each menu option has one underscored letter or number, indicating a keyboard shortcut. This keyboard shortcut can be used only while the menu is displayed. To use a shortcut or a specific menu option, press its underscored letter or number.

EXERCISE 1 • 3   WORKING WITH MENUS

1. Display the Help menu.

   a. Select the About Program Manager option by pressing the letter [A].

   b. Close the window by clicking on OK or pressing [Enter].

2. Select the Accessories option from the Window menu. Did you notice that the Accessories window was added to the Program Manager window?

3. Select the Games option from the Window menu.

4. Select the Tile option from the Window menu, or use the keyboard shortcut ([Shift]+[F4]). The windows are now arranged differently; they are arranged in a tiled format.

5. Select the Cascade option from the Window menu, or use the keyboard shortcut ([Shift]+[F5]). The tiled windows are now arranged in a cascade format.

VIEW 5
DIALOG BOXES AND MESSAGES

PREVIEW

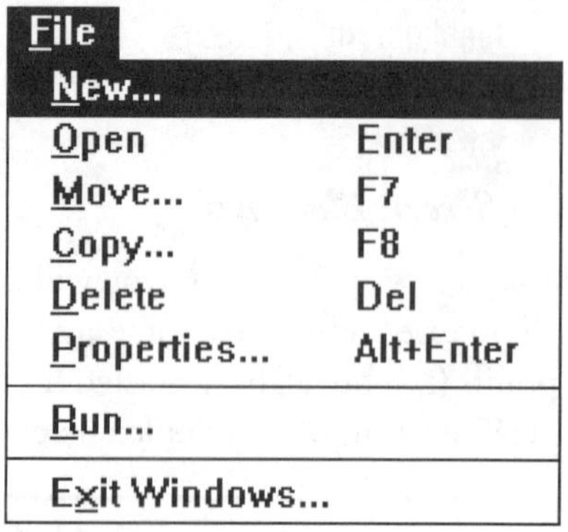

Figure 1.7

File menu

File	
New...	
Open	Enter
Move...	F7
Copy...	F8
Delete	Del
Properties...	Alt+Enter
Run...	
Exit Windows...	

Some menu options, like most of those on the File menu (Figure 1.7), need more information before they can be executed. For example, before Windows can run (start) a program, it needs to know the program name. When an option needs additional information before the command can be executed, the menu option is followed by an ellipsis (...) (see Figure 1.7). How does it get that information? It does so in the form of a **dialog box**, which is shown in Figure 1.8.

A dialog box is itself a window. For example, when you select the Run... option, you'll see the Run dialog box (illustrated in Figure 1.8). When you select the Properties... option, you'll see the Properties dialog box.

Figure 1.8

Run dialog box from the File menu

```
┌──────────────────────────────────────────────────────────┐
│ ▬                         Run                              │
├──────────────────────────────────────────────────────────┤
│                                            ┌──────────┐    │
│ Command Line:                              │    OK    │    │
│ ┌──────────────────────────────────┐      └──────────┘    │
│ │                                  │       ┌──────────┐    │
│ └──────────────────────────────────┘      │  Cancel  │    │
│                                            └──────────┘    │
│ ☐ Run Minimized                            ┌──────────┐    │
│                                            │ Browse...│    │
│                                            └──────────┘    │
│                                            ┌──────────┐    │
│                                            │   Help   │    │
│                                            └──────────┘    │
└──────────────────────────────────────────────────────────┘
```

Dialog Box Elements

Now that you know how dialog boxes are named, take a look at the elements you will find in dialog boxes—buttons and boxes.

Buttons. Windows contain two types of buttons—command buttons and option buttons.

COMMAND BUTTON
Figure 1.9

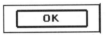

Command buttons carry out your instructions, using the information selected in the dialog box. Command buttons are always rectangles. When you press a command button, the program accepts your instructions and the dialog box closes.

OPTION BUTTON
Figure 1.10

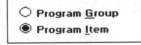

Option buttons (sometimes called *radio buttons*) allow you to choose one option from a group. You may change your selection by choosing a different button.

Boxes. Windows contain four types of boxes—check boxes, list boxes, text boxes, and drop-down list boxes.

CHECK BOX
Figure 1.11

⊠ Double-sided
☐ Restart page numbering

Check boxes also allow you to make choices from a group. However, unlike an option button, you can check more than one box to select a variety of options. When an X appears in the box, the option is selected. Clicking with the mouse selects or deselects a check box.

LIST BOX
Figure 1.12

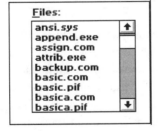

List boxes present a set of options in a list format. List boxes are found in both windows and dialog boxes. Often, a list of options is too lengthy to fit in a box. In such cases, scroll bars are used to allow you to scroll through the items. Items are arranged alphabetically.

TEXT BOX
Figure 1.13

Filename: ┌─────────────────────┐
Directory: C:\WINDOWS

Text boxes are found in dialog boxes and as part of Windows applications. A text box is an area in which you key in information. A blinking insertion point shows you where your keyed text will be displayed. You can move the insertion point with a mouse click. If the box already has text, the previous text will be highlighted and will automatically erase when you begin to key in new text. To work with text in a text box, you will need to select it. Text that is selected appears in a different color, usually white text on a black background.

DROP-DOWN LIST BOX
Figure 1.14

P<u>a</u>ge: | Letter | ↓

A drop-down list box lists only one option and a special arrow symbol. Click on the arrow symbol to reveal the entire list box.

EXERCISE 1 • 4   DIALOG BOXES AND MESSAGES

1. Select Run... from the File menu. The Run dialog box that is displayed contains a text box, a check box, and four command buttons (see Figure 1.8).

2. Key your first name in the text box—do not press [Enter]. Notice the blinking cursor where you are to begin keying.

3. Click on the Run Minimized check box. Notice that the item is checked (selected).

4. Click on the OK command button. You now see a message box similar to the one illustrated in Figure 1.15. This message box is displayed to communicate with you. In this case, Windows is telling you that it cannot locate the file you asked it to run. Later you will run files using the Run dialog box, but for now cancel your instruction.

5. Click on the OK command button to cancel the message display.

6. Click on the Cancel command button to cancel the Run command.

Figure 1.15

Message box

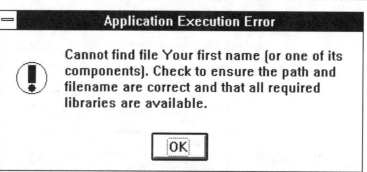

Application Execution Error

Cannot find file Your first name (or one of its components). Check to ensure the path and filename are correct and that all required libraries are available.

OK

VIEW 6
GETTING HELP

PREVIEW

If you need assistance while working in Windows, use Windows Help, a built-in help facility designed to provide you with information about Windows and its applications. The Windows Help facility looks and acts the same in each application, but the information is specific to that application.

To access Help, press [F1] or select Help whenever you see a Help command button, or Help as an item on an application's menu bar (almost every menu bar has one). Locate the Help menu on the Program Manager menu bar. You will be working with this menu in the next exercise.

Figure 1.16

Help menu

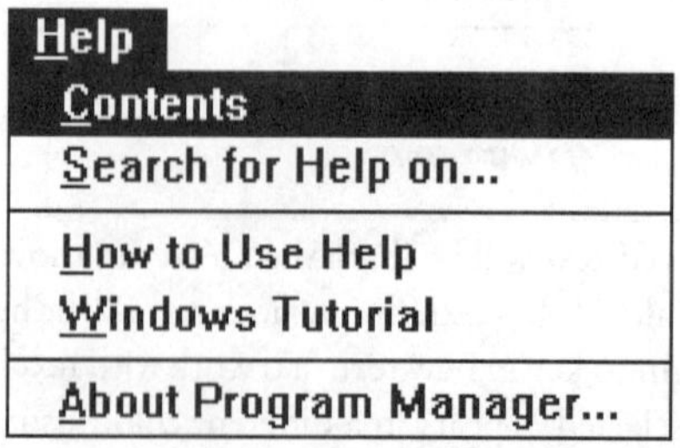

<u>H</u>elp
<u>C</u>ontents
<u>S</u>earch for Help on...

<u>H</u>ow to Use Help
<u>W</u>indows Tutorial

<u>A</u>bout Program Manager...

Different menu bars give different types of Help. Each Help menu has a list of options similar to the ones shown in Figure 1.16. You may also see a Help button in dialog boxes, as in Figure 1.17.

Figure 1.17

Note the Help button in this dialog box.

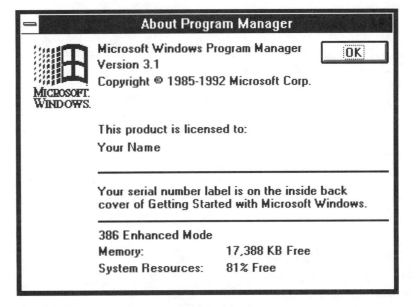

Notice that the Help menu shown in Figure 1.16 is divided into three sections. The top section provides help that is specific contents of the current application in use—in this case, the Program Manager. When displayed, it is an alphabetic list of all Help topics available for the active application. The middle section of this Help menu provides information on how to use the Windows Help system and also provides access to an interactive tutorial on the Windows environment. (*To use the Windows Tutorial, you need a mouse and a VGA monitor.*) The bottom section contains an About option that, when selected, provides version and copyright information about the current application as well as the other useful information shown in Figure 1.18.

Figure 1.18

The About Program Manager Window lists very useful information.

Look more closely at Figure 1.18. The title bar reads "About Program Manager" because this window was displayed by selecting the About... option on the Program Manager Help menu. For the Program Manager (and other applications as well), the About... command also displays useful information such as the operating mode, the name of the registered user of the software, the amount of memory available, the available disk space, and the percentage of system resources available. Most of this information may not mean much to you now; however, when you learn more about Windows, you will find this information useful for troubleshooting certain problems you may encounter.

Think of the Help system as an electronic reference book complete with table of contents, text, index, and glossary. Whenever you press [F1], select an option from the Help menu, or click on a Help button, you activate the Help system.

When Help is active, a Help window is displayed, as shown in the Program Manager Help window in Figure 1.19. Notice the menu bar and the option buttons (Contents, Search, Back, History, and Glossary) just below the menu bar. These buttons help you navigate through the Help system.

Figure 1.19

In this Help window, note the option buttons under the menu bar.

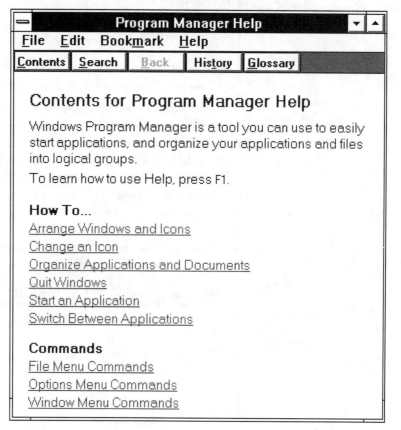

In the Help text, you will notice that the underlined words are cross references and that words with a broken underline are terms. When you move the pointer over the underlined words, the pointer changes from an arrow to a hand icon. Selecting a cross reference will take you to a screen with information about that reference. To select a cross reference, point to the underlined word and click.

Figure 1.20

A Help term description provides a brief definition in a small box.

> **scroll bar**
> A bar that appears at the right and/or bottom edge of a window whose contents aren't completely visible. Each scroll bar contains two scroll arrows and a scroll box, which allow you to scroll within the window or list box.

Selecting a term will display a small box with a definition or short description (Figure 1.20). Selecting a term will not advance you to another screen. To select a term, point to the word and click the mouse button. When you are finished viewing the information, click the mouse button.

EXERCISE 1 • 5   USING THE HELP SYSTEM

Before we explore the Windows Help system, select the Always on Top option from the Help menu on the menu bar. When this option is selected, a checkmark appears in front of the option, as shown in Figure 1.21. By selecting Always on Top, you ensure that the Help window remains in front of all other windows open

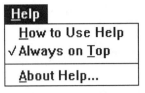

on the screen. If this option is not selected, the Help
window could "disappear" behind another window.
Since you are new to Windows, disappearing windows
could be a bit confusing. You will learn to control the
display of windows a little later.

1. Click on the Help menu in the Program Manager window.

2. Click on the Contents option—the Program Manager Help window opens.

3. Point on the Help menu option on the Help window. If the Always on Top
   option is not checked, click on it to select this option. If the Always on Top
   option is checked, release the mouse button—do not highlight the option or
   you will deselect it. (Hint: If you accidently deselect the option, choosing it
   again will reselect it.)

The Contents Option

4. Select the Contents button on the Help window. The table of contents for the
   Help file will be displayed with its text divided into two categories: (a) How
   To... and (b) Commands.

5. Point on the Arrange Windows and Icons topic (green underscored words if
   you have a color monitor). Notice that the pointer changes to a hand with a
   pointing finger.

6. Click the mouse button. Notice that the text page for the Arranging Windows
   and Icons topic is displayed.

7. Click on the broken underscored words *title bar*. (Hint: The words *title bar* are on
   the last line of the first paragraph.) A definition of *title bar* will be displayed.

8. Click anywhere on the screen to close the definition window.

The Search Button

Clicking on the Search button will open the Help Search dialog box shown in
Figure 1.22. Once you key a word or phrase in the box or select one from the list

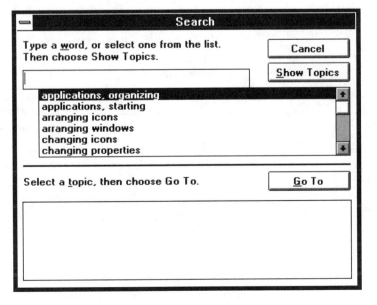

and click on
the Show
Topics but-
ton, a list of
related top-
ics will be
displayed in
the list box
at the bot-
tom of the
window.
You can dis-
play the text
page for any
of the listed
topics by
clicking on
the topic

then clicking on the Go To button. The Help text will be searched and the topic you have requested will be displayed.

9. You should still have the Help window displayed on your screen. Click on the Search button.

10. Key the word *creating* in the text box.

11. Click on the Show Topics button. All the topics with the word *creating* in their title will be displayed in the list box just below the text box. (Six topics are shown in Figure 1.22. The number of topics displayed on your system may vary.)

12. Click on the Creating Icons topic, then click on the Show Topics button. The appropriate help topic will be displayed in the list box. You can display the text for this topic by clicking on the Go To bottom or by double-clicking on the topic.

13. Click on the Go To button to display the text.

Notice that the corresponding text is displayed. When a window is too small to show all of its contents, scroll bars will be displayed so you can scroll the text into view (Figure 1.23). You can also resize the Help window by dragging on the borders, or you can use the maximize button to enlarge the window to a full screen view.

Figure 1.23

Help window with scroll bar

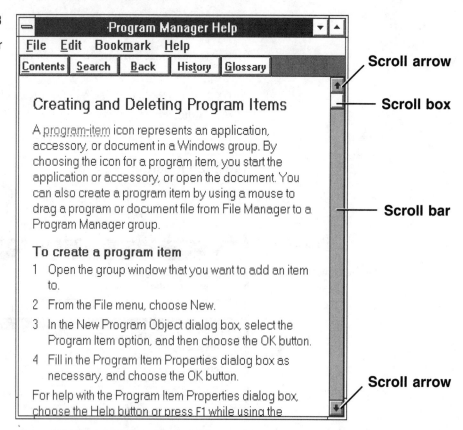

Scrolling the Help Text

To scroll text, you can click on the up or down scroll arrow. Each time you click on the scroll arrow, the text will scroll up or down one line (depending on which arrow you use). If you continue to hold the mouse button down while pointing on a scroll arrow, the text will continue to scroll.

The scroll bar also has a scroll box. You can move through the text quickly by dragging the scroll bar to a position that corresponds approximately with the location you want to view. For example, if you want to view the middle of the text, move the scroll box to the middle of the scroll bar.

14. Point on the down arrow on the vertical scroll bar and click once. Notice the text scrolls up one line.

15. Point on the down arrow on the vertical scroll bar and click once again.

16. Point on the down arrow on the vertical scroll bar and hold down the mouse button until the scroll box reaches the bottom of the vertical scroll bar. You should now be viewing the bottom (last) line of the text.

17. Point on the scroll box, press and hold the mouse button, drag the scroll box to the middle of the scroll bar, and release the mouse button. (The scroll box will not actually move to the pointer location until you release the mouse button.) Notice the text moves up several lines.

18. Point on the up arrow on the vertical scroll bar and click once. Notice the text scrolls down one line.

19. Point on the up arrow on the vertical scroll bar and hold down the mouse button until the scroll box reaches the top of the vertical scroll bar. The top of the text is now again in view.

The Back Button

The Back button takes you back to the previous page of text contained in the Help system. When you click on the Back button, you will see the Help topic that was most recently on the screen. When you click a second time, the next-most-recent topic will be displayed.

The Help system keeps a record of every text page you have displayed for each Windows session. The Back button will trace your steps through all the topics. When you have backed up as far as you can go, the Back button will be "grayed out," indicating that you cannot back up any further.

20. Click on the Back button. Notice that the previous text page is displayed. Continue to click on the Back button until it is no longer accessible (that is, until it is grayed out).

The History Button

While the Back button traces your steps through all the topics you have displayed since starting Windows, the History button displays a listing of each of the Help topics you have displayed in the order in which they were displayed. You can go directly to any of these topics by double-clicking on the desired topic in the listing.

21. Click on the History button.

22. Double-click on the Arranging Windows and Icons topic in the History window. Notice that the text for this topic is now displayed in the Help window.

Glossary Button

The Glossary button displays a list of commonly used words and phrases within the Help system. Think of the glossary as an electronic dictionary. When you click on the Glossary button, you see a list of terms like *active* and *application window,* and when you click on one of these terms, you will see its definition. The definition is the same as the one you see when you click on broken underscored text in the text window.

23. Click on the Glossary button. The Glossary window similar to the one in Figure 1.24 is displayed.

Figure 1.24

Glossary window

24. Click on the term *active* to display its definition; then click anywhere on the screen to close the definition window.

25. Double-click on the Glossary window's Control-menu box to close the Glossary window.

Creating Bookmarks

Just as you use bookmarks to mark places in printed matter, you can place "electronic" bookmarks in the Windows Help system to locate frequently used topics quickly and easily. For example, if you notice that you must often look up the same procedure in a particular application, you could create a bookmark for that topic instead of using the Search or Contents function to locate it.

Creating a bookmark is simple. First, locate the topic you wish to mark, then select the Define option from the Bookmark menu. The Bookmark Define dialog box shown in Figure 1.25 will display up to 20 characters of the topic title in the Bookmark Name text box. If this name is too long, or if you wish to create your own bookmark name, simply key your bookmark name in the text box. Once you have the name you wish to use in the text box, clicking on the OK button will add the topic to the list of bookmarks at the bottom of the Bookmark menu.

Figure 1.25

Bookmark Define dialog box

Bookmark Define

Bookmark Name:

Contents for Program Manager Help

OK

Cancel

Delete

EXERCISE 1 • 6   CREATING AND USING BOOKMARKS

1. Click on the Contents button to display the Help system table of contents.

2. Click on the Switch Between Applications topic in the How to... listing. (Hint: It is the last item in the first group.) The text screen will display, as shown in Figure 1.26.

Figure 1.26

Switching Between Applications text

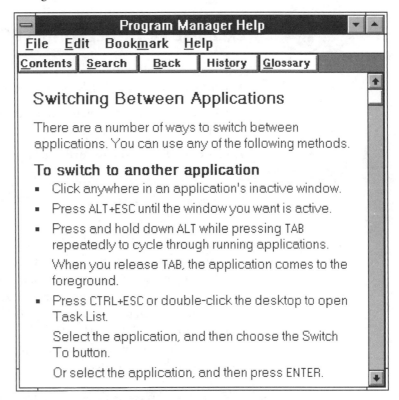

3. Select the Define option from the Bookmark menu.

4. Key your name in the Bookmark Name text box after the words *Switching Between Applications*, as illustrated in Figure 1.27, and click on OK. After the first letter of the name is keyed, the existing text will be erased and will be replaced with the new text being keyed.

Figure 1.27

In this Bookmark Define text box, note the insertion point (the vertical line) after *Switching Between Applications*.

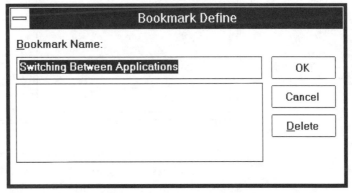

To use the bookmark, you only need to open the Bookmark menu and click on the defined bookmark name (or key the number next to the bookmark).

5. Click on the Back button to return to the previous text page.

6. Select Your Name from the Bookmark menu. The topic containing your bookmark (Switching Between Applications) will be displayed in the Help window.

Deleting Bookmarks

To delete bookmarks you no longer need, select the Define option from the Bookmark menu. When the Define dialog box is displayed, simply select the bookmark name(s) you no longer need from the listing, click on the Delete button, and then click on OK to return to the Help window.

EXERCISE 1 • 7   DELETING A BOOKMARK

1. Select the Define option from the Bookmark menu.

2. Click on the bookmark labeled with your name in the list box.

3. Click on the Delete button to remove the bookmark—the selected bookmark will be removed from the list box.

4. Click on OK to close the dialog box.

Customizing the Help Files

Have you ever found it helpful to make notes or highlight passages of text as a reminder? In most Windows applications, you can add a note to a selected topic to summarize that topic in your own words or to place a reminder to someone about the topic. For example, if you want a reminder that you must check your printer's status before you print, you can add this note to the printer topic by selecting the Annotate... command on the Edit menu. Look at the Annotate dialog box in Figure 1.28 and locate the large text box where some sample text has been keyed. When the dialog box first appears, the insertion point will be at the beginning of the text box ready for you to key your note.

Figure 1.28

Help Annotate dialog box

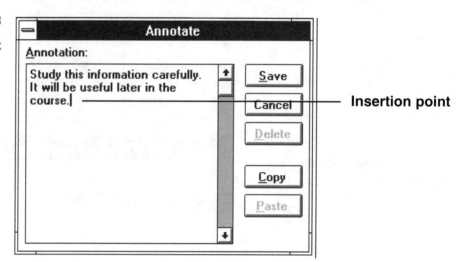

When you key text in this text box, the text will automatically wrap to subsequent lines if necessary. Do not press [Enter] because pressing [Enter] is the same as clicking on Save; both will close the dialog box and add your note (annotation) to the topic. You can have only one annotation for each Help topic.

As shown in Figure 1.29, a Help topic with a custom note attached has a paper clip icon next to the topic's title. To read a note that has been attached to a topic, display the topic and click on the paper clip next to the topic's title.

Figure 1.29

The paper clip shows that this Help
topic has a custom note attached.

Paper clip —————————

```
┌─────────────────────────────────────────────────────┐
│ ▭              Program Manager Help            ▼  ▲   │
│  File   Edit   Bookmark   Help                        │
│ │Contents│ │Search│ │Back│ │History│ │Glossary│       │
│─────────────────────────────────────────────────────│
│                                                       │
│  ⌕ Contents for Program Manager Help                  │
│                                                       │
│  Windows Program Manager is a tool you can use to     │
│  easily start applications, and organize your         │
│  applications and files into logical groups.          │
│  To learn how to use Help, press F1.                  │
│                                                       │
│  How To...                                            │
│  Arrange Windows and Icons                            │
│  Change an Icon                                       │
│  Organize Applications and Documents                  │
│  Quit Windows                                         │
│  Start an Application                                 │
│  Switch Between Applications                          │
│                                                       │
│  Commands                                             │
│  File Menu Commands                                   │
│                                                       │
└─────────────────────────────────────────────────────┘
```

EXERCISE 1 • 8   USING THE ANNOTATION FEATURE

1. Click on the History button to display the Windows Help History box.

2. Double-click on Contents for Program Manager Help in the listing.

3. Select the Quit Windows topic from the table of contents.

4. Select the Annotate... option from the Edit menu.

5. Key the following text in the text box (do not press [Enter]):

   Study this information carefully. It will be useful later in this session.

6. Click on Save. Notice that a paper clip has been placed in front of the topic title to indicate that a note has been attached to this topic.

7. Click on the paper clip to display the annotation.

8. Click on the Save button to close the Annotate window. (Or click on the Delete button to delete the annotation.)

9. Select the Annotate... option from the Edit menu.

10. Click on the Delete button. Notice the paper clip is removed, indicating that the note has been deleted.

Printing Help Files

When you are working with a new Window's program or feature, you may find it handy to have a hard copy (a printout) of selected Help topics so you do not have to keep Help open while you are learning.

If your printer is set up to work with Windows, you can print a chosen topic by accessing the topic and then selecting Print topic from the File menu. A

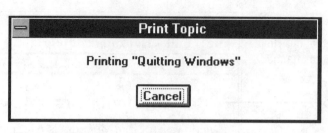

Figure 1.30

Print Topic message box

message box like the one in Figure 1.30 notifies you that the topic is being printed. (Your printout may not look like the text on your screen if your printer has a different font from the one that Help uses.) While the topic prints, the message box will disappear.

If you change your mind and want to cancel the Print Topic command, simply click on the Cancel button in the message box, or press the [Esc] key while the message box is displayed.

EXERCISE 1 . 9   PRINTING A HELP TOPIC

In order to complete this exercise, you must have a printer connected to your computer system and your printer must be set up to work with Windows. If you are sharing a printer, be sure you have access to the printer and be sure it is online. If you do not know how to access your printer, ask for assistance before you begin this exercise.

1. Verify that the Quitting Windows topic is displayed, then select the Print Topic option from the File menu.

2. Remove the page from the printer when printing is finished. When you are finished with the Help system, you should deselect the Always on Top option so the window or Help program icon does not remain on the screen.

3. Select the Always on Top option from the Help menu in the Help window.

Other Help Features

Help features and topics vary from one Windows application to another. Some of the Help commands not discussed in this sesion are listed below:

Menu	Command	Purpose
Edit	Copy	Copies information in the active Help window to be used in another document.
Edit	Paste	Places information that has been copied from an active Help window.
File	Open	Opens a Help file from another Windows program.

VIEW 7	

CLOSING AND EXITING WINDOWS

PREVIEW

When you have finished working with a window and no longer need it on your desktop, you should close that window. A window can be closed four ways:

- Double-click on the Control-menu box,
- Select Close from the Control menu,
- Press [Ctrl]+[F4], or
- Select Exit Windows... from the Program Manager File menu.

When you select Exit Windows... from the File menu, you close the Program Manager, and when you close the Program Manager, you also close all active windows and quit Windows.

EXERCISE 1 • 10 CLOSING A WINDOW

1. Click on the Help window to select it.

2. Click once on the Control-menu box, then select the Close option. The Help window will close.

3. Click on the Accessories window to select it.

4. Double-click on the Accessories window Control-menu box. You must double-click quickly for the command to take effect. The Accessories window will close, and its icon will appear at the bottom of the desktop.

5. Click on the Main window to select it.

6. Press and hold the [Ctrl] key, then press the [F4] key. The Main window will close, and its icon will appear at the bottom of the desktop.

Exiting Windows

Exiting Windows is a two-step process. First, you should close any programs you have been running in the Windows session. (As with any application software package, closing an application before you turn off the computer will guard against losing current work.) Second, once you have closed all applications that have been running, close the Program Manager.

Figure 1.31

Exit Windows prompt box

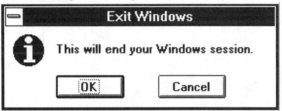

To end a Windows session, select the Exit Windows... command from the File menu in the Program Manager. Each time you exit (quit) Windows, the prompt box shown in Figure 1.31 will be displayed—asking you to verify that you want to quit Windows. To confirm that you really wish to quit, click the OK button or press [Enter]. (If you issue the quit Windows command by mistake, click on the Cancel button or press [Esc] to remain in Windows.)

EXERCISE 1 • 11 EXITING WINDOWS

1. Select the Exit Windows option from the File menu. The Exit Windows dialog box will appear.

2. Click on OK to exit Windows.
(When you exit Windows, you return to the DOS prompt.)

SUMMARY

In this introduction to Windows, you discovered basic terms, practiced some of
the beginning procedures used to navigate in the Windows environment, and
learned how to modify the appearance of the Windows desktop. You also learned
how to access and use the Windows Help feature. The exercises provided practice
in working with menus, menu bars, dialog boxes, and messages. You will use these
features in the remaining sessions of this book as you continue working in the
Windows environment.

OBJECTIVES

When you complete this session, you will be able to:

- Discuss the purpose and function of the Program Manager.

- Name five program groups that the Program Manager may contain and identify programs in each of the five groups.

- Differentiate between program groups, group windows, group icons, and application program item icons.

- Distinguish between Windows applications and non-Windows applications.

- Customize the Program Manager by copying, moving, and adding program item icons and program groups.

- Switch between groups and create a new group window.

- Run programs indirectly using the Run. . . command.

- Use Task List to monitor and control currently running applications.

- Open and close an application.

- Exit the Program Manager and Windows.

SESSION 2 *THE PROGRAM MANAGER*

27

THE PROGRAM MANAGER

GROUP WINDOWS

PREVIEW

You learned in Session 1 how Windows acts as an interface between you and your computer. In order to do this, it uses a shell program—a visual interface between you and Windows. Windows contains two shell programs—Program Manager and File Manager. Each Windows session begins and ends in one of the shells. The shell is the program that begins automatically when you run Windows. Unless you specify otherwise, Program Manager is Windows' center of operations. The first screen you see when you begin Windows for the very first time is the Program Manager window with the Main group window opened inside it (see Figure 2.1). The Program Manager starts and appears automatically each time you begin a Windows session. It remains open while Windows is running so that you can use its commands to control your programs and files.

Figure 2.1

Windows' opening screen shows the Program Manager window with the Main window open inside it.

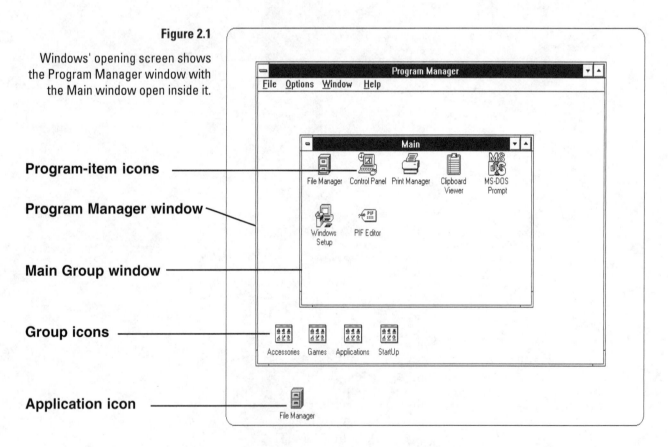

Program-item icons

Program Manager window

Main Group window

Group icons

Application icon

Program Manager is a utility, a tool that allows you to take full advantage of the power of Windows. How? By helping you direct the movement of information from one window to another and keeping track of what is happening within Windows. For instance, Program Manager lets you run the various programs; remembers which window contains which program and which window is active; controls the printer, hard disk, and RAM; and switches between tasks.

And as you will see later, you must use the Program Manager both to start Windows and to exit Windows.

NOTE: Each time you start Windows and as you use Windows, your screen displays may not match exactly the ones shown in the textbook exercises and figures. The differences are due to the fact that Windows can be configured differently on various computer systems.)

Program Manager is very flexible: You can set it up in a configuration that best suits your working style, and you can easily modify your setup if you need to. Program Manager lets you organize applications and documents in logical groups. These groups have nothing to do with the directory structure on your hard disk.

When you start your Windows software, your screen will display the **program groups** that were created when Windows was installed. The Program Manager window shown in Figure 2.1 contains five program groups labeled Main, Accessories, Games, Applications, and StartUp. (The actual number and names on your system may vary, depending on what was installed.)

In Figure 2.1, the Main program group has been opened. Once a program group is opened, it is called a **group window** because it organizes within itself a group of application programs within the Program Manager window. For example, the Main group window in Figure 2.1 has seven programs organized within it. Each group window has its own Control menu but no menu bar; a group window is controlled by commands from the Program Manager's menu bar. Group windows cannot be moved outside the workspace of the Program Manager. A group window can cover the entire screen or a portion of the screen, or it can appear simply as a **group icon**.

How do you open a group window? You open a group window by double-clicking on its group icon. In Figure 2.1, four program groups are shown not as fully opened windows, but as identical group icons. These four group icons are labeled Accessories, Games, Applications, and StartUp. Group icons, therefore, are reduced (minimized) to identical symbols of group windows within the Program Manager. A group icon may be located at the bottom of the window until it is opened. (Remember: To open a group window, double-click on the group icon. For example, if you double-click on the Accessories group icon, the screen will then display the Accessories group window. Likewise, double-clicking on any other group icon in the Program Manager window will open that group window.)

Before you continue, you must know about two more icons—the **application icon** and the **program item icon**:

Application icons represent programs that are running and have been minimized. These icons are generally arranged along the bottom edge of the desktop. The programs represented by application icons are still running and may be performing complex functions. They do not take much memory since they do not need to show their contents in an open window.

Program item icons represent application programs that are not currently running. These symbols identify application programs that exist within and can be started from the group window. The program item icons shown in Figure 2.1 are File Manager, Control Panel, Print Manager, Clipboard Viewer, MS-DOS Prompt, Windows Setup, and PIF Editor. When you double-click on a program item icon, it will start the application program and load any related documents. The program item icon will then be referred to as an application icon.

Main Group Applications

Programs that you will use routinely to manage the Windows environment are located in the Main group window.

Figure 2.2

File Manager icon

File Manager. The File Manager will help you manage your computer files and your hard disk. For example, it makes it easy to access different disk drives as you find, move, copy, delete, rename, or print files.

Figure 2.3

MS-DOS Prompt icon

MS-DOS Prompt. As you know, DOS is the powerful operating system that Windows uses. The MS-DOS Prompt gives you *direct* access to DOS *from within Windows.* To return to Windows, key *Exit* and press [Enter]. As you use DOS Prompt, you will see a number of advantages that result from running DOS from within Windows.

Figure 2.4

Print Manager icon

Print Manager. The Print Manager monitors all printing activity: It coordinates print jobs, sends them to the printer(s) to print, and allows you to continue doing other work while Print Manager does the printing.

Figure 2.5

Control Panel icon

Control Panel. The Control Panel lets you adjust the appearance of your desktop, install printers and fonts, and configure your system. For example, it lets you adjust the spacing between items on your desktop, and if you have a color monitor, it lets you change the colors of the screen elements.

Figure 2.6

Clipboard Viewer icon

Clipboard Viewer. The Clipboard Viewer shows you what is currently on the Clipboard. The Clipboard allows you to move or copy text and graphics from one Windows application and insert it into another Windows application.

Figure 2.7

Windows Setup icon

Windows Setup. The Windows Setup program helps you install ("set up") new applications and change hardware configurations.

Figure 2.8

PIF Editor icon

PIF Editor icon. The PIF (Program Information File) Editor program allows you to establish special settings so that your non-Windows applications (DOS programs) can run correctly under Windows.

Accessories Group Applications

Windows accessories are very useful in doing routine work and include the following applications:

Figure 2.9

Write program icon

Write. Write is an easy-to-use word processing program that lets you key, edit, save, and print documents. Write is not as powerful as commercial software packages such as *Word for Windows* or *WordPerfect for Windows*; it is intended to help you work on simple word processing tasks.

Figure 2.10

Paintbrush program icon

Paintbrush

Paintbrush. Paintbrush is a drawing program that allows you to create images (in color if you have a color monitor) that can be placed in documents and printed (in color if you have a color printer).

Figure 2.11

Calendar program icon

Calendar

Calendar. The Calendar program is a daily appointment book or monthly organizer that contains an alarm.

Figure 2.12

Clock icon

Clock

Clock. The Clock program provides a time display (in analog or in digital format).

Figure 2.13

Cardfile icon

Cardfile

Cardfile. Cardfile provides an electronic "Rolodex" file for storing, sorting, and selecting data.

Figure 2.14

Notepad icon

Notepad

Notepad. The Notepad is a mini word processor with limited capabilities; it is used for jotting down short notes and messages.

Figure 2.15

Calculator icon

Calculator

Calculator. The electronic calculator program provides the capability for doing a variety of mathematical calculations.

Figure 2.16

Character Map icon

Character Map

Character Map. This utility permits you to insert special characters into documents—characters not available on most keyboards (♦, ®, and ½, for example). These characters must, however, be among the available fonts installed in your printer in order to be printed.

Figure 2.17

Media Player icon

Media Player

Media Player. The media player is a Windows multimedia feature. This program permits you to run one of many media players compatible with your system.

Figure 2.18

Object Packager icon

Object Packager

Object Packager. This program enables you to show in a document that represents an object an icon. For example, you can use the Object Packager to create a personal note and place (package) it as an icon in a document. The message will be displayed only when you double-click on the icon. The icon is like an electronic "Post-It Note" attached to your document.

Figure 2.19

Recorder icon

Recorder

Recorder. Recorder permits you to record and play back Windows activities. Recorder is Windows' equivalent to the macro recorder in many DOS applications.

Figure 2.20

Sound Recorder icon

Sound Recorder

Sound Recorder. Sound Recorder is another Windows multimedia feature that allows you to play, record, and edit sound files. However, you must have special sound hardware installed before you can use Sound Recorder. Sound Recorder uses command buttons that are similar to buttons on a tape recorder, such as reverse, fast forward, play, pause, microphone, and others.

Figure 2.21

Terminal icon

Terminal

Terminal. Terminal provides terminal-emulation (communications) capabilities that permit you to access other computers by modem or serial port connections.

Games Group Applications

Playing Solitaire and Minesweeper (included in the Games group) will help you become familiar with Windows buttons, boxes, menu bars, and scroll bars and help develop your skill in using the mouse.

Figure 2.22

Solitaire game icon

 Solitaire. Solitaire is a computerized version of the popular card game.

Figure 2.23

Minesweeper game icon

 Minesweeper. Minesweeper is an electronic board game.

Windows Start-Up Group

This group does not contain any programs when Windows is first installed. You can move or copy any program item icon to the Start-Up group. When you do, any programs that are represented by icons in this group will be loaded each time Windows is launched.

Applications Group

The Applications group contains all of the other applications installed on your hard disk (see Figure 2.24). For example, if *Microsoft Word for Windows* and *Microsoft Excel for Windows* are installed on your computer, their program item icons will appear in the Applications group window when it is opened. Therefore, the number of icons in the Applications group window depends on how many applications are installed on your system.

NOTE: Windows applications can be run *only* from within the Windows program. If you tried to run a Windows application from DOS, you would see a message that says *This program requires Microsoft Windows.*

If you have DOS-based programs such as **WordPerfect** or **Lotus 1-2-3**, they may also be located in this group.

To see the program item icons and start the applications, you must open a group window by double-clicking on its icon. Once the window is opened, you can arrange the position of the window on the desktop and the window layout to suit your taste.

Figure 2.24

The Applications group window displays all the applications installed on your hard disk.

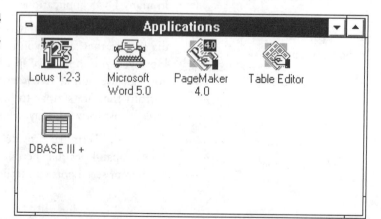

EXERCISE 2 • 1   OPENING, ARRANGING, AND CLOSING GROUP WINDOWS

1. Start Windows if it is not already active.

2. Open the Accessories group window by double-clicking on the Accessories group icon at the bottom of the Program Manager window. You can see which applications are grouped under Accessories by looking at the program icons in the Accessories window.

NOTE: If your Accessories group window is opened automatically when you start Windows, make it the active window now.

3. Open the Games group window by double-clicking on the Games group icon at the bottom of the Program Manager window. You now have two or three group windows opened, as shown in Figure 2.25.

NOTE: If your Games group window is opened automatically when you start Windows, make it the active window now.

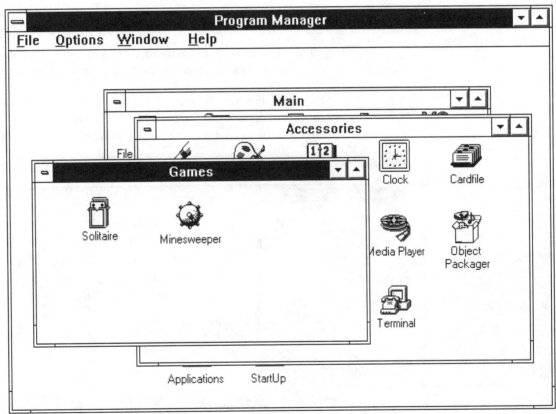

Figure 2.25 This Program Manager window has the Main, Accessories, and Games windows opened within it.

You can arrange Windows in tile or cascade format by (a) selecting the Window option on the Program Manager menu bar and then (b) selecting the Tile or Cascade option.

4. Select the Cascade option from the Window menu. Figure 2.26 shows group windows displayed in cascade format. As you can see, the Cascade option layers group windows into a stack with titles showing; the active window is always in front of the stack, on the top layer.

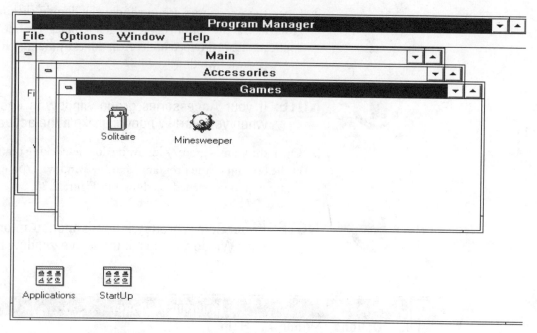

Figure 2.26 Here the Main, Accessories, and Games group windows are arranged in cascade format within the Program manager window.

5. Select the Tile option from the Window menu. As shown in Figure 2.27, the Tile option divides the Program Manager window evenly among the open group windows and shows the windows side by side, rather than overlapping.

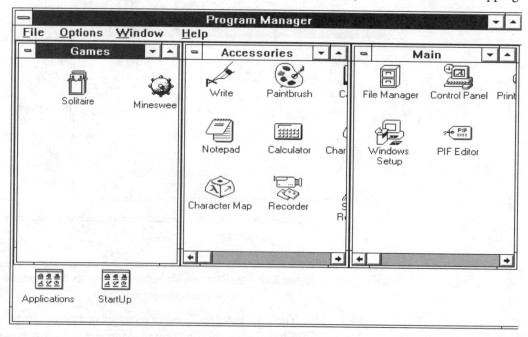

Figure 2.27 In this Program Manager window the Main, Accessories, and Games windows are arranged in tile format.

6. Open the Applications group window by double-clicking on the Applications group icon at the bottom of the Program Manager window.

7. Select the Tile option from the Window menu. The open group windows are now evenly distributed in the Program Manager window.

8. Close the Games group window.

   a. Click on the Games window to select it.

   b. Double-click on the Control-menu box to close the Games window.

9. Close the Applications group window by double-clicking on its Control-menu box. You now have two group windows open--Main and Accessories.

10. Move the windows so that they are placed in the locations shown in Figure 2.28, if they do not already appear as shown.

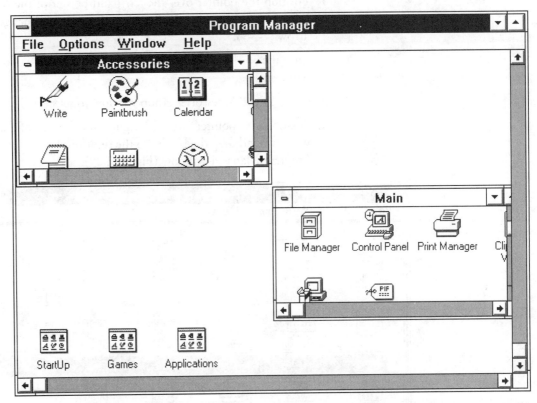

Figure 2.28 The Accessories and the Main group windows are open.

Modifying Group Windows

So far you have been working with group windows created when Windows was installed on your hard disk. Some day you will, no doubt, install new programs or add, remove, or change a group window or program item. To do so, you can use either the Control Panel or the Program Manager. Later you will learn to use the Control Panel. For now, use the Program Manager to modify the group windows.

Resizing Group Windows. When you cascade or tile windows, the software determines the window size. (Whenever software makes a predetermined choice for you, that choice or setting is called the **default**.) At times, however, you will want to control the size of your windows, that is, change the default settings. You can resize windows to suit your needs by clicking on and dragging one of the three types of window borders (horizontal, vertical, or corner):

● If you drag on a horizontal border, you will make the window taller or shorter.

● If you drag on a vertical border, you will make the window wider or narrower.

● If you drag from one of the corners, you can change two window dimensions with one movement.

EXERCISE 2 ● 2   RESIZING A WINDOW

1. Position the pointer over the left-hand border of the Main group window. When the pointer is in the correct position, it will change to a double-headed arrow (<—>).

2. Drag the border to the left until it is at the left margin of the Program Manager window.

3. Click on the Accessories group window to select it.

4. Position the pointer over the right-hand border of the Accessories group window, and drag the border to the right until it is at the right margin of the Program Manager window (Figure 2.29).

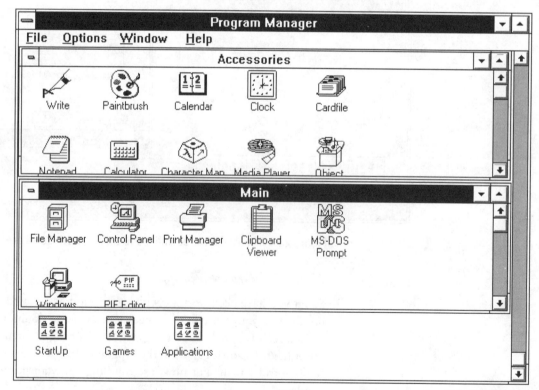

Figure 2.29 The Accessories group window and the Main group window are arranged one beneath the other.

Minimizing, Maximizing, and Restoring Windows. As you have already seen, it is easy to size individual windows within the Program Manager. At times, however, you will want to temporarily enlarge an individual window to fill the entire screen. Three sizing functions are available from each window to help you quickly minimize, maximize, or restore a window:

● **Minimize.** Minimize reduces the active window to an icon, which is placed inside the Program Manager window. The window is still available but is covered, allowing more room on your desktop.

● **Maximize.** Maximize enlarges the active window to its maximum size so that it fills the entire window—helpful if you need a larger view of one window.

● **Restore.** When a window has been minimized or maximized, Restore returns the window to its original size.

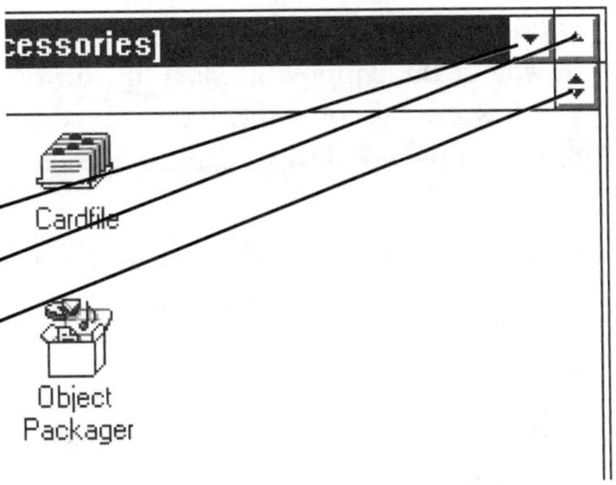

Figure 2.30

The minimize, maximize, and restore buttons are located at the upper-right-hand corner of a window.

Minimize button

Maximize button

Restore button

Cardfile

Object Packager

If you are using a mouse, you can use the three sizing buttons located in the upper-right-hand corner of the window as shown in Figure 2.30. Clicking on a button activates it. For example, clicking on the minimize button will minimize the window to an icon, and clicking on the maximize button will enlarge the window to fill the entire desktop. Once you select the maximize button, it is replaced by the Restore button, which appears below the title bar.

EXERCISE 2 ● 3   MINIMIZING, MAXIMIZING, AND RESTORING GROUP WINDOWS USING THE SIZING BUTTONS

1. If necessary, double-click on the Main window to open it.

2. Click on the minimize button. The window will shrink to an icon at the bottom of the Program Manager window.

3. Click on the Program Manager's maximize button. Notice that the maximized window has no borders and that its maximize button has changed to a Restore button (note the double arrow), which can restore the window to its original size and location.

4. Click on the Restore button. The Program Manager's window will be restored to its size and location before it was maximized.

Using the Control Menu

The Minimize, Maximize, and Restore options on the Control menu can also be used to perform the same functions as the sizing buttons.

5. Click on the Games group window icon to display the Control menu.

6. Select the Maximize option. Notice that the window fills the entire screen and covers up the other open windows.

7. Click on the Restore button. The Games window is restored to an open window in the Program Manager.

8. Click once on the Control-menu box of the Games group window to display the Control menu.

9. Select the Close option.

Rearranging the Program Item Icons. As you resize windows, use a mouse to rearrange them, and work with program item icons, your active window can become disorganized. The Program Manager includes an option on two drop-down menus, the Options menu and the Window menu, that assist you in arranging the program item icons. The Arrange Icons option on the Window menu organizes all the program item icons in the active window and "squares up" all the icons, saving you the time and trouble.

When resizing windows, it is important to have the Auto Arrange option on the Options menu *active*. This option automatically rearranges the icons in the window to fit the new window's size. In this way, this option helps you determine how large the window needs to be during resizing. Of course, you can make a window any size you want. If the icons do not fit, a scroll bar appears at the bottom or side of the window so you can view icons not visible in the window.

EXERCISE 2 • 4   ARRANGING WINDOWS AND GROUP ICONS

Figure 2.31

The check mark indicates that the Auto Arrange option is selected on this Options menu.

Options
√ Auto Arrange
Minimize on Use
Save Settings on Exit

When the icons in a window are not neatly arranged, you can reorganize them by selecting the Arrange Icons option on the Window menu. Or if you prefer, you can have them reorganized automatically by checking the Auto Arrange option on the Options menu, as shown in Figure 2.31.

The Auto Arrange option, like many of the Options menu items, can be toggled on and off. If the option is active (checked), it is toggled on; selecting it again will toggle it off, making it inactive. If the option is inactive (not checked), selecting it will make it active.

Practice using both these options.

Using the Arrange Icons Option

1. Click on Options to display the menu.

2. Verify that the Auto Arrange option is <u>in</u>active (<u>un</u>checked). (a) If it is active, click on the option to make it inactive. (b) If it is not active, just close the menu by clicking on the desktop—not the menu.

3. If necessary, double-click on the Accessories group window to open it. Click on the Accessories maximize button.

4. Drag the program icons so they are randomly placed around the screen.

5. Select the Arrange Icons option on the Window menu. The icons will jump into an orderly line.

Using the Auto Arrange Option

6. Click on the Auto Arrange option on the Options menu and verify that it is *de*selected (that is, *un*checked).

7. Drag the program icons in the window so that they are arranged in two columns the left side of the screen.

8. Click on the Restore button on the menu bar. Notice that the icons remain in two columns. Since you cannot see all the icons, scroll bars are displayed at the right side of the window.

9. Maximize the Accessories window.

10. Select the Auto Arrange option from the Options menu. Notice that the icons are automatically arranged across the top of the window.

11. Click on the Restore button. Notice the icons are again arranged across the window. Since all the icons are in view, scroll bars are not displayed.

VIEW 2
WORKING WITH GROUPS

PREVIEW

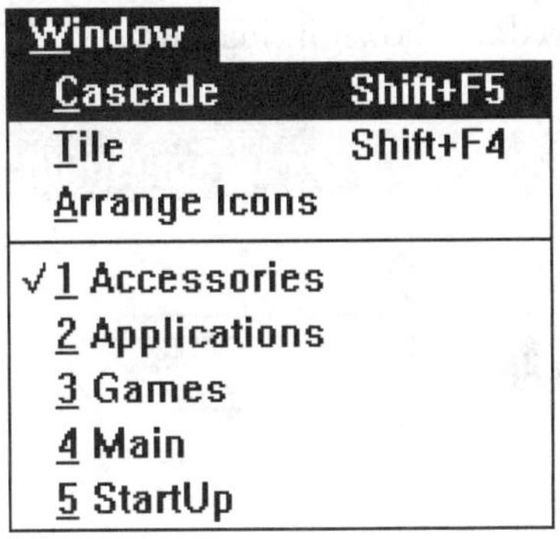

Figure 2.32

In this Window menu from the Program Manager, the checkmark indicates the active group.

Window	
Cascade	Shift+F5
Tile	Shift+F4
Arrange Icons	
√ 1 Accessories	
2 Applications	
3 Games	
4 Main	
5 StartUp	

As you have seen, at times the active window covers up some or all of the other group windows, making it difficult to access the other windows. To eliminate this problem, the Window menu lists all the groups that have been created, thereby letting you quickly switch between groups. A check mark will be placed on the menu next to a window's name when it has been activated (see Figure 2.32). To make another group active, just click on its name on the menu. If the chosen window is minimized, it will also be opened. If the layout of the windows is in cascade format, the window selected will be brought to the front of the stack of windows.

EXERCISE 2 • 5   SWITCHING BETWEEN GROUPS

1. Select the Games group from the Window menu. The Games group window is opened and displayed as an active window.

2. Select the Main group from the Window menu. The Main group window is opened over the other windows.

3. Select the Tile option from the Window menu.

4. Minimize the Games group window by clicking on the minimize button.

5. Select the Tile option from the Window menu to rearrange the open windows.

Creating Group Windows

In Windows, you have the ability to customize your groups and the programs within the groups to fit your special needs. One way to customize Windows is to add or create a new group or a new group item. The process for both adding a new group and a new item is similar, but we will look at each one separately. First, look at adding or creating a new group.

Creating a new group window will place a new, empty group in the Program Manager window. For example, you could create a new group window named *Word Processing* and insert related items into it.

SESSION 2

EXERCISE 2•6   CREATING A NEW GROUP WINDOW

1. Select New... from the File menu. The New Program Object dialog box will appear, as shown in Figure 2.33.

Figure 2.33

New Program Object dialog box

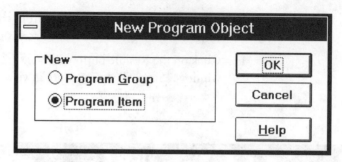

2. Click on the Program Group option button.

3. Click on the OK button. The Program Group Properties dialog box will be displayed, as shown in Figure 2.34.

Figure 2.34

Program Group Properties dialog box

Program Group Properties

Description: _____   OK

Group File: _____   Cancel

Help

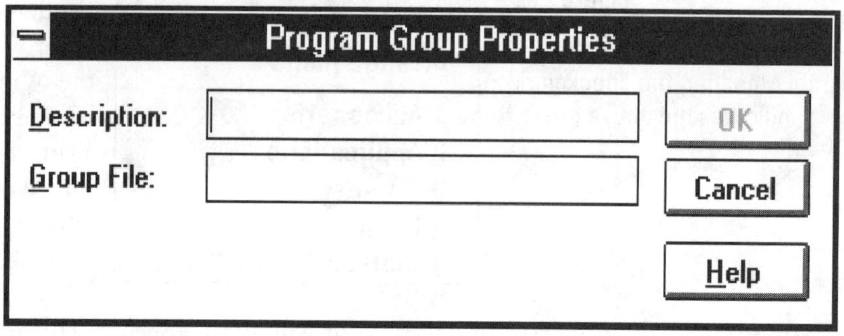

4. Key *Word Processing* in the Description text box to name the new group window. You do not need to fill in the Group File text box (the purpose of this box will be explained later).

5. Click on the OK button. The new program group will be added and displayed as the active window, as shown in Figure 2.35. Notice that the title on the title bar is the same as the description you keyed in the Description text box.

Figure 2.35

Word Processing group window

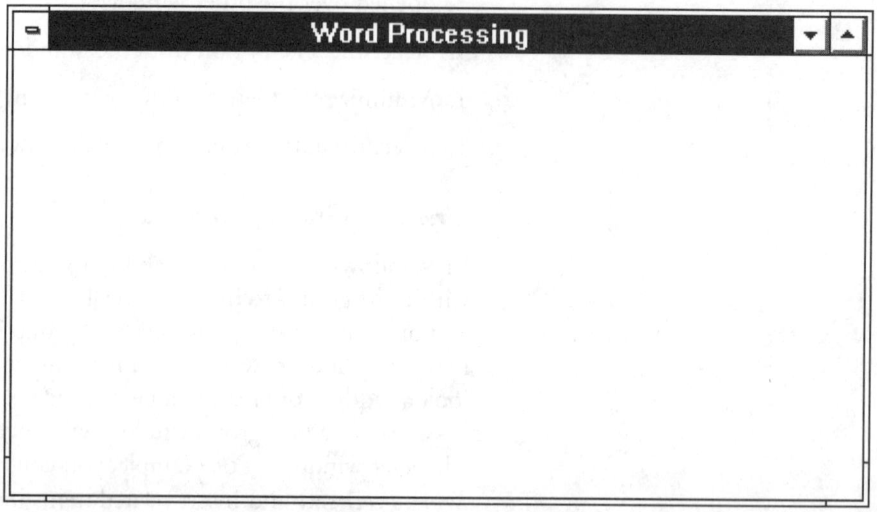

Word Processing

Adding Applications to a Group

You can add applications to a program group in three different ways:

- By copying a program item icon from one group to another
- By moving a program item icon from one group to another
- By adding a new program item icon to a group

Copying a Program Item Between Groups

To copy a program item between groups, you can (1) use the Copy option available on the File menu, or (2) use the mouse to drag a program item icon from one group window to another—a process that actually copies the program item.

EXERCISE 2 • 7   COPYING A PROGRAM ITEM BETWEEN GROUPS

Using the Mouse

1. Select the Tile option on the Window menu to display the three open windows.

2. Press and hold [Ctrl].

3. Place the mouse pointer on the Write program item icon in the Accessories group window and click on the mouse button. (You may need to use the scroll bar to bring the Write program icon into view.)

4. Drag the Write program item icon to the Word Processing group window and release the mouse button and [Ctrl]. The Write program item icon now appears in both the Accessories group window and the Word Processing group window. The Write program can be accessed from either group (Figure 2.36).

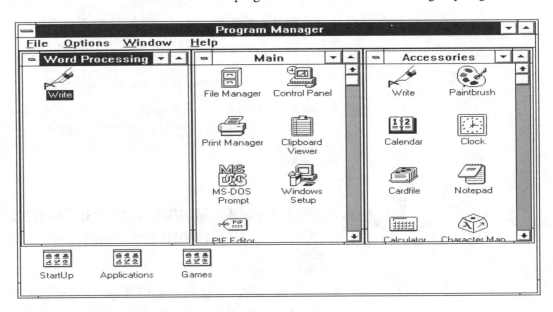

Figure 2.36 Because the Write program item has been copied, the Write program item icon appears in both the Word Processing group window and the Accessories group window.

Using the Copy Option

5. Click on the Notepad icon in the Accessories group window to select it. (You may have to use the scroll bar to bring it into view.)

6. Select the Copy... option from the File menu. The Copy Program Item dialog box with a drop-down box inside will be displayed (Figure 2.37).

Figure 2.37

The Copy Program Item dialog box has a drop-down box inside.

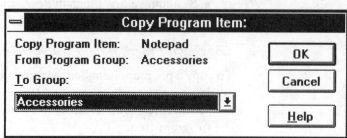

7. Click on the down arrow of the drop-down box to display the list box.

8. Scroll the list box until the Word Processing group name is in view (Figure 2.38).

Figure 2.38

Scrolling the list box shows the Word Processing group name.

9. Select the Word Processing group name, then click on the OK button. As before, the selected program item is copied to the Word Processing group window.

Moving a Program Item Between Groups

Earlier you learned to move a program item by dragging its icon to a new location. When a program item icon is dragged from one group window to another, it is moved, not copied. In other words, the program item icon will appear only in the new location.

EXERCISE 2 • 8   MOVING A PROGRAM ITEM BETWEEN GROUPS

Using the Mouse

1. Point on the Notepad icon in the Word Processing group window and drag the icon to the Main group window. Notice that the Notepad program item is "removed" from the Word Processing window and placed in the Main group window.

Using the Move Option

2. Select the Notepad icon in the Main group window.

3. Select the Move option from the File menu.

4. Click on the down arrow of the drop-down box to display the list box.

5. Scroll the list box until the Word Processing group name is in view.

6. Select the Word Processing group name, then click on the OK button. Notice that the Notepad icon has moved as you directed.

Adding a New Program Item to a Group

On occasion, you may need to add a new program item (a program item that does not currently exist somewhere in the Program Manager) to a program group. This would be the case if:

- A program item has been deleted from the Program Manager.

- A new application has been installed on your system's hard disk.

- The Windows program was not instructed to create a program item for the application during the installation process.

You can create a new program item if you know (1) the directory in which the application program has been saved and (2) the command that is keyed to run the program. For example, assume you want to install a new word processing program called Micro Writer in the Windows directory on your hard disk, and the command needed to run this new program is WRITE.EXE.

Knowing this information, you select the New... command from the File menu and click on the Program Item option button, then click on the OK command button. In the Program Items Properties dialog box, you enter the description of the new item (the name to be given to the icon), and in the Command Line text box, you enter the command needed to run the application. In our example, you know the command is WRITE.EXE, but if you cannot remember (or do not know) the exact location on your hard disk, you can click on the Browse... command button to display the Browse dialog box.

The Browse dialog box contains a listing of files and directories that you can scroll through until you locate the command. When you select the appropriate command, it will be placed in the appropriate text box. Clicking on the OK command button will return you to the Program Item Properties dialog box, and clicking on the OK command button again will record your selections and create the new program item.

EXERCISE 2 • 9   ADDING A NEW PROGRAM ITEM TO A GROUP

1. Select the Word Processing group window.

2. Select the New... option from the File menu.

3. Verify that the Program Item option button is selected, then click on the OK command button.

4. Key the program name *Micro Writer* in the Description text box.

5. Click on the Browse... option button to display the Browse dialog box.

6. Verify that the directory containing the Windows program is selected. In our example, this is the C:*WINDOWS* directory, as shown in Figure 2.39.

Figure 2.39

The Browse dialog box contains a listing of files and directories that you can scroll through.

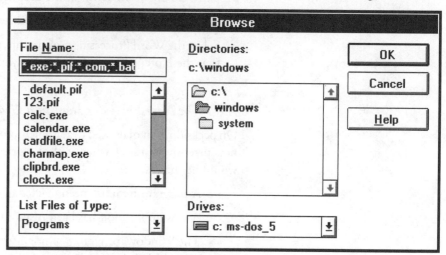

The Browse dialog box has four parts: (1) File Name, (2) List Files of Type, (3) Directories, and (4) Drives. First, make sure the correct drive is selected in the Drives list box; if not, click on the down arrow in the Drives list box and select the correct one. Then verify that the appropriate directory (folder) is open, and finally select the appropriate filename from those listed in the File Name list box. By default, only valid program files will be displayed (those with the extensions EXE, PIF, COM, and BAT).

7. Select the WRITE.EXE file from the File Name list box. You will need to scroll to locate the file at the bottom of the list. Notice that the filename WRITE.EXE is transferred to the File Name text box (Figure 2.40).

Figure 2.40

In this Browse dialog box, the File Name text box shows WRITE.EXE.

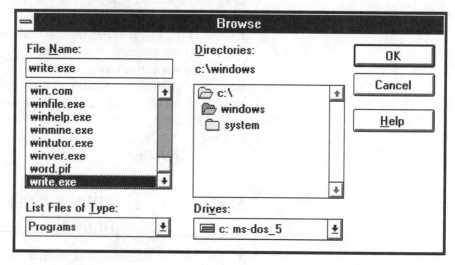

8. Click on the OK command button.

9. Verify that the Program Item Properties dialog box contains the text lines similar to those shown in Figure 2.41. (We'll learn about the other text boxes and the check box later.)

Figure 2.41

Completed Program Item Properties
dialog box

Program Item Properties

Description:	Micro Writer	OK
Command Line:	C:\WINDOWS\WRITE.EXE	Cancel
Working Directory:		
Shortcut Key:	None	Browse...
	☐ Run Minimized	Change Icon...
		Help

10. Click on the OK command button. The new program item icon Micro Writer should be displayed in the Word Processing group window.

Adding DOS Program Items

At times you want to add a DOS program to the Program Manager. While the Windows installation program provides an automatic routine for creating program item icons for DOS programs, it rarely finds all the programs, so you will want to add those programs you currently have on your system. Also you may purchase a DOS program and wish to run it from Windows.

Most Windows programs automatically install an icon as part of their setup routine—DOS programs do not. To create a program item icon for a DOS program, you will need to know three things: (1) the directory in which the application program has been saved, (2) the command that is keyed to run the program, and (3) the directory where you will keep the document files, if any, created by this program. You will have to decide on (1) the icon and (2) the shortcut key, if any, you wish to use to run the program.

Unlike Windows programs, most DOS programs do not have unique icons. When you create a program item for a DOS program, Windows automatically assigns it the same generic icon that all DOS programs get. It looks like a computer screen displaying the letters *DOS*. You can change this icon by selecting the Change Icon command button in the Program Item dialog box.

EXERCISE 2 • 10 ADDING A DOS PROGRAM

In this exercise we will assume that you have installed a new DOS program called *Micro Speller* on your hard disk in the C:\WINDOWS directory and that the command used to run the program is <u>DEFAULT.PIF</u>.

1. Select the Word Processing group window.

2. Select the New... option from the File menu.

3. Verify that the Program Item option button is selected, then click on the OK command button.

4. Key the program name *Micro Speller* in the Description text box.

5. Press [Tab] to move the cursor to the Command Line text box.

6. Key *C:\WINDOWS\DEFAULT.PIF*. Remember, if your Windows program has been installed in a directory other than C:\WINDOWS, you must key the appropriate drive and directory.

7. Press [Tab] to move the cursor to the Working Directory text box.

8. Key *C:*

Now you can create a shortcut key for running the Micro Speller program. You can enter only one character. Windows will automatically assign [Ctrl][Alt] as the first two characters.

9. Press [Tab] to move the cursor to the Shortcut Key text box.

10. Key *S*. Notice that Windows added [Ctrl][Alt] as you keyed the letter *S*.

Windows permits you to create a shortcut key using the sequence [Ctrl][Alt] followed by a key of your choice. When you press and hold this combination of keys, the program will run, even if the program item is not visible.

If you add a generic DOS application icon for the program, it will be displayed in the lower-left corner of the dialog box. If you want to use this generic icon, click on the OK command button. If you do not see a generic icon displayed or wish to change the default icon, click on the Change Icon button on the Program Item dialog box. When you issue the Change Icon command, Windows will search the current file for additional icons, and if no available icons are found, the message box shown in Figure 2.42 will display, informing you that no icons were found. Once you clear the message box by clicking on the OK button, Windows will display a list box of icons. You can scroll the list box to select the icon of your choice. After you choose OK in the Change Icon dialog box, the new icon will take effect.

11. Click on the Change Icon command button. The Change Icon message box shown in Figure 2.42 is displayed.

Figure 2.42

Change Icon message box

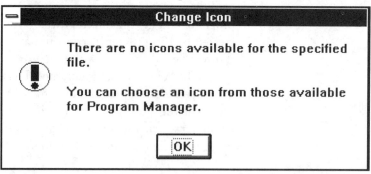

12. Click on the OK command button to display the Change Icon list box shown in Figure 2.43.

Figure 2.43

Change Icon listing box

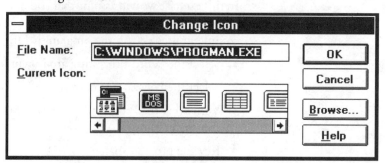

13. Scroll the listing and select the typewriter by double-clicking on the typewriter icon in the list box. The typewriter icon will display in the lower left corner of the Program Item Properties dialog box, as shown in Figure 2.44.

Figure 2.44

The typewriter icon in this completed Program Item Properties dialog box will serve as an icon for a DOS program.

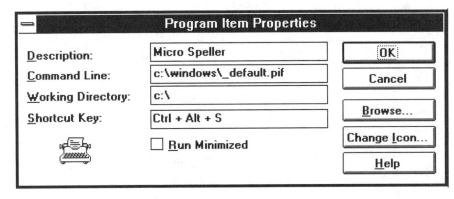

Figure 2.44

The typewriter icon in this completed Program Item Properties dialog box will serve as an icon for a DOS program.

14. Click on the OK command button. The program item Micro Speller with the typewriter icon is added to the Word Processing Group window.

Changing the Properties of Groups and Items

Another way to customize the Program Manager is to change the icon of a program item or change the title of a group or program item. This is called *changing a group's or an item's properties.* Changing properties is appropriate when you find that a group's title is not descriptive enough or an item's icon is not representative enough to make the icon easy to recognize.

EXERCISE 2 • 11   CHANGING GROUP PROPERTIES

1. Minimize the Word Processing group window to an icon.

2. Click on the Word Processing group icon name to display the Control menu. (Make sure you click on the group name, not just on the group icon.)

3. Select the Properties... option from the File menu. The Program Group Properties dialog box will be displayed (Figure 2.45). You change the group name by keying in the new name in the Description text box.

Figure 2.45

Program Group Properties dialog box

Program Group Properties	
Description: Word Processing	OK
Group File: C:\WINDOWS\WORDPROC.GRP	Cancel
	Help

4. Key the new name *Publishing* and click on the OK command button. Notice that the group icon has been renamed.

Just as you can change the properties of a group, you can change the properties of a program item—its name and its icon. For the next exercise, pretend that the Control Panel program is actually a desktop publishing program. We will copy the Control Panel icon to our publishing group and change its properties—its name and its icon.

EXERCISE 2 • 12   CHANGING PROGRAM ITEM PROPERTIES

1. Open the Publishing group window by double-clicking on the Publishing group icon.

2. Copy the Control Panel icon from the Main group to the Publishing group. (Remember: Press and hold [Ctrl] while you drag the icon.)

3. Verify that the Control Panel program is selected in the Publishing group.

4. Select the Properties option from the File menu. The Program Item Properties dialog box is displayed.

5. Key the new description *Easy Publisher* in the Description text box (see Figure 2.46).

6. Click on the Change Icon command button. Notice that only one icon is available in this file.

7. Click on the Browse command button to display a file listing.

8. Scroll the File Name listing box until the file *MORICONS.DLL* is in view.

9. Double-click on the *MORICONS.DLL* filename.

10. Scroll the Icon list box, locate the icon illustrated in the lower left corner in Figure 2.46, and double-click on it.

Figure 2.46

Note the item in the lower left corner of this Program Item Properties dialog box.

11. Click on the OK command button on the Program Item Properties dialog box. The Item Properties are now displayed in the Publishing group window.

Deleting a Program Item and a Group

Program groups are nothing more than a convenient way to organize your Windows desktop. As you learned earlier, you do not have to keep the program groups arranged as they were installed. For example, if you expect to have little use for any of the programs in the Accessories group, you can place those program item icons in their own group and keep the group reduced to an icon at the bottom of the Windows desktop. If you believe you will never use a program, you can remove its icon from the program group and *not* delete it from your hard disk. You can always start any application program that is on your hard disk by using a Run... command from the File menu. So, you can safely remove any unwanted program item icons from the Program Manager without fear of losing access to the program. When you delete an application program or a group of application programs from your system, you should also delete the corresponding program item icons. When you delete a program group, you also delete all the program item icons within that group.

EXERCISE 2 • 13   DELETING A PROGRAM ITEM AND A PROGRAM GROUP

Deleting a Program Item

1. Select the Easy Publisher icon in the Publishing Group window.

2. Select the Delete option from the File menu. The Delete message box will be displayed. Clicking on the Yes command button will activate the command; clicking on the No command button will cancel the command.

3. Click on the Yes command button. The Easy Publisher program item will be removed from the Publishing group window.

Deleting a Group

4. Reduce the Publishing group to an icon.

5. Select the Publishing group by clicking on its icon.

6. Select the Delete option from the File menu. The Delete message box will be displayed.

7. Click on the Yes command button to delete the group. As shown in Figure 2.47, the Publishing group has been deleted.

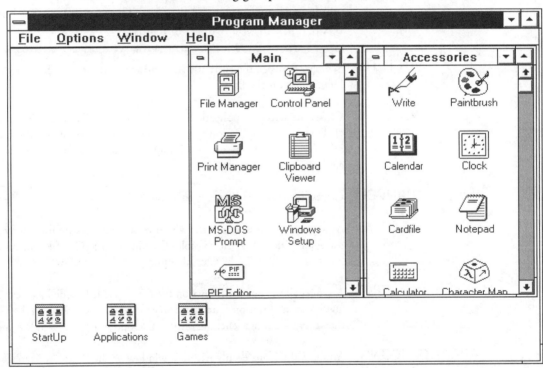

Figure 2.47 This screen shows that the Publishing group has been deleted.

VIEW 3
TASK MANAGER

PREVIEW

Up to now, you have been switching between open windows, arranging items on the desktop, and closing windows using Program Manager menu options.

Figure 2.48

To display this Task List dialog box, double-click on any unoccupied desktop area or press [Ctrl] + [Esc].

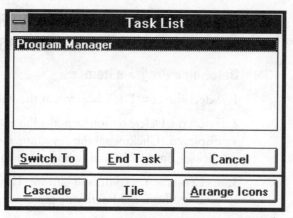

Windows has a built-in feature, the Task Manager, that allows you to perform these tasks quickly and easily. Unlike the Program Manager, the Task Manager does not have its own icon; *it is an integral feature of Windows and is available at all times while Windows is running.* When accessed, the Task Manager displays a Task List dialog box similar to the one illustrated in Figure 2.48. How do you display the Task List dialog box (or Task List, as it is more commonly called)? You can display the Task List by either (1) double-clicking on any area on the Windows desktop that is not already occupied by an icon or a window or (2) pressing [Ctrl]+[Esc].

If you look closely at the Task List shown in Figure 2.48, you will see that the commands and items listed resemble those on the Program Manager's Window menu. At the top of the dialog box is a listing of the currently running applications, with the active application window at the top of the list. Group windows do not show in the Task List. The six buttons at the bottom of the dialog box perform the following commands:

SWITCH TO
: Switches between the currently running applications. The currently active application is highlighted on the list.

END TASK
: Closes the selected application. Clicking on End Task has the same effect as double-clicking on the application's Control-menu box. Clicking on the End Task button is a safe way to exit an application without losing any changes you may have made while the application was running.

CANCEL
: Closes the Task List dialog box.

CASCADE
: Arranges the appearance of the windows on your desktop into an overlapping stack and leaves the title bar of each visible. Clicking on the Cascade button performs the same function as selecting the Cascade option on the Window menu.

TILE
: Arranges all the open windows on the desktop side by side in a clear and accessible way, giving each application equal space on your desktop. Clicking on the Tile button performs the same function as clicking on the Tile option on the Window menu.

ARRANGE ICONS
: Arranges the icons evenly within a window or the Program Manager. Clicking on this button performs the same function as the Arrange Icons option on the Window menu.

When multiple windows are open on your desktop, the one you are working with at the present time is called the **active window**. The active window is easy to recognize because its title bar is a different color or intensity. The active window is always highlighted on the Task List; inactive windows are not highlighted. Using the Task List is a three-step process: (1) display the Task List, (2) select the desired application (if not already selected), and (3) click on one of the command buttons at the bottom of the dialog box. When you are finished working with the Task List, close it by clicking on the Cancel button or clicking anywhere on the Windows desktop.

In the next exercise you will open several program items that are located in the Main and the Accessories groups. You will not be using the features of these applications, so do not worry if you do not understand their functions. These applications will be for illustration purposes only; you will learn to use them in later sessions.

EXERCISE 2 • 14   USING THE TASK MANAGER

Switching Between Application Windows

1. Open the Main and the Accessories windows if they are not already open.

2. Activate the **Calendar** by double-clicking on its icon in the Accessories group. The Calendar window will cover a portion of the Program Manager. (Note: You can use the keyboard shortcut [Alt][Tab] to cycle through the active windows. If you press [Alt][Tab] now, a window will display listing the Program Manager and displaying its icon. When you release the keys, the Program Manager will come to the top with the Calendar window hidden beneath it. Pressing [Alt][Tab] again will display a window listing the Calendar window and its icon; when you release the keys, the Calendar window will be on top.)

3. Press [Alt][Tab] until the Program Manager is listed in a window in the center of the screen; then release the keys.

4. Activate the **Notepad** application from the Accessories group. Don't worry if your screen looks cluttered—we'll rearrange it later.

   Use the [Alt][Tab] shortcut to display the Program Manager.

5. Activate the Print Manager application from the Main group.

6. Minimize the Program Manager.

7. Double-click on a vacant area on the desktop to display the Task List dialog box. Be careful not to click on an icon or any open window! If you do not have a vacant space on your desktop, use the keyboard shortcut [Ctrl]+[Esc]. The currently active application will appear in the Task List dialog box, listed at the top, with other currently running applications listed in the order in which they were activated.

8. Click on Notepad on the Task List to highlight it, then click on the Switch To command button. The Task List will close and the Notepad application window will come to the front as the active window on your screen.

9. Display the Task List by double-clicking on a vacant area on the desktop, select Calendar, then click on the Switch To command button. Again, the Task List will close and the Calendar application window will display as the active open window on the desktop.

10. Display the Task List.

11. Click on Print Manager, then click on the Switch To command button. The Print Manager application window will be displayed as the active window.

Arranging Application Windows

12. Display the Task List, then click on the Tile command button. The three open windows (Notepad, Calendar, and Print Manager) will be displayed in a tiled format with Print Manager as the active window.

Closing an Application Window

13. Display the Task List, click on Calendar, then click on the End Task command button. The Calendar window will close.

Rearranging the Icons

14. Display the Task List, then click on the Arrange Icons command button. You may not notice any difference if your icons were already arranged neatly.

15. Close all open applications using the Task List. Program Manager should remain open.

16. Restore the Program Manager.

VIEW 4
RUNNING APPLICATIONS

PREVIEW

Earlier you learned to manipulate group windows and program item icons. Now you will learn how to use these windows and icons to start or *run* your application programs.

There are two ways you can start an application—directly and indirectly.

• You start an application directly by clicking on the program item icon or by keying in the WIN command followed by the application name when you start Windows from the DOS prompt.

• You start an application indirectly by using the Run... command on the File menu.

EXERCISE 2 • 15 STARTING AN APPLICATION DIRECTLY

You can start an application directly in one of two ways: (1) from the DOS prompt or (2) from the Program Manager. You can exit to DOS from the Program Manager; however, in the following exercise, you will Exit Windows so that you can simulate how to start a program directly—without Windows running.

Exiting Windows

Program Manager remains running in the background while you run applications. Thus, you do not quit Program Manager until you are ready to quit Windows, and then you do so as follows: (1) Exit all applications that are running, (2) select Exit Windows from Program Manager's File menu, and when the Exit Windows message box appears, (3) click on OK to end this Windows sessions.

(Remember: If you want to save the arrangement of the Program Manager's group windows and icons, open the Options menu and make sure that Save Settings on Exit is checked. This means that the next time you start Windows, the Program Manager workspace will look identical to when you last used it. Everything you have done during your last work session will be permanently saved until you make more changes to the Program Manager workspace and save your settings again.)

Starting an Application Directly from the DOS Prompt

1. Display the Options menu on the Program Manager window and verify that the Save Settings on Exit option on the Options menu is unchecked.

2. Choose Exit Windows on the File menu. When the dialog box appears, click on OK to return to the system DOS prompt (usually C:>).

3. Key the command *WIN*, space once, key the application name *Write*, and press [Enter]. Your command should look like this: C:>WIN WRITE[Enter].

   You will see the Write application program, as shown in Figure 2.49. You will learn to use this application later. For now, just close the application.

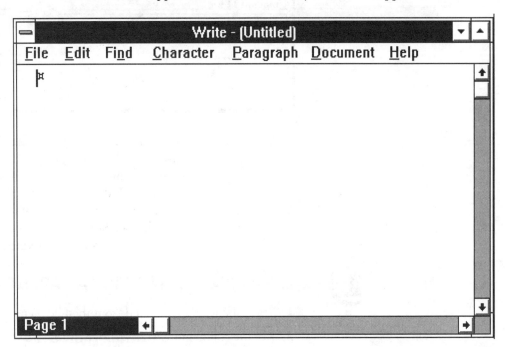

Figure 2.49 Opening screen for Windows Write

4. Select the Exit command from the File menu. You should always select the Exit command because Exit will prompt you about saving your work (if you have started a document) before you issue the Close command. Once the application is closed, you will be returned to the Program Manager.

5. Double-click on the Program Manager icon to open it, if it is not already opened.

6. Double-click on the Accessories group icon to open the Accessories group window.

Starting an Application Directly from the Program Manager

7. Double-click on the Write program icon in the Accessories window. The application will begin as before.

8. Select the Exit command from the File menu. The application will be closed, and you will be returned to the Program Manager.

Starting an Application Indirectly

You can start any application from the Program Manager, whether it has an icon or not. The Run... command on the File menu allows you to start an application indirectly by giving the Program Manager the details it needs to execute the command. For example, if you want to use a program you do not work with very often, a program you did not bother adding to a group window, you can start it indirectly by selecting the Run... command, which brings up the Run dialog box, shown in Figure 2.50.

Figure 2.50

Run dialog box

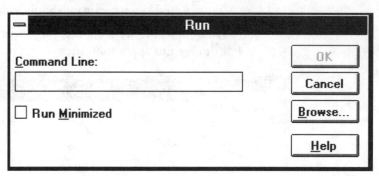

When you use the Run... command, you need to know (1) where the application program is saved on the hard disk (the path) and (2) the command that starts the application. For example, if you have installed the Write program in the C:\WINDOWS directory and the command that starts the application is WRITE.EXE, you would key *C:\WINDOWS\WRITE.EXE* in the Command Line text box. When you click on the OK command button, your application will run. When you exit the application, you will be returned to the Program Manager.

EXERCISE 2 • 16   RUNNING AN APPLICATION INDIRECTLY

1. Select the Run... command from the File menu.

2. Key the command *C:\WINDOWS\WRITE.EXE* (or key the correct path for your system) in the Command Line text box and press [Enter]. Again, the Write program is opened.

3. Select the Exit command from the File menu. The application will be closed, and you will be returned to the Program Manager.

SUMMARY

In this Session you learned the purpose and function of the Program Manager and learned about several programs in the Main group window that help you manage the Windows environment. You practiced organizing group windows and application program icons. You also customized the Program Manager by copying, moving, and adding program icons and group windows. You learned about one of the strengths of Windows when you switched between groups and created a new group window.

The ability to minimize, maximize and restore group windows became clearer while doing the exercises in Session 2, as did arranging windows and group items, and deleting program items and a group. Finally, you learned how to start and quit an application, and exit Windows.

OBJECTIVES

When you complete this session, you will be able to:

- Explain the use of the Windows Control Panel.

- Describe the Control Panel menu bar and explain its two options.

- Identify the Control Panel icons and explain the general purpose of each.

- Change the Windows color scheme.

- Change the desktop wallpaper.

- Switch between running applications.

- Use the screen saver.

SESSION 3 *THE CONTROL PANEL*

57

THE CONTROL PANEL

VIEW 1
WORKING WITH THE CONTROL PANEL

PREVIEW

The more you use Windows, the more you realize how its *graphical user interface* provides a desktop environment complete with icons, color, sound, and a mouse. But this environment is not static. You can change it to suit your taste or needs! How? By using the *Control Panel.*

The Control Panel contains built-in tools to give you *control* of the way Windows looks, feels, and sounds. These tools permit you to customize both the desktop environment and several of your system's original hardware and software settings. Windows implements Control Panel changes immediately, without requiring you to reboot (turn your computer off and start it up again), unlike most other software programs.

The Control Panel is located in the Main program group. You start the Control Panel by double-clicking on the Control Panel icon.

NOTE: Do not confuse the Control Panel with the Control-menu box found in the upper left corner of every window. If you have forgotten what the Control-menu box looks like, refer back to Figure 1.1.

When you start Control Panel, you will see a Control Panel window such as the one shown in Figure 3.1. The number and types of icons in your Control Panel window may vary, depending on several factors:

If your system is on a network, you will see a network icon.

If Windows is running in the 386-Enhanced mode, you will see the 386 Enhanced Icon (shown in Figure 3.1).

If you have any multimedia devices in your system, you will see additional icons.

Figure 3.1

This Control Panel window includes the 386 Enhanced icon.

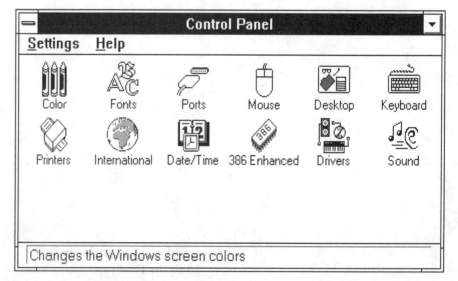

EXERCISE 3 • 1   STARTING THE CONTROL PANEL

1. Launch Windows if it is not running.

2. Open the Main group if it is not currently open.

3. Double-click on the Control Panel icon to display the Control Panel window. A Control Panel window similar to the one in Figure 3.1 is displayed on your screen.

Looking at the Control Panel Window

A quick glance at the Control Panel window in Figure 3.1 shows that it is similar to other windows. It incorporates the Windows elements that you have seen in other windows: a menu bar, a title bar, the Control-menu box, a minimize button, and icons.

The Control Panel Menu Bar

A closer look shows that the Control Panel menu bar contains only two items—Settings and Help. The Help menu is typical of other Help menus. The Settings menu, illustrated in Figure 3.2, lists the name of each Control Panel icon. You can access any of the Control Panel items by (1) double-clicking on an icon, or (2) selecting the item name from the Settings menu.

Figure 3.2

Use the settings menu to access any of the Control Panel icons.

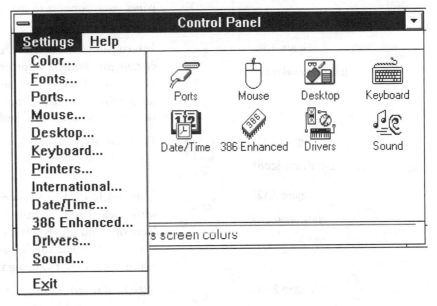

The Control Panel Icons

Each icon in the Control Panel enables you to customize one particular aspect of Windows. Look at the illustration of each icon as you read its purpose and use.

Figure 3.3

Color icon

Color Icon. This icon sets the color scheme of nearly every Windows screen element on your desktop. Not happy with the color combinations you see on screen? Create your own combinations instead!

Figure 3.4

Fonts icon

Fonts Icon. The Fonts icon permits you to add or remove fonts. A *font* is the complete set of characters for a particular typeface. Which font do you want Windows to use to display text on your screen? To print text on your printer?

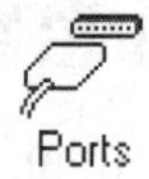

Figure 3.5

Ports icon

Ports Icon. A *port* is a physical connection between your computer and a printer or a communicating device. Serial ports and parallel ports are the two types of ports that are available. The difference between the two is in the method used to transfer information across the port. The Ports icon permits you to configure serial ports. (Your computer probably has at least one serial port.)

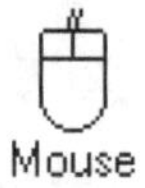

Figure 3.6

Mouse icon

Mouse Icon. The Mouse icon permits you to tailor the way your mouse performs under Windows. You can adjust the speed of the mouse's movement across the screen as well as the speed of the double-clicking action. You can also switch the functions of the left and right buttons.

Figure 3.7

Desktop icon

Desktop Icon. This icon changes the appearance of the outermost Windows screen. It also changes the appearance of the icons and their titles and allows you to adjust their alignment on the desktop. The Desktop icon also lets you set the speed at which the cursor blinks.

Figure 3.8

Keyboard icon

Keyboard Icon. The Keyboard icon adjusts the speed settings for the "typematic" (repeating) keys.

Figure 3.9

Printers icon

Printers Icon. This icon lets you use Print Manager, add or remove a printer, assign ports, specify graphics resolution, choose paper sizes, connect to network printers, and choose the default printer.

Figure 3.10

International icon

International Icon. You use the International icon to tailor your system for use in a number of different countries. Using the International Icon, you can set a different currency symbol, format times and dates, choose between the metric or the English system of measurement, and otherwise tailor your system.

Figure 3.11

Date/Time icon

Date/Time Icon. This icon enables you to set the date and time that will be displayed by the system.

Figure 3.12

Network icon

Network Icon. The Network icon lets you control how Windows works when it is installed on a network. For example, the Network Icon allows you to control how users sign on and off and lets you change a user's password. This icon appears only if Windows is told it is being used on a network.

Figure 3.13

386 Enhanced icon

386 Enhanced Icon. This icon allows you to adjust how programs work with Windows in an Enhanced mode, that is, if you are running Windows on an Intel 80*386*-based computer. This icon will only appear if Windows itself is operating in the Enhanced 386 mode.

Figure 3.14

Drivers icon

Drivers Icon. The Drivers icon allows you to install and configure drivers for optional services such as a pen tablet or a sound card.

Figure 3.15

MIDI Mapper icon

MIDI Mapper Icon. *MIDI* is an acronym for *Musical Instrument Digital Interface*, which is a set of rules that allows musical instruments and computers to communicate. If you have a MIDI device or a sound card, you can add, configure, or remove sounds.

Sound

Sound Icon. When the computer senses an error, the sound icon turns the beep or sound on and off. If your computer is equipped with a sound board, you can set Windows to respond to various mouse or keyboard actions with selected, prerecorded sound files.

This session covers the Control Panel programs that are common to most computer systems. Later you will see how Control Panel allows you to control hardware settings. First, however, you will see how Control Panel lets you control *appearance*--specifically, how it allows you to control the colors displayed on the screen and customize the items appearing on the desktop.

Controlling Color

One of the first things you notice about the Windows environment is its use of colors (or shades if you have a monochrome monitor). Windows' color scheme features were designed to be used with a color VGA (or better) monitor. So far, you have "accepted" the color scheme as it appears on your screen; however, you have complete control over your monitor's color scheme.

Using the Color option, you can set a color scheme by (1) selecting from a set of predefined schemes or (2) creating your own color scheme. When you select the Color icon, the Color dialog box (shown in Figure 3.17) is displayed. In the center of the dialog box is a sample window with most of the window elements displayed in their selected color. The various colors in this sample box make up a **color scheme**. The name of the color scheme currently displayed is highlighted in the Color Schemes list box. For example, the color scheme used in Figure 3.17 is called *Practice*.

Figure 3.17

In this Color dialog box, note that the Color Schemes text box shows the name *Practice*.

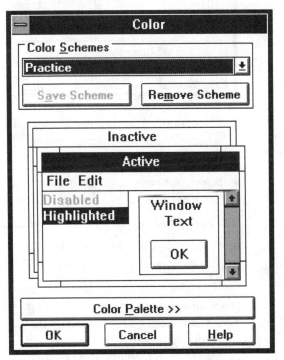

Using a Predefined Color Scheme. If you wish, you can change the color scheme currently displayed on your screen without taking the time to create a custom one. Instead, just select from a list of **predefined color schemes**.

To access a list of predefined color schemes, click on the down arrow to the right of the Color Schemes list box. As you click on a name on the list, that color scheme is displayed in the sample window. This way, you can review the selections available. When you make your choice, click on the OK command button and your selection will become the new default color scheme.

EXERCISE 3 . 2   USING A PREDEFINED COLOR SCHEME

1. Double-click on the Color icon to display the Color dialog box.

2. Click on the down arrow to the right of the Color Schemes list box and scroll, if necessary, to bring the Arizona color scheme into view (Figure 3.18).

Figure 3.18

In this Color dialog box, the Arizona color scheme is selected in the Color Schemes list box.

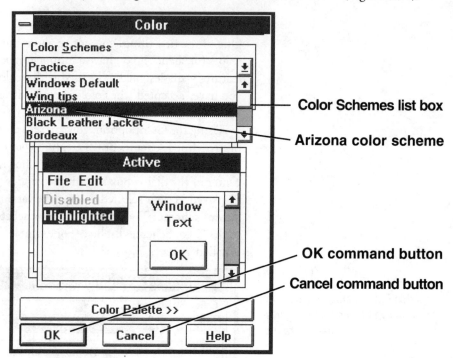

3. Click on the Arizona color scheme. Take some time to study the new color scheme. While this color scheme will display in the sample window, it will not take effect unless you click on the OK command button.

4. Select a different color scheme from the Color Scheme list box (use the up and down arrows to scroll through the list).

5. Continue to sample the predefined color schemes, then go to Step 6.

6. Click on the Cancel command button. This action will close the Color Scheme dialog box and return the window display to its default color scheme.

Creating a New Color Scheme. If you do not find a predefined color scheme you want to use, you can use the color palette to create your own custom scheme. To access the color palette, click on the Color Palette >> command button. The Color dialog box will enlarge and will show a color palette editor with three sections (Screen Element, Basic Colors, and Custom Colors), as shown in Figure 3.19.

Changing a color scheme is a two-step process: (1) select a screen element whose color you want to change, then (2) select a color. The simplest way to select a screen element is to click on that element in the sample window. However, if you know the element's name, you can select the element from the Screen Element

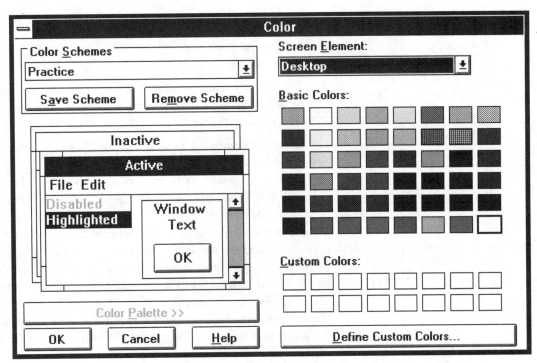

Figure 3.19 The color palette editor is opened in this Color dialog box.

drop-down list box in the upper-right corner of the Color window. The change is immediate; you can see it in the sample window.

After you "color" your screen elements, either (1) click on the OK command button to implement your color scheme without saving it to disk, or (2) click on the Save Scheme command button to save the color scheme and return to the former color scheme.

EXERCISE 3 • 3   CREATING A NEW COLOR SCHEME

This exercise assumes that you have a color monitor. If you have a monochrome monitor, select a shade or pattern in place of a color.

One quick way to develop a new color scheme is to select a predefined color scheme that is similar to what you like, then change that scheme to suit your taste.

1. Open the Control Panel if it is not already opened.

2. Double-click on the Color icon, then click on the Color Palette >> button to display the color palette editor (Figure 3.19).

3. Click on the down arrow in the Screen Element list box, then scroll down the element list until the Active Title Bar element appears. Select the Active Title Bar element. If you look closely at the Basic Colors palette, you will see that the active color is outlined with a thick black rule.

4. Click on a color other than the current color. The selected color will become outlined (it is now the active color), and the screen element will display in this color in the sample window.

5. Click on Inactive Title Bar in the sample window. Note that the name of the screen element changes in the Screen Element box when the Inactive Title Bar is clicked.

6. Click on a second color of your choice on the Basic Colors palette.

7. Continue selecting screen elements and colors until you have a pleasing color scheme.

8. Click on the Cancel command button. When you leave the Color window, you will be returned to the Control Panel window, which will revert to the original color scheme.

Saving or Removing a Color Scheme. When you change a screen element's color, you must either (1) click on the OK command button to use the color scheme on a temporary basis or (2) click on the Save Scheme button to save the color scheme. You can save a color scheme with or without a name.

To save the color scheme *with a name*, select the Save Scheme button, then key a name in the text box of the Save Scheme dialog box that appears. A prompt appears asking for a name to assign to the new color scheme. The name can be up to 32 characters long, and you can use any character (including spaces) in the name. If you click on the OK command button after saving your color scheme, the color scheme will take affect. If you click on the Cancel command button, the color scheme will be *saved*, but the previous color scheme will remain *displayed*.

When you select the OK command button, the color scheme settings are stored on the hard disk as the new default color scheme. As a result, the next time you launch Windows, the new color scheme will display.

EXERCISE 3 • 4   SAVING AND REMOVING A COLOR SCHEME

1. Double-click on the Color icon.

2. Click on the Color Palette >> button to display the color palette editor.

3. Save the current color scheme using the name *Current Colors*.

   a. Click on the Save Scheme command button.

   b. Key the Color Scheme name, Current Colors, in the Save Scheme dialog text box.

   c. Click on the OK command button.

4. Select the Rugby color scheme from the Color Schemes list box.

5. Make the following changes to the Rugby color scheme:

   a. Change the Active Border to red.

   b. Change the Application workspace to blue (select a shade of blue other than the one used by the Active Title Bar).

   c. Change the Desktop to blue (select a shade of blue not already used).

   The color scheme sample should have only red, white, and blue elements while the text remains black.

6. Click on the Save Scheme command button. The Save Scheme dialog box will display with the current scheme name, Rugby, highlighted.

7. Key the name *Fourth of July* in the Save Scheme text box as illustrated in Figure 3.20, then click on the OK command button.

Figure 3.20

The Save Scheme dialog box
shows a new color scheme, Fourth
of July, keyed in the text box.

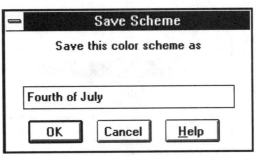

Figure 3.20

The Save Scheme dialog box
shows a new color scheme, Fourth
of July, keyed in the text box.

Once you have saved your new color scheme, you have the option to use it immediately or continue using the former color scheme. If you click on the OK command button, you will invoke the new color scheme; if you click on the Cancel command button, you will close the Color Palette and use the former color scheme.

8. Click on the OK command button. Your screen elements should now display using your Fourth of July color scheme.

Removing a color scheme is easy: Simply select the color scheme to be deleted from the Color Schemes list box and click on the Remove Scheme command button. Of course, if you are currently using the color scheme, you must select another before exiting the Color dialog box.

9. Remove the Fourth of July color scheme from the Color Schemes list box.

   a. Double-click on the Color icon.

   b. Verify that Fourth of July is selected on the Color Scheme list box.

   c. Click on the Remove Scheme button.

   d. Click on the Yes command button in the message box (Figure 3.21) that appears.

Figure 3.21

This Control Panel message box
asks if you want to remove the
Fourth of July color scheme.

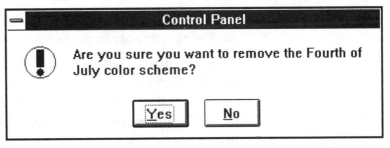

10. Select the Current Colors color scheme from the Color Schemes list box, then click on the OK command button.

VIEW 2

CUSTOMIZING THE DESKTOP

PREVIEW

Windows applications run on the **desktop**, and Windows icons rest on the **desktop**. When you install Windows, the original desktop you see is rather plain, but you can customize it to suit your personal tastes! You customize, of course, using the Control Panel.

Selecting Control Panel's Desktop option displays the dialog box shown in Figure 3.22. The Desktop dialog box has seven option sections you can use to change the appearance and the behavior of your desktop:

Figure 3.22

The Desktop dialog box allows you
to adjust seven desktop settings:
Pattern, Applications, Screen
Saver, Wallpaper, Icons, Sizing
Grid, and Cursor Blink Rate.

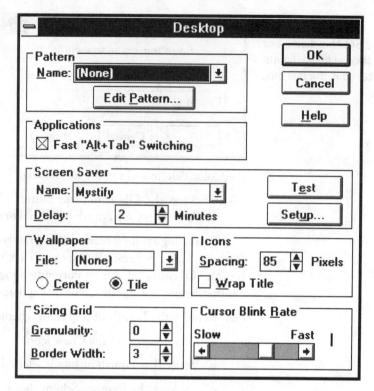

- The **Pattern** section permits you to place a background pattern on your desktop. You can use one of the patterns that comes with Windows or create one of your own.

- The **Applications** check box allows you to select a "fast" method of scrolling the active applications while Windows is running.

- The **Screen Saver** section allows you to prevent screen burn-in by permitting you to display a moving graphic or blank screen while your computer system is on and you are not actively using it.

- The **Wallpaper** section allows you to place an image on top of a background pattern. You can use one of the graphics that comes with Windows or create one using a program such as Paintbrush.

- The **Icons** section allows you to set the amount of space between icons and display long titles under icons.

- The **Sizing Grid** section has two features: (1) The **granularity** setting activates an invisible set of grid lines. Objects placed or moved on the screen automatically align with one of the invisible grid lines. (2) The **Border Width** setting determines the thickness of most window borders.

- The **Cursor Blink Rate** controls the speed that the on-screen cursor line flashes within the various applications.

Setting the Background Pattern

When Windows is first installed, your desktop has no background pattern; your desktop is a solid color. However, you can change the desktop to a predefined background pattern, create your own background pattern, or use a graphic file created by a paint program.

Selecting a Predefined Background Pattern. Windows provides *predefined background patterns*, available on the Pattern Name drop-down list. You simply scroll through the list and select one of the patterns listed, then click on the OK button. If you want to see the patterns before applying any of them, start by clicking on the Edit Pattern button. You will get the Edit Pattern dialog box, which is shown in Figure 3.23. As you scroll the list, you will see a sample of each in the sample window. Clicking on the OK command button twice—once in the Edit Pattern dialog box, and once in the Desktop dialog box—will place the pattern on the your desktop.

Figure 3.23

This Edit Pattern dialog box displays the Boxes desktop pattern.

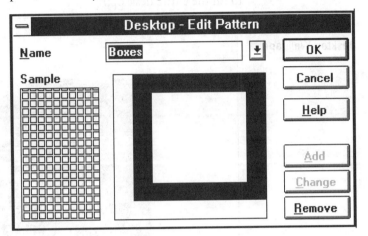

EXERCISE 3 . 5   SELECTING A PREDEFINED BACKGROUND PATTERN

Since a background pattern lies behind all open windows, in order to see the results of this exercise, you must minimize all windows except the Control Panel window.

1. Open the Control Panel window if it is not already opened.

2. Minimize all windows except the Control Panel window.

3. Double-click on the Desktop icon to display the Desktop dialog box as shown in Figure 3.22.

4. Select the Boxes background pattern:

   a. Write the name of the pattern currently listed in the Pattern Name box.

   b. Click on the down arrow to the right of the Pattern Name drop-down list box to display a list of stored patterns.

   c. Click on the pattern you would like to use. In this case, click on Boxes.

   d. Click on the OK command button. After you view the effect of the boxes background, go to step 5.

5. Repeat Steps 3 and 4 above to select the Weave background pattern.

NOTE: With dark desktop colors certain patterns may not be visible.

6. Repeat Steps 2 through 4. This time, select the pattern you wrote in Step 4a.

Hanging Desktop Wallpaper

The Desktop Wallpaper option allows you to place drawings (graphic files) on the desktop background. You can select from the graphic files that come with the Windows program, or you can create your own. Any bitmapped (.BMP) graphic file can be used as a wallpaper. If you create your own or have a favorite graphic file you wish to use, you can bring it into the Paintbrush program in Windows and save it as a .BMP file. (This process will be discussed more in a later session.) A wallpaper can be centered on the desktop, as in Figure 3.24, or it can be tiled to fill the entire desktop.

Figure 3.24

Desktop Wallpaper

EXERCISE 3 • 6   HANGING DESKTOP WALLPAPER

1. Double-click on the Desktop icon.

2. Select the Paper wallpaper:

   a. Click the down arrow in the Wallpaper drop-down list box to display a list of available graphic files.

   b. Click on the PAPER.BMP file. By default, Windows centers the wallpaper file (the Center button is highlighted). Accept this default.

3. Click on the OK command button to "hang" the wallpaper (see Figure 3.24). (Hint: You may need to minimize all of the windows on your screen in order to see the wallpaper.)

Notice that the wallpaper is centered on the desktop. If you have selected a background pattern, the background pattern fills the area of the desktop not covered by the wallpaper. Now see what wallpaper looks like when it is tiled to fill the desktop area.

4. Open the Desktop application.

5. Change the wallpaper to Zigzag and tile the wallpaper to fill the desktop area:

   a. Click on the down arrow button in the Wallpaper drop-down list box and select the ZIGZAG.BMP file.

   b. Click on the Tile button to select it.

   c. Click on the OK command button to "hang" the wallpaper.

   The Zigzag wallpaper now covers the entire desktop. If you look closely at the desktop, you will see that the graphic has been duplicated enough times to fill the area.

6. Reset the wallpaper to None:

   a. Click on the Desktop icon to open the application.

   b. Click on the down arrow button in the Wallpaper drop-down list box and select [None].

   c. Click on the OK command button.

   Keep in mind that a wallpaper background takes up memory. If you want to use your computer's memory to its best advantage, do not use a wallpaper desktop.

Other Desktop Custom Options

The Desktop dialog box allows you to customize three additional desktop features: the cursor blink rate, the icon spacing, and the sizing grid.

The Cursor Blink Rate. The Cursor Blink Rate option adjusts the speed at which the cursor blinks. The cursor blink rate has no effect on the operation of any Windows program; it is an individual preference.

Icon Spacing. The Icon Spacing feature regulates how closely icons will be placed together on the desktop. If you think your program item icons are too crowded in an application window or at the bottom of the desktop when you minimize a window, you can move the icons farther apart by increasing the number in the Icon Spacing box. The value in this box specifies the width of each icon. The space between icons is determined by the number of pixels (screen dots) that separate them. The largest value you can enter, 512, will place one icon on a line. The smallest value depends on the monitor you are using. For example, on a VGA monitor, the minimum value is 32, which will place the icons next to each other without any space between them. In addition, you can reduce the spacing required by each icon even more by checking the Wrap Title box. This will cause the title of the icon to wrap to the next line, thereby reducing the amount of horizontal space used by the icon.

Sizing Grid. The sizing grid has two features: **granularity** and **border width**. The Granularity value controls the spacing of an invisible set of grid lines that help control the positioning and alignment of certain windows on the desktop. Any value greater than zero turns the grid lines on. With grid lines turned on or set to a number greater than zero, whenever you size or move application windows or application icons that appear at the bottom of your screen, the windows or icons automatically snap into place to the nearest "invisible" grid line. The smaller the number you have set, the smaller increments you can move; the larger the number set, the bigger the jump from one location to another.

Window borders can be enlarged or reduced to make more or less room for your desktop by keying a value in the Border Width text box. Again, this value is measured in pixels, and increasing or decreasing the number will change the size of the borders. You can adjust the border width of all windows on your desktop except fixed-size windows, such as most dialog and message boxes. To use the Border Width feature, click on the up or down arrows in the Border Width text box in the Desktop dialog box.

Using Screen Saver

Screen saver programs were written to protect monitors. Because of the way the image is projected on the screen, a screen image can be permanently "burned" on the screen—quite distracting! You can see the image even when the screen is turned off.

Here is how screen saver programs work. You specify a period of time at the end of which the screen should change to a blank screen or a moving image (moving images will not burn into the screen and they are fun!). If, during this time, you do not move the mouse or press a key, the screen saver takes over the display. As soon as you touch a key or move the mouse, the original screen returns. Figure 3.25 shows a screen with the Mystify screen saver active.

Windows provides several different screen savers:

<u>Screen Saver</u>	<u>Image Displayed</u>
Blank Screen	A blank screen.
Flying Windows	Various sizes of the Windows logo in different colors.
Marquee	A text message of your choice.
Mystify	Random shapes created with a combination of lines (see Figure 3.25).
Starfield Simulation	A simulation of flight through a starfield.

Figure 3.25

The Mystify screen saver is running while the system is on but not in use.

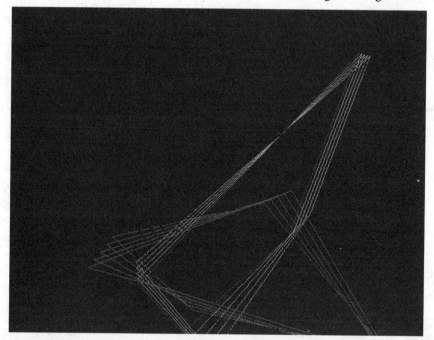

To select a screen saver, open the Screen Saver drop-down list box and make your choice. The Delay option lets you specify the amount of time that must elapse without mouse or keyboard movement before the screen saver begins. To change the delay, click on the up or down arrow to increase or decrease the amount of time, or key the desired delay time in minutes. You may enter from 0 to 99 minutes.

Three of the screen savers, Marquee, Mystify, and Starfield Simulation, can be customized; each has its own Setup dialog box. In the following exercise the Marquee Setup dialog box (Figure 3.26) is used as an example of how these three screen savers can be customized.

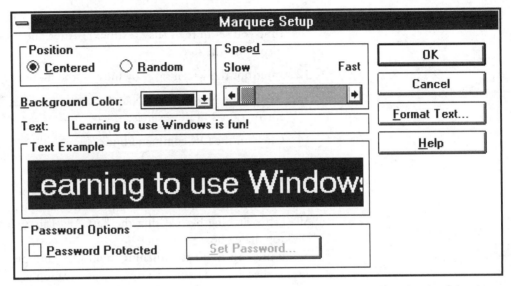

Figure 3.26 You can customize the Marquee screen saver by selecting from the options available in the Marquee Setup dialog box.

EXERCISE 3 • 7   CUSTOMIZING AND TESTING THE MARQUEE SCREEN SAVER

1. Open the Desktop application if it is not already opened.

2. Write the name shown in the Screen Saver Name text box.

3. Select the Marquee screen saver and click on the Setup command button to display the Marquee Setup dialog box shown in Figure 3.26. Watch the Text Example box; it illustrates the results of your selections.

4. Click on the Centered button in the Position section. (If you want the text to scroll at random heights from the bottom of the screen, you would click on the Random button.)

5. Move the Scroll box on the Speed scroll bar to the middle of the scroll bar.

6. Click on the Background Color drop-down list box and select Black.

7. Key the text *Learning to use Windows is fun!* in the text box. The Text Sample box will display your text as you key it in.

8. Click on the Format Text command button and make the following settings in the Format Text dialog box, then click on the OK command button.

Font: MS Serif
Font Style: Italic
Size: 24
Color: Fuchsia

When you return to the Marquee Setup dialog box, you will see the results of your format changes in Text Example box.

9. Click on the OK command button to return to the Desktop dialog box.

10. Double-click in the Delay text box in the screen saver Delay text box and key the number *1*, then click on the OK command button.

11. Sit back and do not touch the keyboard or mouse for at least one minute (the time you set in the Delay text box). After one minute, your marquee will display on the screen.

12. Interrupt the screen saver by moving the mouse or pressing a key.

13. Return the Screen Saver Name to its original setting as it was written in Instruction 2 of this exercise.

14. Click on the OK command button.

Switching Between Running Applications

Want a quick method of switching between running applications? Enable Fast Alt+Tab switching by selecting the Fast Alt+Tab Switching check box in the Desktop dialog box.

To use Fast Alt+Tab switching, hold [Alt] and press [Tab]. Windows will display the icon and name of a running application in a window in the middle of the screen (Figure 3.27). While still holding down [Alt], press [Tab] again and the icon and name of the next running application appears. Continue until the window shows the application you want to switch to, then release [Alt]. The selected application window will become the active window.

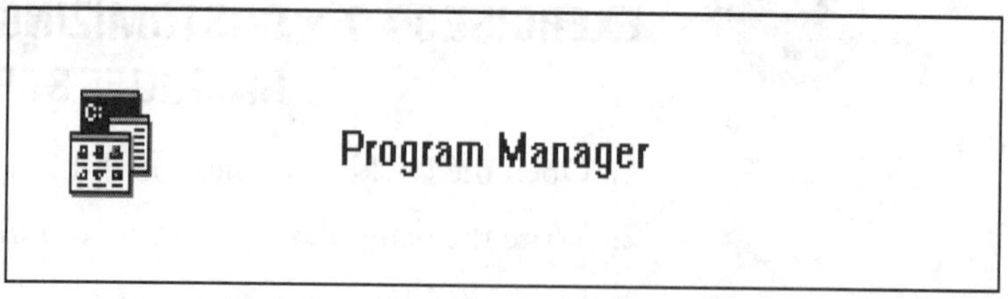

Figure 3.27

When you enable Alt+Tab Switching, you can quickly switch to a selected application by holding [Alt] while pressing [Tab].

 Program Manager

EXERCISE 3 • 8   USING FAST ALT+TAB SWITCHING

To see the real benefit of the Fast Alt+Tab Switching feature, you need to have several applications running. In the following exercise, you will launch several applications (You will learn more about how to use the applications later in this text.)

1. Open the Desktop application if it is not currently running.

2. Verify that the Fast Alt+Tab check box is selected (checked). If it is not checked, click on the box to select it.

3. Click on the OK command button to close the Desktop application.

4. Hold [Alt] and press [Tab] until the Program Manager icon and name appear in a window similar to the one shown in Figure 3.27, then release [Alt]. The Program Manager will become active and will be displayed on the screen.

5. Launch the following applications by double-clicking on their icons in the Accessories window:

   Paintbrush
   Write
   Calculator

6. Switch to the Program Manager application by holding down [Alt] and pressing [Tab] until the Program Manager icon and name appears in a window in the center of the screen.

7. Switch to each of the following applications in the order listed. Do not switch until you have each application active on the screen.

   Paintbrush
   Calculator
   Write
   Program Manager

8. Switch to each of the following applications and double-click on its Control-menu box to close the application. When you are finished, only the Program Manager and the Control Panel should be open.

   Paintbrush
   Write
   Calculator

9. Make the Control Panel active and minimize the Program Manager application.

VIEW 3
CUSTOMIZING PRINTER SETTINGS

PREVIEW

One key area in which Control Panel lets you customize Windows is printer settings. You can use Windows with most printers, but first you must install the printer and make some printer settings in Windows, called **configuring** the printer.

Configuring a printer may be as simple as selecting a name from a list of available printers. On the other hand, the installation may be more complex for an additional printer. You will be working with printers that have already been installed.

Selecting the Active and Default Printer

Windows provides a Printers icon for adding a printer, choosing an installed printer, and changing the settings on an already-installed printer. Double-clicking on the Printers icon in the Control Panel will display the Printers dialog box (Figure 3.28) in which these settings are made.

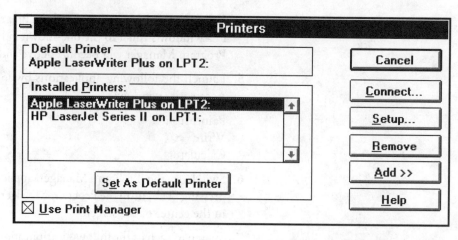

Figure 3.28

The Printers dialog box is used to
add and configure printers for use
with Windows.

Selecting the Active Printer. As you see in Figure 3.28, Windows can have multiple available printers. However, only one printer can be active at a time. To make an inactive printer active, you must click on the printer you wish to be active.

EXERCISE 3.9   SELECTING THE ACTIVE PRINTER

1. Double-click on the Printers icon to display the Printers dialog box.
2. Click on the printer you wish to make the active printer. (If you have only one printer, click on this printer—it will not change anything, but you will see how the process works.)
3. Click on the Cancel command button (if you do not have a Cancel command button, click on the Close command button).

Changing the Default Printer. Windows will automatically use one printer it calls the default printer. Each time you launch Windows, the default printer is the active printer. Whenever you need to change the default printer, just double-click on the printer name in the Printers list box, then click on Close. That is all there is to it!

EXERCISE 3.10   CHANGING THE DEFAULT PRINTER

1. Double-click on the Printers icon to display the Printers dialog box.
2. Write the name of the printer currently listed as the default printer.
3. Click on a printer name that is not highlighted (if you have more than one printer) to make it the default printer, then click on the Set As Default Printer button. Unless you specify otherwise, anything you send to the printer will be directed to the default printer.
4. Click on the Close command button.
5. Open the Printers dialog box and set the default printer back to its original setting (if necessary, refer to the name of the printer you wrote in Step 2).
6. Click on the Close command button.

SUMMARY

In this session you learned how to use the Control Panel, which provides capabilities different from most of the other Windows applications. The Control Panel allows you to customize Windows by changing the default settings, the settings originally set by the software developer, and therefore control the Windows environment.

You learned that the Control Panel gives you an easy way to: change the color scheme, change the icon spacing, and increase or decrease the window border widths. In addition, the Control Panel provides access to the Screen Saver utility, and even lets you incorporate a personal message into the Marquee screen saver.

The Control Panel also provides a means to customize other aspects of your Windows environment, such as the mouse speed, keyboard repeat rate, fonts, printer connectors, and so on. The Control Panel does indeed let you *control* your environment!

• • • • • • • • • • • • • •

OBJECTIVES

When you complete this session, you will be able to:

- Start and exit File Manager and explain its purpose and function.
- Expand and collapse the Directory Tree.
- Open and close a directory window.
- Format and label disks.
- Create directories and subdirectories.
- Search a directory or a disk.
- Search by using wildcard characters.
- Select and deselect files.

SESSION 4 *FILE MANAGER PART I*

VIEWS
Understanding the File Manager
Working with Disks and Disk Drives
Creating Directories and Subdirectories

FILE MANAGER PART I

UNDERSTANDING THE FILE MANAGER

PREVIEW

In order to understand the File Manager, you must understand something about computer memory and storage. Your computer manipulates and processes data in electronic memory called **RAM** (**R**andom **A**ccess **M**emory). The application programs and contents of the documents you use in Windows reside in RAM when they are active. When you exit a program, turn your computer off, or lose power to your computer, the content of RAM is erased.

The two drawbacks of electronic memory are that (1) it is limited in size and (2) it is erased when the power is turned off. For these reasons, magnetic storage is used to save application programs and data documents for extended periods or when the computer is not in operation. Magnetic storage may be in the form of a hard disk inside your computer or as an external floppy disk.

Think of a disk as a kind of electronic file cabinet. The files in this electronic file cabinet are the program instructions or data documents saved on the disk. Thus, computer files are categorized as program files or data files. While file cabinets have drawers and folders to help organize their contents, computer disks rely on **directories** and **subdirectories** to organize their magnetic files.

Figure 4.1

File Manager icon

File Manager

The File Manager is designed to help you find, view, manage, and use your files easily and efficiently. That is why the File Manager icon is a file cabinet (Figure 4.1). With the File Manager, you are able to get a graphic view of your disk's contents. It shows you all the directories and how they relate to each other in a window known as the **directory window**. In addition, you can view the contents of multiple directories at the same time. You can even change the type and amount of directory information that is displayed.

Starting File Manager

When you start File Manager, you see a window with the familiar title bar, menu bar, and status bar (see Figure 4.2.). The menu bar is used to select menu options. The status bar at the bottom of the screen tells you how much space is available on your disk and offers other information as well.

As you see in Figure 4.2, a second window within the File Manager window—the directory window—appears. The directory window helps you see the contents of directories and subdirectories by giving you a graphic view of the disk's contents. The directory window has its own set of scroll bars, borders, and sizing buttons.

As you complete Exercise 4.1, you will see the graphical display that File Manager presents. Then, after the exercise, you will learn more about the directory window.

EXERCISE 4 • 1   STARTING FILE MANAGER

This exercise assumes that when Windows was installed on your system, File Manager was installed in the Main program group. If File Manager is not in the Main group, ask your instructor for assistance.

Figure 4.2

A directory within the File Manager application window.

File Manager menu bar

Directory window

Application window

File Manager status bar

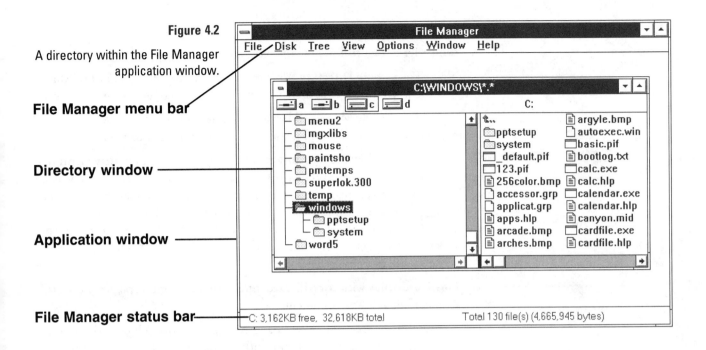

1. Start Windows if it is not currently running.

2. Verify that the Main window is the active window.

3. Double-click on the File Manager icon. As illustrated in Figure 4.2, the File Manager now displays two open windows--the File Manager application window and a directory window.

4. Click on the directory window maximize button to enlarge the directory window. Note that the title bar changes to reflect the new combination: It displays *File Manager [C:\WINDOWS*.*],"* as illustrated in Figure 4.3 Your screen may appear somewhat different, but the basic window is the same.

Figure 4.3

When maximized, the directory window enlarges and its title bar reflects the new combination.

Title bar

Disk drives icon bar

Display window

Directory tree

Directory contents

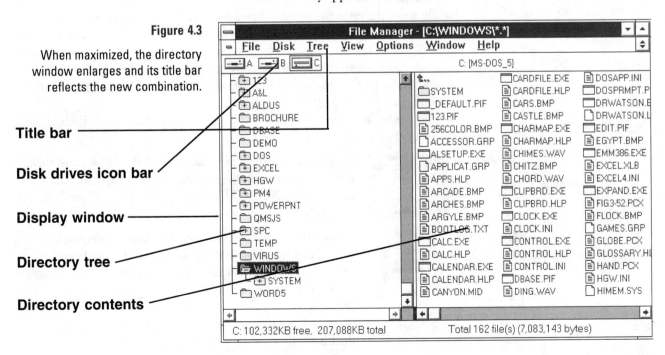

Viewing the Directory Window

As you refer to Figure 4.3, note the parts and the icons in the directory window.

The Parts of the Directory Window. The directory window has a **title bar** at the top, followed by the **disk drive icon bar**, and then the large **display window**.

- Below the File Manager title bar is the **directory window title bar**. Like all other title bars, it has a Control-menu box and minimize and maximize buttons.

- Directly below the directory window title bar is the **disk drive icon bar**, which identifies by letter and type the disk drives that you can access. (The icons displayed will vary, depending on the computer system.) Of these drives, the icon of the <u>active</u> drive is outlined (with a box), and its letter is shown at the right, over the second half of the display window (see Figure 4.3). Note that the icons simulate the look of floppy disk drives and hard disk drives. To change the active drive, click on another drive icon.

- The **display window** is divided into two panes—one displaying a directory tree, the other a directory contents:

  Directory tree. The left pane of the directory window displays the directory structure for the currently selected disk. This structure is called the **directory tree**. Think of the directory tree as an upside-down tree; its main root (C:\) is at the top and its major branches (directories) and lesser branches (subdirectories) flow downward toward the bottom.

  Directory contents. The contents of the directory that is currently selected in the left pane is displayed in the right pane—that is, in the **directory contents**. Optional detailed information about the files may also be displayed. (Later you will learn how to control this display using File Manager's View menu options.)

The Icons in the Directory Window

In the directory tree (the <u>left</u> pane in Figure 4.3), each directory is identified by a file icon; the *open* file is the *active* directory. In the listing of the directory contents (the <u>right</u> pane in Figure 4.3), a file icon represents a *sub*directory of the open directory. At the top left of the directory contents listing, you may see an upward-pointing arrow with two dots to the right of the arrow. This arrow, called the **up icon**, represents the parent of the *current* directory. Double-click on the arrow and you will "go back" one directory.

Four additional icons are used in the directory contents pane. Each of these icons distinguishes a different type of file:

Figure 4.4

Icon for a program file

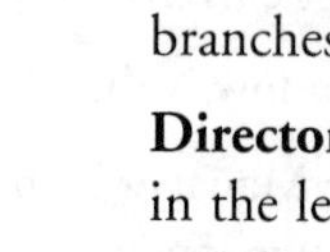

Program file icon. The rectangle with the stripe across the top indicates an executable or *program* file—files that have the extension .BAT, .COM, .EXE, or .PIF. These files will launch an application or program.

Figure 4.5

Icon for an associated document file

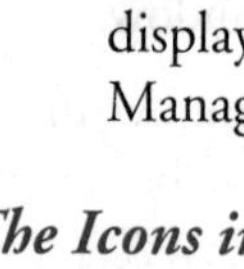

Associated document file icon. The page icon with one corner turned down and horizontal lines across it identifies an *associated document file*. These files are data files that can be launched by an application and commonly have the extension .TXT, .DOC, .BMP, .HLP, or .INI. The Associate command, described in the next session, allows you to launch this type of document file by double-clicking on its icon.

Figure 4.6

Icon for an unassociated document file

Unassociated document file. The page icon without the horizontal lines represents an *unassociated* data file. The data contained in such a file cannot be viewed or edited directly, so these files are not associated with an application. Unassociated data files have extensions such as .GRP, .FON, or .DLL.

Figure 4.7

Icon for a file containing a special attribute

Special attribute file. A page symbol with an exclamation point inside represents a file that has one or more *special attributes*. These attributes are generally attached to files that are critical to the operation of the computer system. Special attribute files are sometimes "hidden," that is, they do not show in the directory contents display.

Collapsing and Expanding the Directory Tree

Each time you access File Manager, the directory tree will display the root directory and all of the root's immediate subdirectories of the selected drive. As you noticed before, the directory tree shows the subdirectory of the Windows directory. You can *collapse* (decrease the levels) the directory tree so that the subdirectory does not appear. You can also *expand* (increase the levels) the directory tree so that subdirectories at all levels will show. How do you know whether a directory has any subdirectories? If you select the Indicate Expandable Branches option from the Tree menu, then you will see a plus (+) sign in a file icon in the directory tree window. The plus sign tells you that a directory *does* have subdirectories. If no plus sign appears, then no subdirectories exist (see Figure 4.8).

Figure 4.8

In the left pane, the plus (+) sign in the Windows directory file icon tells you that this directory does have subdirectories.

Directories with subdirectories

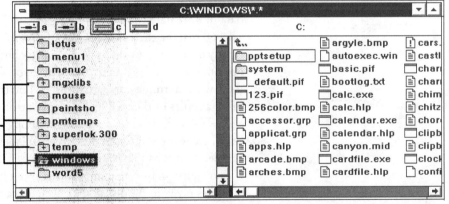

Double-clicking on an icon acts as a toggle: If the directory is expanded, double-clicking will collapse it; if the directory is collapsed, double-clicking will expand it. Use File Manager's Tree menu (Figure 4.9) to speed expanding and collapsing of multiple directories.

Figure 4.9

File Manager's Tree menu

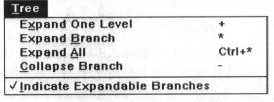

(Hint: While you can change directories quickly by using the mouse, this is one activity where you may find it easier and quicker to use the keyboard.) Directories that share the same level in the directory tree are always listed alphabetically, and you can move between them the same way you move in any other Windows list—by pressing the first letter of the directory name you want to move to.

EXERCISE 4 • 2   EXPANDING THE DIRECTORY TREE

The exercises in this session assume that Windows has been installed in a Windows subdirectory on drive C. If this is different for your system, your instructor will give you alternate instructions.

1. Verify that the Indicate Expandable Branches option is selected (checked) on the Tree menu.

2. Find the WINDOWS directory, and note whether its file folder shows a plus (+) or a minus (-) sign.

3. Double-click on the WINDOWS directory icon. If the file icon has a plus sign, the directory tree will expand showing the subdirectories below WIN-DOWS; if the file icon displays a minus sign, the directory tree will collapse.

4. Select the Expand All option from the Tree menu. The directory tree will display the root and all its directories and subdirectories. Scroll bars will be displayed if the directory tree is too large to display in the directory tree pane.

5. If necessary, scroll the directory tree using the scroll bar, then return to the root of the active drive by double-clicking on the up button at the top of the scroll box until the root (that is, C:\) is displayed.

VIEW 2	

WORKING WITH DISKS AND DISK DRIVES

PREVIEW

Like paper files, data files tend to accumulate. Again like paper files, disorganized data files are hard to find and frequently lost. In Windows, the process of saving a data file (it may be a word processing document, a spreadsheet, or data generated by any other application program) is easy enough: You use the Save or Save As... option from the File menu. But where you save your files and how you organize them will determine how easily you can find them when you want them. You must maintain files or they will get out of control. File Manager makes disk handling easy. Whether you are formatting a floppy disk (you will learn more about this later), accessing a different disk drive, or labeling a disk, each process is quick and simple, thanks to File Manager.

To maintain files, you must know about hard disks and floppy disks. You can save files on your hard disk, but even a spacious hard disk can quickly become filled. On the other hand, floppy diskettes (or simply disks) are easy to use and portable; they can be carried to other machines. In this view, you will learn to prepare floppy disks to save files; that is, you will learn to **format** floppy disks.

Choosing Floppy Disks

What kind of floppy disk should you use with your computer? The answer depends on the kind of disk drive or drives your system contains.

Floppy disk drives come in two commonly-used sizes: 3 1/2 inch and 5 1/4 inch. Your computer may have one size floppy drive, or it may have one of each. Check it now.

How much data can a disk store? That depends on the disk *and* the disk drive in which it was formatted. Two types of disk drives and disks exist: high-density (also called "high capacity") or double-density (also called "low density"). The "density" determines the maximum amount of data that a disk can store. High-density disks will store approximately twice as much data as double-density disks.

Unfortunately, you cannot mix and match disks and drives randomly. You should match disks and disk drives not only by size but also by density: Use a high-density disk in a high-density drive and a double-density disk in a double-density drive. Now, that is easy enough, right? (Actually, you *can* use a double-density disk in a high-density drive, but not vice versa. You will master the differences with some experience.)

Formatting a Floppy Disk

Formatting prepares a disk for use on a specific type of drive—that is, it imprints a disk with the information it needs to work in that particular kind of drive. The formatting process also erases all the information on a disk and is therefore potentially dangerous. As you will see in the exercise below, File Manager uses dialog boxes to protect you from erasing data accidently and to ask you for information about your disk drive or diskette.

EXERCISE 4 • 3   FORMATTING A DISK

In this exercise you will format a disk, preferably a high-density (or high-capacity) disk.

1. Using a felt pen, label a floppy disk (preferably a high-density disk) *Win Practice*. It is good practice to write on the label before your place it on the disk. Figure 4.10 shows you where to place the label on both 3 1/2- and 5 1/4-inch disks.

Figure 4.10

Note how labels are placed on 3 1/2- and 5 1/4-inch diskettes.

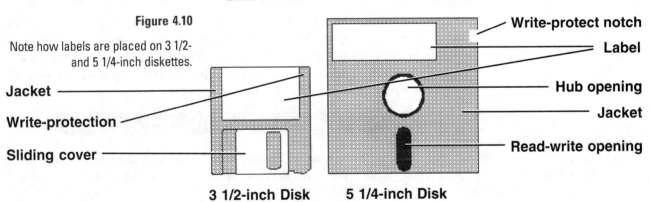

2. Start the File Manager if it is not already running.

3. Select the Format Disk... option from the Disk menu. The Format Disk dialog box will appear (see Figure 4.11), asking you to select the drive that contains the disk to be formatted (if you have more than one floppy drive) and to indicate the capacity of the disk. This dialog box also gives you several formatting options: Label, Make a System Disk, and Quick Format.

Label. The text you key in the Label text box will be used as an "electronic" disk label and will appear whenever you access the drive containing the disk. (The Label Disk command can also be used to label a disk or to change an existing label.)

Make System Disk. This option will transfer the appropriate DOS files to the floppy disk so that you can use this floppy disk to boot the system. But

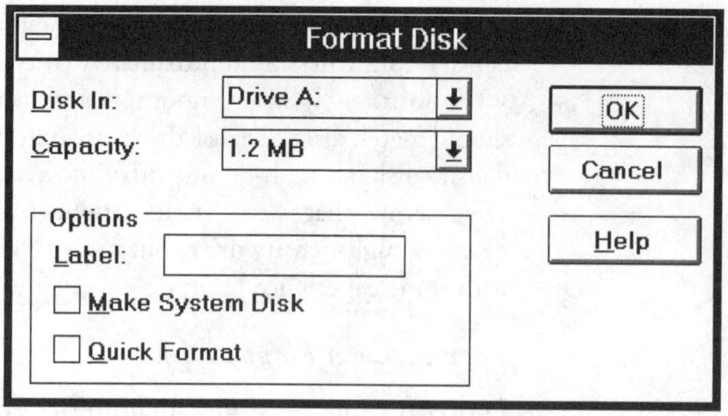

Figure 4.11

The Format Disk dialog box gives
you several formatting options.

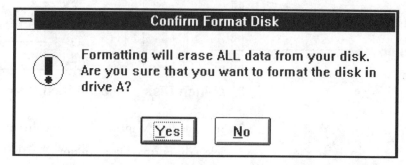

remember, these files fill space on the disk, so do not check this option unless
you need to make a bootable disk.

Quick Format. The Quick Format command formats a disk more quickly
than normal because it does not check the disk for problem areas before it
prepares the disk for use. This option can be used only with disks that have
been previously formatted and you are *sure* they are in good condition. Do not
use this option with new disks because many new disks contain areas that are
unusable; the normal Format command will find these areas and prevent you
from storing data on faulty disks.

4. If you have more than one floppy disk drive and you must change the drive,
   click on the arrow to the right of the Disk In text box and select from the listing
   box. Then in the Capacity text box, indicate the capacity of the disk (360K
   or 1.2MB for 5 1/4-inch disks; 720K or 1.44MB for 3 1/2-inch disks).

5. Verify that none of the option check boxes are checked, then click on the OK
   command button. Next you will see the Confirm Format Disk message box
   (Figure 4.12) warning you that all data will be erased from the disk when it is
   formatted. Click on the Yes button to begin formatting; if you do not wish
   to format your disk, click on the No button.

Figure 4.12

The Confirm Format Disk message
box warns you that all files will be
erased during the formatting
process.

> **Confirm Format Disk**
>
> (!) **Formatting will erase ALL data from your disk.
> Are you sure that you want to format the disk in
> drive A?**
>
> [Yes]   [No]

6. Insert your Win Practice disk in the correct disk drive label-side up, with the
   oblong read/write slot facing the drive. (Hint: Hold the disk in your right
   hand with your thumb on the label.)

7. Verify that the appropriate capacity is indicated:

   High-density: 1.44MB for 3 1/2-inch disk; 1.2MB for 5 1/4-inch disk.
   Double-density: 720K for 3 1/2-inch disk or 360K for 5 1/4-inch disk.

   Then click on the OK command button. A Formatting Disk window will
   open and display a "progress report" (in percent formatted) as the task is

completed (see Figure 4.13). You can cancel the format operation at any time by clicking on the Cancel button. If you cancel the format command during the formatting process, you cannot use the disk to store data.

Figure 4.13

Formatting Disk message box

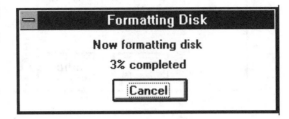

When formatting is complete, a Format Complete message box similar to the one shown in Figure 4.14 is displayed. This message box indicates the available disk space on the formatted disk (in bytes) and asks if you want to format another diskette.

Figure 4.14

Formatting Disk Complete message box

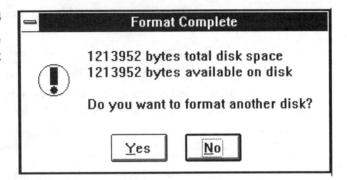

8. Click on the No command button to end formatting.

Accessing Disk Drives

All disk operations except formatting require that you first select the drive you want to use. Floppy disk drives are generally drive A and drive B (if the system has a second floppy drive); hard drives are designated drive C, D, E, and so on. Each disk drive available on your computer is represented by an icon on the directory window's drive icon bar.

You can select a drive by clicking once on an icon on the disk drive icon bar in the directory window (see Figure 4.15). You can also access a drive by selecting the Select Drive... option from the Disk menu.

Figure 4.15

On this disk drive icon bar, the outline indicates which disk is selected.

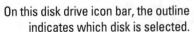

EXERCISE 4 • 4   SELECTING A DISK DRIVE

1. Select the drive that contains your newly formatted Win Practice disk. The disk drive icon for that drive becomes highlighted.

If you forget to insert the disk into the drive, an Error Reading Directory message box will tell you that the drive is not ready (Figure 4.16). Insert the disk, close the drive gate (if necessary), and click on the Retry command button. If you wish to cancel, click on the Cancel command button.

Figure 4.16

When you forget to insert a disk
into the drive, you will get this Error
Reading Directory message box.

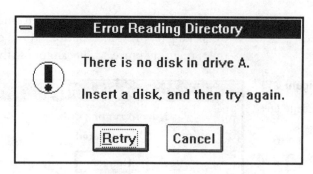

2. Select drive C, then remove your Win Practice disk from the drive.

3. Select the drive that contained your Win Practice disk. Wait until the Error
   Reading Directory message box is displayed.

4. Reinsert your Win Practice disk into the same drive.

5. Click on the Retry command button to select the drive once again.

Labeling Disks

Just as a paper label identifies a disk on the outside, a **disk label** identifies a disk
on the inside, that is, electronically, with a magnetic label. The label is displayed
on the directory window just below the drive icon bar, as shown in Figure 4.17.

Figure 4.17 In this directory window, note the disk label following the disk drive
letter A.

EXERCISE 4 . 5   LABELING A DISK

1. Verify that your Win Practice disk is in one of the floppy drives. Then select
   that drive.

2. Select the Label Disk... option from the Disk menu. The Label Disk dialog
   box, shown in Figure 4.18, will be displayed with the cursor already in the
   Label text box.

Figure 4.18

Label Disk dialog box

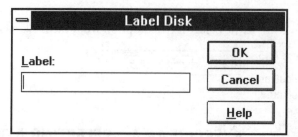

3. Key your last name. If your last name is longer than 11 characters, use a
   shortened version for this exercise. If the disk already has a label, the Label Disk
   text box will display it. (If you then key a new label, the new name will replace
   the former name.)

4. Click on the OK command button to record the label (if you do not wish to
   label your disk, click on the Cancel button to close the dialog box with no
   further action).

5. Verify that the disk label is displayed on the directory window to the right of the disk drive icon bar (see Figure 4.17).

6. Double-click on the File Manager Control-menu box. If a dialog box appears, click on the OK command button to close File Manager.

Naming Directories and Files

Rules, of course, exist for naming files and directories. Knowing and applying these rules will help you organize your directories and find your files. If you have some experience with computers, perhaps you are familiar with **DOS** (**d**isk **o**perating **s**ystem). If so, you have a head start in using the File Manager to name directories, find files, and more.

First of all, as shown in Figure 4.19, a directory name or filename consists of three parts: a *name* (from 1 to 8 characters long), a *separator*, and an *extension* (no more than 3 characters long). For example, the filename LETTER.DOC includes the name LETTER, a separator (a period), and the extension DOC. You <u>must</u> name your files, but file extensions are optional (most Windows programs add their own file extensions to filenames).

Figure 4.19

Note these conventions in naming directories and filenames.

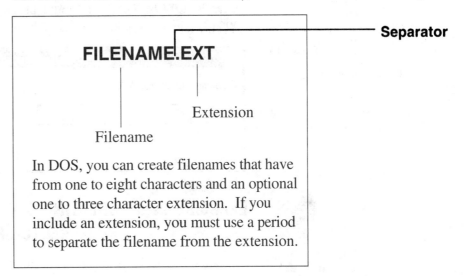

Separator

FILENAME.EXT

Extension

Filename

In DOS, you can create filenames that have from one to eight characters and an optional one to three character extension. If you include an extension, you must use a period to separate the filename from the extension.

You can use any letter of the alphabet, any number, and some symbols in your names, but you cannot use a space--use a hyphen (-) or an underscore (_) instead. An remember, use no more than 8 characters. If you do use more than 8 characters, the extra letters will be ignored.

—	**VIEW 3**	▼ ▲

CREATING DIRECTORIES AND SUBDIRECTORIES

PREVIEW

Think of a **directory** as a file drawer that holds a group of file folders on one subject, each folder labeled for a certain kind of file. You might have a drawer (a **directory**) labeled 1993TAX, another labeled 1994TAX, and so on, one for each year. In each drawer you might have different folders (**subdirectories**) labeled RETURNS, RE-CEIPTS, and so on. In each folder you might have dozens of papers (**files**), all related. Now, to appreciate the value of directories and subdirectories, imagine having no file drawers and no folders—just a mess of loose papers!

In File Manager, you can create directories and subdirectories when you are in the directory window. First, what is the difference between a directory and a subdirectory? A directory comes straight from the root (that is, from A:\ or B:\ or C:\, for example), but a *sub*directory comes from a directory. In the next exercise, you will create a directory with two subdirectories beneath it. The directory comes from the root--A:\ or B:\, depending on which drive you put your Win Practice disk in. The two subdirectories come from the directory—that is why they are called *sub*directories.

In either case, the process of creating a directory or a subdirectory is the same. First, you must make a decision. If you are creating a directory, decide which disk you will place the new directory. If you are creating a subdirectory, decide under which parent directory you will place the new subdirectory. Then, whether you are creating a directory or a subdirectory, pull down the File menu and select the Create Directory... option. The Create Directory dialog box, shown in Figure 4.20, will show you where the new directory or subdirectory will be placed. Above the Name text box in Figure 4.20 you see *Current Directory: A:*. If you key a name in the Name text box and click on the OK command button, you will create a directory. If, on the other hand, the line above the name box said *Current Directory: C:\1993TAX*, you would be creating a subdirectory beneath the 1993TAX directory, which comes from the root C:\.

Figure 4.20

Create Directory dialog box

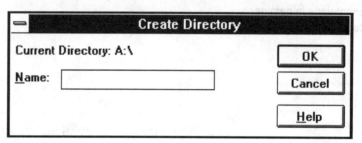

EXERCISE 4 • 6   CREATING DIRECTORIES AND SUBDIRECTORIES

1. Start Windows if it is not already started. Double-click on the File Manager icon.

2. Verify that your Win Practice disk is in one of the floppy drives. Then select that drive.

3. Verify that the Indicate Expandable Branches command is selected on the Tree menu.

4. Select the Create Directory... option from the File menu.

5. Key the directory name *DTP* (for desktop publishing) in the Name text box. You can use lowercase letters; File Manager will convert them to capital letters.

6. Click on the OK command button. Notice that the root directory of your Win Practice disk is an open folder with a minus (-) sign.

7. Select the DTP directory. Notice that an arrow pointing upward with two dots to the right of it is displayed in the directory contents pane (the right pane in the directory window). This symbol indicates that you have accessed a directory under the root directory.

8. Select the Create Directory... option from the File menu.

9. Key the name *STORIES* in the Name text box, then click on the OK command button.

10. Double-click on the DTP directory icon to collapse the directory tree one level. The DTP icon should remain selected and the STORIES subdirectory will be displayed in the directory contents pane.

11. Select the Create Directory option... from the File menu.

12. Key the name *GRAPHICS* in the Name text box, then click on the OK command button. The DTP directory will expand to display its two subdirectories in the directory tree pane. The two subdirectories are also shown in the directory contents pane.

Controlling File Displays in the Directory Contents Pane

So far, we have used File Manager's defaults to display directories and files in the directory contents pane. But at times you may want to change the display format—for example, when you are searching for a particular file or group of files.

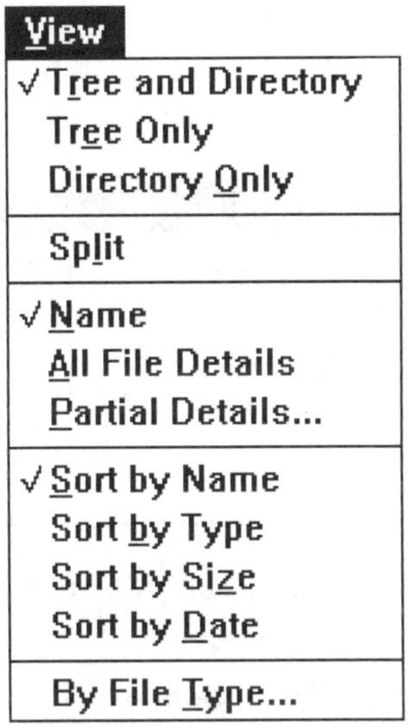

Figure 4.21

View menu

```
View
√ Tree and Directory
  Tree Only
  Directory Only

  Split

√ Name
  All File Details
  Partial Details...

√ Sort by Name
  Sort by Type
  Sort by Size
  Sort by Date

  By File Type...
```

The View menu options, shown in Figure 4.21, allow you to control how files are displayed in the directory contents listing. The first three options control what will be displayed in the directory window: (1) the directory tree alone, (2) the contents alone, or if you prefer, (3) both in a split window.

Tree And Directory. This is the default option. When the Tree And Directory option is selected, the directory window is divided into two panes—one for the directory tree, the other for directory contents.

Tree Only. When this option is selected, only the directory tree is displayed in the directory window.

Directory Only. Selecting this option displays only the directory contents pane in the directory window.

The Split option permits you to move the line that divides the directory window between the tree and the directory contents. When you select the Split option, the scroll bar that divides the directory window becomes a solid line known as the **split bar** (see Figure 4.22) which can move with the mouse or with the right or left arrow keys. You can also move the split bar at any time in the same way you can change the window border. Move the mouse slowly across the split bar until it becomes a black double-headed arrow, press the mouse button, and drag the split bar to the right or left. You can reposition the split bar to show any amount of the directory tree pane or the directory contents pane.

The next three View options determine the file details you will see in the directory contents pane.

Name. This is the default. When Name is selected, information about the file, other than its name, will not be listed.

Figure 4.22

You can move the split bar to
change the directory tree pane or
the directory contents pane.

Split bar

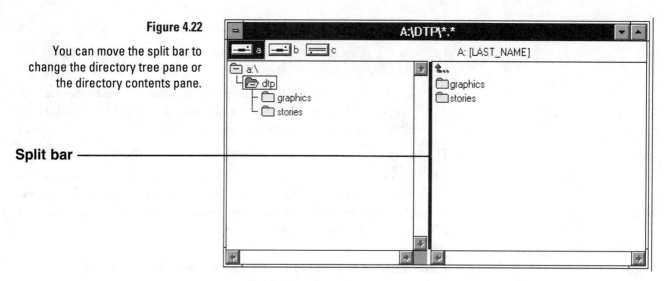

All File Details. When this option is selected, the following details are listed to the right of the file name: size (in bytes), date created, time created, and file attributes (a hidden code that identifies the type of file).

Partial Details. The Partial Details... option permits you to select only certain file details. The Partial Details dialog box will display (see Figure 4.23), allowing you to make your selections by clicking on the appropriate check boxes.

Figure 4.23

Partial Details dialog box

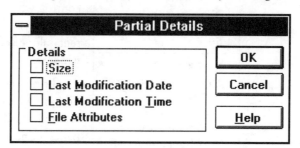

The next four View options determine how the directory contents listing is sorted:

Sort by Name. This option sorts files in normal alphabetic order by filename (with symbols first, then numbers, and finally letters). Subdirectories will be placed before files following this same sequence.

Sort by Type. This option displays files first by alphabetic order according to the extension and then by filename within each extension group.

Sort by Size. The Size option lists files in order by descending size.

Sort by Date. This option will display the files by their creation date or the date the file was last modified. The files are listed in descending date order.

The last menu option, **By File Type**..., permits you to specify the file type you want to display. To do this, you enter a file type in the Name text box (see Figure 4.24).

Now that you know all these View options, you can control file displays in a listing—a handy tool for searching a directory or a disk.

Searching a Directory or a Disk

To locate a directory or a file, use the Search... option on the File menu. Search allows you to locate:

Figure 4.24

By File Type dialog box

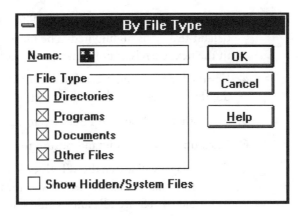

- one file among many within a directory,
- one directory among many on a disk,
- all the directories and files with similar names, and
- all the files with a common extension.

Using the Search Option

When you select Search..., the Search dialog box is displayed (see Figure 4.25). If you are searching for a specific file, key the name in the Search For text box. If you do not know the exact name, or want to search for a group of files, you can use the asterisk (*) as a wildcard character. This is explained in more detail later in this session. You can also key several filenames in the text box, leaving a space after each filename to create a list of files. The text box will accommodate long lists and it will keep scrolling the filenames as you add to the list.

Figure 4.25

Search dialog box

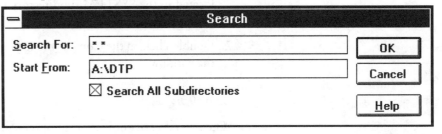

If you select Search All Subdirectories (or simply allow the X to remain in this box) and then click on the OK button, File Manager will search the selected directory and all its subdirectories (if any) for the search text. If you do not select Search All Subdirectories, the search will be limited to the currently selected directory; its subdirectories will not be searched.

EXERCISE 4 • 7   SEARCHING AN ENTIRE DIRECTORY FOR A SPECIFIC FILE

Locate the WIN.CNF file, which is stored somewhere in the Windows directory.

1. Select drive C (or the drive that contains the WINDOWS directory).

2. Select the WINDOWS directory in the directory tree listing.

3. Select the Search... option from the File menu. In the Search For text box, the default text *.* is highlighted. The meaning of this symbol will be explained in the next exercise. For now, remove it by keying new text.

4. Key the filename and extension *WIN.CNF* in the Search For text box. As you do, this text replaces the default text.

5. Verify that the Search All Subdirectories check box is selected (checked).

6. Click on the OK command button to start the search.

   File Manager will search the WINDOWS directory and all of its subdirectories for all files that match the search specifications. When the search operation is completed, a Search Results window similar to the one illustrated in Figure 4.26 will display an icon and the complete directory path for each file that matches your search specifications.

Figure 4.26

The Search Results window displays an icon and the complete directory path for each file that matches the Search specifications.

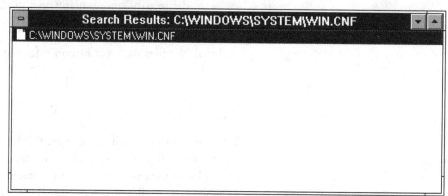

As illustrated in Figure 4.26, only one match was found. The directory path C:\WINDOWS\SYSTEM\WIN.CNF indicates that the WIN.CNF file is located in the SYSTEM subdirectory in the WINDOWS directory on drive C.

7. Double-click on the Control-menu box of the Search Results window to close the window.

Searching with Wildcards

When you do not know (or cannot remember) the exact name or extension, you can use the **wildcard character** * to assist you with your search. In File Manager, an asterisk (*) means *any filename* or *any extension*, depending on where you place the asterisk.

Here are some examples that show how you might use wildcards effectively:

- If you know the filename (README) but not the extension, you would enter README.* in the Search For text box. This search would find all README filenames, such as README.DOC, README.TXT, or README.WRI.

- If you know the extension (TXT) but not the filename, you would enter *.TXT in the Search For text box. This search would find all filenames with the extension .TXT, such as CHAPTER1.TXT, README.TXT, or REPORT.TXT.

- If you know a portion of the filename (READ) but not the entire name or extension, you would enter READ*.* in the Search For text box. This search would find filenames that begin with the letters READ, such as README.DOC, READER.TXT, or READY.WRI.

• If you know neither the filename nor the extension, use two asterisks separated with a period (*.*), which is the default text that appears in the Search For text box each time the Search... option is selected. The symbol *.* instructs File Manager to search for all files, regardless of filename or extension.

EXERCISE 4 • 8   SEARCHING WITH WILDCARDS

Use the wildcard character feature to locate all the files in the WINDOWS directory that have a .BMP extension.

1. Verify that the WINDOWS directory is selected.

2. Select the Search option from the File menu.

3. Key the filename wildcard and extension *.BMP in the text box.

4. Verify that the Search All Subdirectories check box is checked.

5. Click on the OK command button to start the search.

The Search Results dialog box now lists every file in the WINDOWS directory and subdirectories that matches the search specifications. The number of files located will display at the bottom of the File Manager window. If the listing is too long for all the files to be seen, scroll bars will be displayed in the window.

6. Double-click on the Search Result window's Control-menu box to close the window.

Selecting Directories and Files

You generally search a disk to locate a directory or file you wish to copy, delete, or rename. The first step in performing any of these functions is to *select its icon*. From the directory tree (the left pane of the directory window), you can select only one directory. But from the directory contents pane (the right pane of the directory window), you can select single or multiple directories and files.

A number of techniques are available that allow you to select multiple directories or files:

• To select a single directory or file, click on it.

• If the files are randomly scattered through the directory, press *and hold* [Ctrl] while you click on each of the desired files. As shown in Figure 4.27, the selected files will be highlighted.

Figure 4.27

Multiple files with .BMP extensions are selected in the directory contents pane. Note that the Windows directory is selected in the directory tree pane.

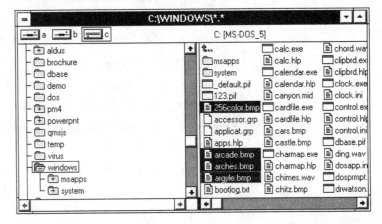

• For consecutive files, press *and hold* [Shift] while you (1) click on the first file and then (2) click on the last file to be included. Again, the selected files will be highlighted.

• Another option is to use the Select Files... option on the File menu.

EXERCISE 4 • 9   SELECTING INDIVIDUAL FILES

Since the techniques for manipulating both directories and files are the same, the exercises below use files only.

1. Scroll the directory tree until the WINDOWS directory is in view.

2. Select the WINDOWS directory if it is not already selected.

3. Select the first file in the directory contents pane with a .BMP extension by clicking once on it. (Be careful not to double-click or you may launch an application!)

4. Press *and hold* [Ctrl], then click on the next three files in the contents listing with a .BMP extension.

5. Cancel the first file selected by pressing [Ctrl] and clicking on the file icon. You can use the scroll bars to move around the directory contents pane even though a selected file moves out of view. A file will remain selected until you cancel the selection.

   When you want to cancel all the selections in a contents listing, click on the directory tree pane.

6. Click once in the directory tree pane. All the selected files will be deselected.

EXERCISE 4 • 10   SELECTING MULTIPLE ADJACENT FILES

In this exercise, you will select all files with a .PIF extension. Using the View menu makes them easier to locate.

1. Select the By File Type... option from the View menu. The By File Type dialog box (a) lists the file parameters you can select in the display and (b) provides a text box for you to indicate the file, the extension, or both file and extension.

2. Key the wildcard and extension *.PIF*, then click on the OK command button. Notice that only those files with the extension .PIF are displayed.

3. Click on the first file in the listing.

4. Press *and hold* [Shift], then click on the last file in the listing. All the intervening files will be selected, as illustrated in Figure 4.28.

   You can redisplay the entire directory contents listing with the By File Type... option on the View menu.

5. Select the By File Type... option from the File menu.

6. Press [Backspace] to remove the text in the text box and click on OK. The entire directory contents will redisplay in the directory contents pane.

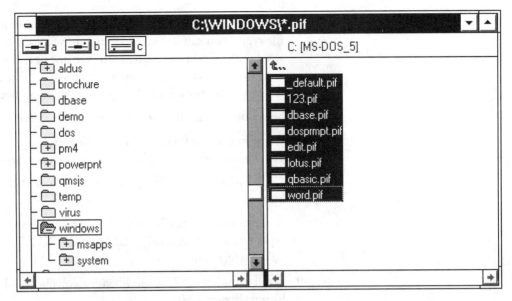

Figure 4.28 Multiple files with .PIF extensions are selected in the directory contents pane.

EXERCISE 4 • 11 SELECTING FILES USING FILE MENU OPTIONS

Use the Select Files option on the File menu either to select or to deselect files (see Figure 4.29).

Figure 4.29

The Select Files dialog box allows you both to select or to deselect files.

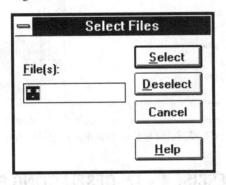

1. Select the Select Files... option from the File menu.

2. Key *.*PIF* in the File(s) text box to indicate you wish to include only those files with a .PIF extension.

3. Click on the Select command button. The Cancel command button will change to a Close command button, and the directory contents listing will be searched. If the contents listing is long, it will scroll to the left. All files matching the selection options will be outlined.

4. Click on the Close command button.

   All files with the *.PIF extension will be highlighted. You may have to scroll the directory contents listing to see all the files.

5. Scroll the directory contents listing until the subdirectory icons are visible.

The Select Files... option can also be used to select more than one filename or file type. You can key several names or wildcard combinations in the File(s) text box, leaving a space after each filename or type to create a list of files. The box will keep scrolling as you add to the list. You can use the arrow keys or the mouse to move back through the list if you need to edit the text.

6. Select the Select Files... option on the File menu.

7. In the File(s) text box, key *.*BMP*, then space once and key *.*TXT* to indicate you wish to select all files with these two extensions.

8. Click on the Select command button, then click on the Close command button.

   Since you did not deselect the selected files, the contents listing will have three types of files selected, .PIF, .BMP, and .TXT. You will have to scroll to see all the selected files.

9. Scroll to the left until the subdirectory icons are visible in the directory contents listing (Figure 4.30).

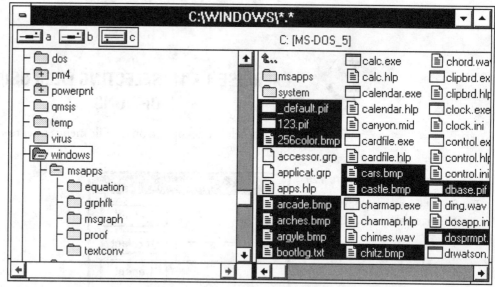

Figure 4.30 Selected files with .PIF, .BMP, and .TXT extensions

EXERCISE 4 • 12 DESELECTING FILES

Once you have selected the desired files, you can manipulate them by issuing various commands. Manipulating techniques will be presented in the next section. For now, deselect the files.

Deselect all the files with the .BMP extension from the listing.

1. Select the Select Files... from the File menu.

2. Key *.*BMP* in the File(s) text box, then click on the Deselect command button.

3. Click on the Close command button. All files with the .BMP extension are now deselected; the other previously selected files remain selected.

4. Double-click on the File Manager's Control-menu box to exit File manager.

5. Exit Windows.

SUMMARY

This session focused on the File Manager, the Windows feature designed to help you find, view, manage, and use your files easily and efficiently by controlling and manipulating the directories and subdirectories on a disk. Fittingly, then, the File Manager icon is a file cabinet.

In this session, you learned how to format a disk, how to add an electronic label to a formatted disk, and how to use File Manager to create directories and subdirectories. You also learned about File Manager's powerful search capabilities, which makes finding files quick and easy.

As you have probably already discovered, the File Manager affects the basic ways in which you save, organize, and view every file you create in Windows. Only by knowing and using File Manager correctly can you get the maximum benefit from the power of Windows. In fact, the more you use Windows, the more important it is for you to understand the File Manager. For this reason, you will learn more about the File Manager in the next session.

OBJECTIVES

When you complete this session, you will be able to:

- Name, rename, copy, move, and delete directories and files.
- Associate and unassociate files.
- Run applications from the File Manager.

SESSION 5 *FILE MANAGER PART II*

VIEWS
Manipulating Directories and Files
Changing the Directory Window Typeface
Running Applications

FILE MANAGER PART II

PREVIEW

You have seen how File Manager permits you to organize and manage files, directories, and disks, but the real power of File Manager lies in its ability to *manipulate* directories and files. The more you use a computer, the more you will need to erase unwanted directories and files, copy files to other disks, or move files between directories and disks. File Manager is an excellent tool for performing these operations.

Displaying Warning Messages

During some operations, File Manager displays a warning message that asks, for example, if you really want to delete a file. Because warning messages give you an opportunity to change your mind before executing certain commands, they are obviously important; once deleted, a directory or file may be lost forever!

On the other hand, too many messages can be annoying. So File Manager gives you a choice: If you wish, you can turn off selected warning messages by checking the appropriate boxes in the Confirmation dialog box (see Figure 5.1).

Figure 5.1

Confirmation dialog box

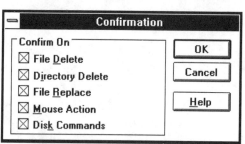

To access the Confirmation dialog box, select Confirmation... from the Options menu. You will see the following options:

Check this . . .	To get confirmation of . . .
File Delete	Each file being erased
Directory Delete	Each directory being erased
File Replace	One file being placed over another with the same name
Mouse Action	Moving or copying any directory or file using the mouse
Disk Commands	Copying or Formatting disks.

Suggestion: Until you become very familiar with Windows 3.1, keep all options in this dialog box checked so that File Manager will warn you if you are about to accidentally delete or overwrite data.

Opening Multiple Document Windows

At times you will need to work with two directories or drives at once. For example, when you want to copy files from a floppy disk to a hard disk, you will need to have each drive in its own document window. File Manager lets you open multiple document windows. You can then use the familiar Windows commands to organize them neatly on your screen.

To open a new window, select the New Window command on the Windows menu. The contents of the new window will be the same as the original window.

EXERCISE 5 • 1 MANIPULATING MULTIPLE DIRECTORY WINDOWS

In the following exercises, if an unexpected warning message box is displayed, you should **not** proceed with the action. Click on the No (Cancel) command button. Reread the instructions and try again.

1. Start Windows if it is not currently running.

2. Open the File Manager.

3. Select the Confirmation... option from the Options menus, and verify that all of the check boxes in the Confirmation dialog box are checked. Click OK to close the Confirmation dialog box.

4. Click on the appropriate drive icon (probably C) and then select the WINDOWS directory.

5. Select the New Window command from the Window menu. A duplicate directory window will be placed in front of the initial window. The initial window will be numbered "1" and the new window will be numbered "2."

6. Click on the SYSTEM subdirectory under the WINDOWS directory in the directory tree pane to change the contents of window #2. Notice that the original window remains numbered 1, but the new window (formerly window #2) is not numbered. Only duplicate directory windows are numbered (see Figure 5.2).

Figure 5.2

Multiple directory windows

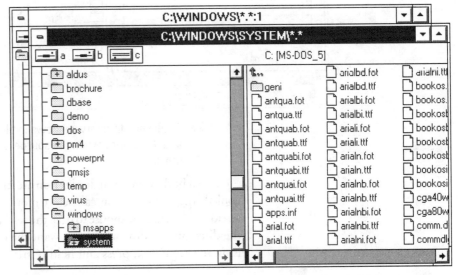

Directory windows can be moved, sized, tiled, and cascaded like any other window.

7. Select the Tile option from the Window menu. The directory windows will display as tiled windows.

8. Double-click on the C:\WINDOWS\SYSTEM*.* directory window's Control-menu box to close the window.

9. Select the Cascade option from the Window menu to adjust the size and position of the C:\WINDOWS*.* 1 window.

Copying Directories and Files

Files are copied *from* a "source" to a "destination." In this case, the source is the file or directory to be copied and the destination is the location to which the file is copied. Whenever you need to copy directories or files, make both the source and the destination directory window visible. In this way, you can see what you are copying and where it is going. If the source and the destination are on different disks, tile the directory windows, as illustrated in Figure 5.3.

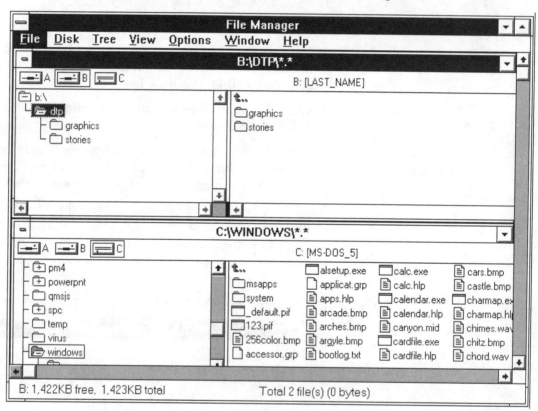

Figure 5.3 Displaying directory windows in tile format makes it easy to copy files and directories when the source and the destination are on different drives.

When both source and destination are in view, select the file or directory to be copied (the source). You can select more than one, as described earlier in this session. Then use the mouse to drag the selected file or directory to its destination, the directory window where you want the copy to be placed. If the destination is on the same disk, press and hold [Ctrl] as you drag the file.

NOTE: If you hold [Alt], the file will be moved, *not copied*, to the destination disk or directory.)

When using a mouse, you can release the icon of the copied directory or file on top of another directory window, on top of a directory icon in the directory tree, on top of a directory icon at the bottom of the File Manager window, or on top of a disk drive icon at the top of the File Manager.

Now, copy all the graphic files in the WINDOWS directory with the extension .BMP to the GRAPHICS directory on your Win Practice disk.

EXERCISE 5 • 2   COPYING FILES

1. Verify that the WINDOWS directory is selected in the directory tree.

2. Place your Win Practice disk in one of the floppy drives.

3. Double-click on the drive (from the disk drive icon bar) in which you have placed your Win Practice disk.

4. Select the Tile option from the Window menu.

5. Double-click on the DTP directory to display the GRAPHICS subdirectory.

6. Double-click on the GRAPHICS subdirectory to open its directory contents pane (destination).

7. Select the C:\WINDOWS*.* directory window.

8. Select the Select Files... option from the File menu.

9. Key the wildcard and extension *.BMP in the text box. Click on the Select command button, and then click on the Close command button.

    Only those files with a .BMP extension will be selected in the WINDOWS directory window. Look at the left side of the status line on the bottom of the File Manager window. Note the number of files that were selected.

10. Point anywhere in the highlighted area of one of the selected files in the C:\WINDOWS*.* contents listing, press and hold the mouse button, then move the mouse slightly. The cursor will change into a graphic that looks like a stack of cards.

11. Continue to hold the mouse button and drag the graphic until it sits inside the GRAPHICS directory contents pane. Release the mouse button. A message box asks you to confirm that you want to copy the files into the directory (Figure 5.4).

Figure 5.4

Confirm Mouse Operation message box

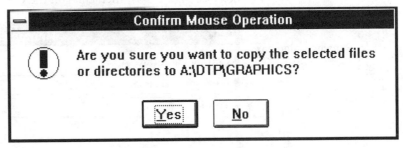

12. Click on the Yes button to copy the files.

13. After the files have been copied, click on the GRAPHICS directory window to select it.

    Notice that the status bar at the bottom of the File Manager window gives you information about the selected drive and its directories and subdirectories. The number of files contained in this subdirectory should equal the number of files selected to be copied.

Moving Directories and Files

Moving a directory or file is similar to copying—the difference is that the Move command *removes* the directory or file from its original location.

EXERCISE 5 • 3   MOVING FILES

1. Double-click on the C:\WINDOWS*.* directory window's Control-menu box to close the window.

2. Select the New Window option from the Window menu.

3. Select the Tile option from the Window menu.

4. Double-click on the STORIES subdirectory on the directory tree in one of the directory windows.

5. Select the ARCADE.BMP file in the GRAPHICS directory contents listing. Be sure you select *only* this file.

6. Press and hold [Alt], then drag the ARCADE.BMP file icon from the GRAPHICS directory window and place it in the STORIES directory contents pane.

7. Release the mouse button and [Alt] when the icon is over the directory contents pane.

8. Click on the Yes button to move the file.

9. Double-click on the STORIES directory window's Control-menu box to close the window.

10. Select the Cascade option on the Window menu to change the size and position of the GRAPHICS directory window.

Renaming Directories and Files

File Manager has a simple process for renaming directories and files: Select the source, issue the Rename... command, key the new name in the Rename dialog box (see Figure 5.5), then click on the OK command button.

Figure 5.5

Rename dialog box

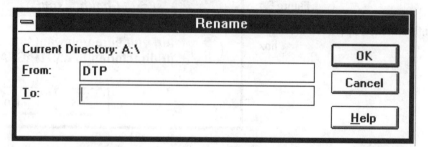

EXERCISE 5 • 4   RENAMING DIRECTORIES AND FILES

Renaming a Directory

1. Select the DTP directory icon on the directory tree.

2. Select the Rename... option from the File menu.

3. Key the new name *DESKTOP* in the To text box, then click on the OK command button.

Renaming Multiple Files

4. Double-click on the DESKTOP directory to display the GRAPHICS subdirectory icon.

5. Double-click on the GRAPHICS subdirectory icon to display its contents in the directory contents pane.

6. Select the Select Files... option from the File menu.

7. Click on the Select command button, then click on the Close command button. All of the files in the directory contents pane will be selected.

8. Select the Rename... option from the File menu.

9. Key the wildcard and new extension *.GRA* in the text box, and then click on the OK command button.

10. Verify that the files have been renamed.

Deleting Directories and Files

With File Manager, you can delete one file or a large group of files in a single action. But note that when you delete a directory or a subdirectory name, you also delete all the files in it! For this reason, you should select the File Delete check box *and* the Directory Delete check box on the Confirmation dialog box. When these check boxes are selected, a message window will be displayed each time you issue the delete command. This message serves as a "double check" that the file or directory should be deleted before it actually happens.

EXERCISE 5 • 5   DELETING FILES

Delete all the files in the GRAPHICS directory. Although you usually want to select the Confirm on Delete box, to increase the speed of this activity, you will *de*select this warning message in this exercise only.

1. Select the Confirmation... option from the Options menu to bring up the Confirmation dialog box.

2. Deselect (uncheck) the File Delete option by clicking on the check box. Leave the other check boxes selected (checked).

3. Click on the OK command button.

4. Select the first filename in the GRAPHICS directory contents window; then press Shift and click on the last filename.

5. Select the Delete... option from the File menu to erase the selected files, then click on the OK command button. The files will be deleted.

6. Select the Confirmation... option from the Options menu and check the File Delete option by clicking on the check box.

7. Click on the OK command button.

VIEW 2
CHANGING THE DIRECTORY WINDOW TYPEFACE

PREVIEW

At times, you may want to get more filenames in a listing without having to scroll, or you may want the listing in uppercase letters. How can you do so? By choosing the Font... option on the Options menu to change the typeface and style in the directory window.

The Font dialog box (Figure 5.6) permits you (1) to change the font, font style, and size and (2) to display in either uppercase or lowercase letters. As you make your selections, a sample is displayed in the rectangular box in the lower-right corner of the dialog box.

Figure 5.6

In this Font dialog box, notice the Sample box in the lower-right corner.

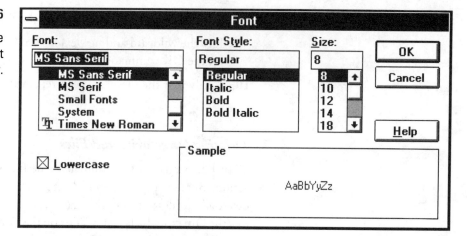

EXERCISE 5.6 CHANGING THE DIRECTORY WINDOW TYPEFACE

1. Double-click on the STORIES subdirectory icon in the directory tree pane to display its contents in the directory contents pane.

2. Select the Font... option from the Options menu. The Font dialog box will display three listing boxes labeled Font, Font Style, and Size:

   a. In the Font listing box, select the MS Sans Serif font if it is not already selected.

   b. In the Font Style listing box, select Bold Italic from the Font Style listing box.

   c. In the Size listing box, select 10 (you may have to scroll to bring the size in view).

3. Click on the Lowercase check box to deselect this option, if it is not already deselected.

4. Click on the OK command button. Notice that the directory window is refreshed using the typeface you specified.

5. Select the Font... option from the Options menu and make the following selections:

   a. In the Font listing box, select MS Sans Serif.

   b. In the Font Style listing box, select Regular.

c. In the Size listing box, select 8.

d. In the Lowercase check box, make sure the box is *not* checked.

6. Click on the OK command button.

Changing File Attributes

If you have ever accidently deleted or changed files, you know how annoying and upsetting that can be. And even if you have not, you surely want to take every precaution to avoid such time-wasting, irritating, and frustrating accidents! Windows can help you.

Windows permits you to place controls on the kinds of operations you are permitted to perform on the file. You place controls by assigning one or more **attributes** to the file. An *attribute* is simply a hidden code or "flag" placed in a file. DOS uses such flags both to identify the type of file and to determine the type of operations you can perform on the file.

For example, your system simply will not operate without certain files; deleting them would make your system permanently inoperable. To avoid the possibility of deleting such files, you can assign them the **hidden attribute**. The files are stored on your disk, but using conventional DOS commands you can not find files flagged with the hidden attribute. If they are difficult to find, they are difficult to delete!

You can assign up to four attributes to a single file. The four attributes, their flag code, and a brief explanation are shown below.

Attribute	Flag Code	Explanation
Read Only	R	A **read only attribute** prevents a file from being changed. It can be read into memory or copied from one location to another, but its contents cannot be changed.
Archive	A	An **archive attribute** is automatically assigned to any file you create or modify. Using DOS utilities such as BACKUP and XCOPY turns off the archive attribute.
Hidden	H	A **hidden attribute** means that the filename will not be listed on a regular directory listing (useful if others use your computer or you are working on sensitive or confidential information). How can you list hidden files? By selecting Show Hidden/System check box in the By File Type dialog box on the View menu.
System	S	A **system attribute** identifies the file as a DOS system file. The system attribute is assigned to those DOS files that are critical to the operation of your system. Like hidden files, files with the system attribute appear only if you select Show Hidden/System check box in the By File Type dialog box on the View menu.

Read only is the most frequently used attribute. Can you guess why?

Say you have created a long report and saved it as a file. You want others to have access to the information in the file, but how can you make sure they cannot change the text? Yes, by assigning the read only attribute you limit other users to only reading, not changing, the file. The read only attribute also helps protect your files from many destructive viruses.

How do you assign a file attribute? By using the Properties... command on the File menu. The Properties dialog box appears, and at the bottom it offers you four check boxes, as shown in Figure 5.7. Just click on any or all of the boxes to assign attributes.

Figure 5.7

The Properties dialog box for the ARCADE.BMP file. Note that only the Archive attribute box is checked.

```
┌─────────────────────────────────────────────────────────┐
│ ▬        Properties for ARCADE.BMP                        │
├───────────────────────────────────────────────────────────┤
│  File Name:     ARCADE.BMP                ┌─────────┐     │
│  Size:          630 bytes                 │   OK    │     │
│  Last Change:   3/10/92  3:10:00AM        └─────────┘     │
│  Path:          A:\DESKTOP\STORIES        ┌─────────┐     │
│                                           │ Cancel  │     │
│  ┌─Attributes──────────────────────┐      └─────────┘     │
│  │  ☐ Read Only    ☐ Hidden         │      ┌─────────┐     │
│  │  ☒ Archive      ☐ System         │      │  Help   │     │
│  └──────────────────────────────────┘      └─────────┘     │
└─────────────────────────────────────────────────────────┘
```

Above the check boxes, the Properties dialog box gives you certain statistics on the selected files. These are the statistics you see when you select the All File Details option from the View menu.

EXERCISE 5 • 7   SETTING FILE ATTRIBUTES

1. Verify that the drive in which you have placed your Win Practice disk is selected.

2. Select the Expand All option from the Tree menu to display the STORIES subdirectory.

3. Select the ARCADE.BMP file.

4. Select the Properties... option from the File menu. The Properties dialog box will display on your screen.

5. Click on the appropriate check box to assign the Read Only attribute (that is, place an X in the Read Only box; see Figure 5.8).

Figure 5.8

This Properties dialog box has the Read Only and Archive file attributes checked.

```
┌─────────────────────────────────────────────────────────┐
│ ▬        Properties for ARCADE.BMP                        │
├───────────────────────────────────────────────────────────┤
│  File Name:     ARCADE.BMP                ┌─────────┐     │
│  Size:          630 bytes                 │   OK    │     │
│  Last Change:   3/10/92  3:10:00AM        └─────────┘     │
│  Path:          A:\DESKTOP\STORIES        ┌─────────┐     │
│                                           │ Cancel  │     │
│  ┌─Attributes──────────────────────┐      └─────────┘     │
│  │  ☒ Read Only    ☐ Hidden         │      ┌─────────┐     │
│  │  ☒ Archive      ☐ System         │      │  Help   │     │
│  └──────────────────────────────────┘      └─────────┘     │
└─────────────────────────────────────────────────────────┘
```

6. Click on the OK command.

Displaying File Attributes

How can you see file attributes in the contents pane of a directory window? By choosing either the All File Details... option or the Partial File Details... option from the View menu: Use the All Files Details... option to display not only the attribute information but also the additional file information shown in Figure 5.9.

Figure 5.9

The contents pane of this directory window shows that the ARCADE.BMP file has two attributes assigned to it--Read Only, which is indicated by the flag code R, and Archive, which is indicatd by the flag code A. What else does this entry tell you about the ARCADE.BMP file?

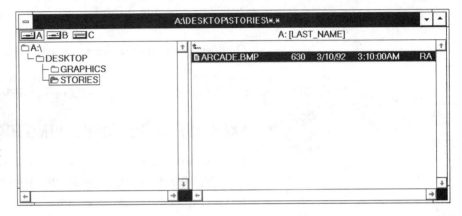

Use the Partial Details dialog box (see Figure 5.10) to select any combination of the four check boxes. Check a box to select it. When you have made all your choices, click on the OK command button.

Figure 5.10

In this Partial Details dialog box, all four of the check boxes are selected.

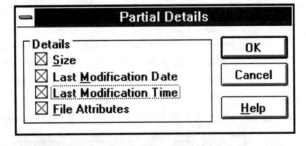

EXERCISE 5 • 8   DISPLAYING FILE ATTRIBUTES

1. Select the ARCADE.BMP file if it is not already selected.

2. Select the All File Details... option from the View menu to display the file attributes as shown in Figure 5.9.

NOTE: You may need to enlarge the window to display the entire listing.

The letters "RA" to the right of the file listing is the flag code, which indicates that this file has been assigned the Read Only and Archive attributes.

Removing File Attributes

File attributes are removed or changed by selecting the Properties... option on the File menu and by checking the appropriate check box or by removing the check from the appropriate check box.

EXERCISE 5 • 9   REMOVING FILE ATTRIBUTES

1. Verify that the ARCADE.BMP file is selected in the contents directory (the right pane) of the STORIES directory window.

2. Select the Properties... option from the File menu.

3. Click in the Read Only and Archive check boxes to remove the check.

4. Click on OK. Since all the attributes were removed from this file, no attributes will be shown in the directory window.

Displaying Hidden Files

Earlier you learned that a file could be hidden from the display listing by checking the Hidden check box in the Properties dialog box.

EXERCISE 5 • 10   DISPLAYING HIDDEN FILES

1. Verify that the ARCADE.BMP file is selected in the contents directory (the right pane) of the Stories directory window.

2. Select the Properties... option from the File menu.

3. Click in the Hidden check box to set the hidden file attribute.

4. Click on OK. The ARCADE.BMP file will no longer be listed in the directory contents listing because it has been assigned a hidden attribute.

   Remember, a hidden file is not deleted from the disk--it is only hidden from view. The By File Type... option on the View menu permits you to indicate which types of files are displayed in your directory listing, including hidden and system files. As you see in Figure 5.11, the By File Type dialog box lists four check boxes under File Type (Directory, Programs, Documents, and Other Files) and a separate check box labeled Show Hidden/System Files (check this box if you want to display hidden and system files).

Figure 5.11

In this By File Type dialog box, note the four check boxes under File Type and the separate check box for Show Hidden/System Files.

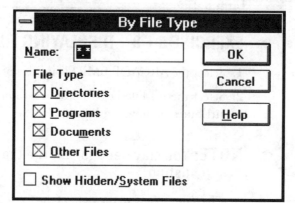

5. Select the By File Type... option from the View menu.

6. Click in the Show Hidden/System Files check box if it is not already checked.

7. Click on OK. The ARCADE.BMP file will display with hidden attribute code "H." Notice the file icon is a page with an exclamation mark (in red if you have a color monitor). These visual clues tell you this is a hidden or system file.

8. Verify that the ARCADE.BMP file is selected.

9. Select the Properties... option from the File menu and remove the check from the Hidden check box.

10. Select the By File Type... option from the View menu and remove the check from the Show Hidden/System Files check box.

11. Double-click on File Manager's Control-menu box to close File Manager.

VIEW 3
RUNNING APPLICATIONS

PREVIEW

You learned in Session 2 how to run applications from the Program Manager. You can also run applications in File Manager. For example, you can open a file in File Manager by:

- double-clicking on selected data file icons,
- by issuing commands from the File menu, and by
- dragging with the mouse.

Associating Files

In File Manager you can create an icon that launches an application and immediately opens a specific document file that was created in that application. To create a launchable data icon, associate files that contain a given extension with the application that supports those files.

For example, .BMP is the standard file extension for Microsoft Paintbrush files. You can create an association between all files with the .BMP extension and the Paintbrush application program. But, remember, that once you associate a selected file with a specific application, you associate *any* other files bearing the same extension with that application too.

Once an association exists, you can double-click on any document file icon with the associated extension (.BMP in our example) in any directory window and automatically start the application *and* load the selected file at the same time.

Figure 5.12

An associated (left) and an unassociated (right) document file icon

As shown in Figure 5.12, an associated document file icon looks like a piece of lined paper; an *un*associated document file looks like a blank sheet of paper.

Files are associated by selecting the Associate... command from the File menu and keying the filename that launches the application (this filename generally has an .EXE extension). Figure 5.13 illustrates the Associate dialog box for the Paintbrush document files used in the example above.

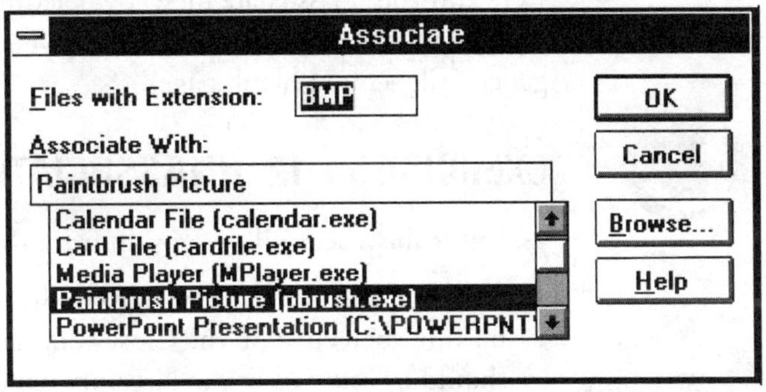

Figure 5.13

In this Associate dialog box, PBRUSH.EXE is highlighted in the Text File text box.

Associate
Files with Extension: BMP
Associate With:
Paintbrush Picture
Calendar File (calendar.exe)
Card File (cardfile.exe)
Media Player (MPlayer.exe)
Paintbrush Picture (pbrush.exe)
PowerPoint Presentation (C:\POWERPNT

OK
Cancel
Browse...
Help

EXERCISE 5 • 11 ASSOCIATING FILES

1. Open File Manager by double-clicking on its icon in the Main group.

2. Select the drive that contains the Windows directory.

3. Verify that the Windows directory is selected.

4. Select the Select Files... option from the File menu. The Select Files dialog box will display.

5. Key the wildcard and extension *.*TXT* in the text box in the Select Files dialog box.

6. Click on the Select command button, then click on the Close command button.

7. Verify that at least one file is selected (you may have to scroll to locate one), then select the Associate... option from the File menu. The Associate dialog box will display with Text File (notepad.exe) highlighted in the text box, as shown in Figure 5.14, indicating that all .TXT document files are associated with the Notepad application.

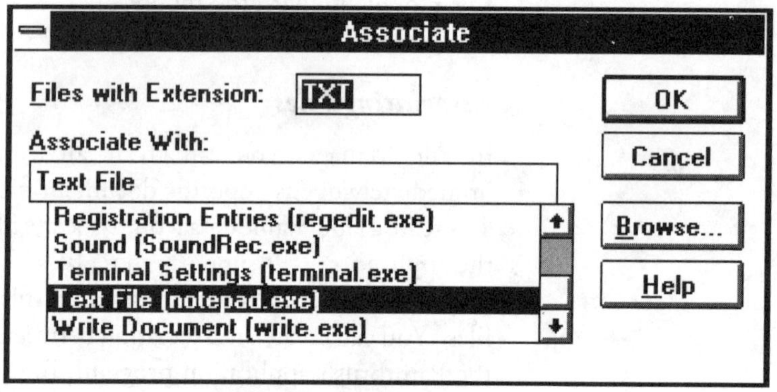

Figure 5.14

In this Associate dialog box, Text File (notepad.exe) is highlighted in the Text Files box.

Associate	
Files with Extension: [TXT]	OK
Associate With:	Cancel
Text File	
Registration Entries (regedit.exe) ↑	**B**rowse...
Sound (SoundRec.exe)	
Terminal Settings (terminal.exe)	**H**elp
Text File (notepad.exe)	
Write Document (write.exe) ↓	

8. Click on the OK button to close the dialog box.

9. Locate one of the document files that is selected. Notice that this is an associated file (the icon is a lined sheet of paper).

10. Double-click on the selected document file icon to launch the Notepad application and load the document.

11. Study the document window, then click on the Control-menu box to close the document window.

Unassociating Files

How can you unassociate files? By deleting the application name in the text box in the Associate dialog box. The File Manager will convert the file's icon into a generic file icon (a blank page).

EXERCISE 5 • 12 UNASSOCIATING FILES

1. Select the Select Files... option from the File menu.

2. Key the filename *WININI.WRI* in the text box and click on Select command button, then click on the Close command button. One file, WININI.WRI, should be selected in the directory window.

3. Select the Associate... option from the File menu. The dialog box shows that the WRI document files are associated with Write.

4. Scroll up the Associate With listing box until the [None] option comes into view, then click on the [None] option. Notice that None is placed in the Associate With text box.

5. Click on the OK command button.

6. Double-click on the document file icon. The message "No application is associated with this file" appears.

7. Click on the OK command button to close the message box.

8. Select the Associate... option from the File menu.

9. Scroll the text box listing and select the Write Document [write.exe] option, then click on OK. Notice the selected document file icon now displays as an associated file icon.

10. Double-click on the selected document file icon to launch the Write program and open the selected file.

11. Double-click on the document window Control-menu box to close the window.

Using File Menu Commands

You can run applications by using commands in the File menu. For example, you can select an executable file (any file with an .EXE extension) in any directory window and select the Open command to run the application. Or if you prefer, you can select the Run... command so that File Manager will display the Run dialog box, as shown in Figure 5.15. When the Run dialog box is displayed, key the path and the name of the application's executable file on the command line, and press Enter. If you want to load a document file for that application as well, key the path and the name of the application's executable file followed by a space, the path, and name of the document file. If the application or its document file is in the current directory, or in a directory that is included in your path, you can simply use filenames without the preceding path information.

Figure 5.15

In this Run dialog box, note that the path and name of the application's executable file are keyed.

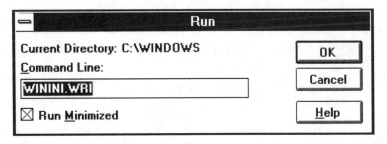

EXERCISE 5 • 13 ISSUING FILE MENU COMMANDS

Using the Open Option

1. Verify that the WINDOWS directory is selected.

2. Select the Select Files... option from the File menu.

3. Key *.*WRI* in the text box and click on the Select command button, then click on the Close command button. Scroll and locate the NETWORKS.WRI file, which is highlighted in the directory window.

4. Select the Open option from the File menu. The NETWORKS.WRI file will open. Notice that the Title bar displays the name of the application, Write, and the name of the document, NETWORKS.WRI.

5. Double-click on the Control-menu box of the NETWORKS.WRI document to close the file and the document window.

Issuing the Run... Command

6. Select the Run... command from the File menu.

7. Key *WRITE.EXE* in the text box and click on OK. The Write program will launch and open an untitled document.

8. Double-click on the Write window Control-menu box to close the untitled document and the Write program.

   If you prefer, you can select the Run Minimize check box to run the application and place it as a application icon at the bottom of your desktop.

Issuing the Run Minimized Command

It is easier to understand the Run Minimized command if the Program Manager is minimized. The File Manager may be covering the Program Manager, so use the [Alt]+[Tab] shortcut to scroll through the active application programs and bring the Program Manager to the front.

9. Use the [Alt]+[Tab] until the Program Manager is selected.

10. Minimize the Program Manager.

11. Select the Tile option from the Window menu.

12. Select the Run... command from the File menu.

13. Key *PRINTERS.WRI* in the text box.

14. Click on the Run Minimized check box to check the box.

15. Click on OK. The Write program is launched, and the PRINTERS.WRI file is minimized at the bottom of the desktop as a Write icon with the filename beneath it.

16. Double-click on the PRINTERS.WRI icon to open the document window.

17. Double-click on the Control-menu box to close the application.

Dragging with the Mouse

Another way to launch a document along with its application program is to drag the document file icon on top of the appropriate application program file. For example, if you want to work with a monthly report named MONTHLY.WRI created in Write, you can simply drag the MONTHLY.WRI document file icon on top of the WRITE.EXE application program filename, as illustrated in Figure 5.16.

   File Manager will verify that you want to start Write with your monthly report as the initial file; specifically, File Manager will display a Confirm message box like the one in Figure 5.17. After you click on Yes, the File Manager will open Write's application windows and immediately open your monthly report. When you exit Write, Windows will return to the File Manager.

Figure 5.16

You can launch a document and its application program by dragging a document file icon over an application program icon.

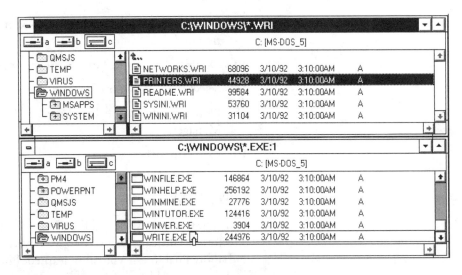

Figure 5.17

Confirm Mouse Operation message box

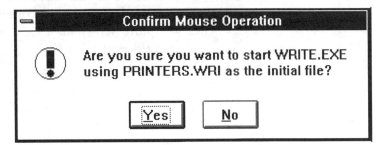

EXERCISE 5 • 14 RUNNING APPLICATIONS BY DRAGGING WITH THE MOUSE

1. Verify that the WINDOWS directory window is selected.

2. Select the By File Type... option from the View menu.

3. Key the wildcard and extension *.EXE in the text box, then click on the OK command button.

4. Select the New Window option from the Window menu.

5. Select the Tile option from the Window menu. If your directory windows do not fill the screen, you may want to maximize the File Manager application window.

6. Select the bottom window if it is not already selected.

7. Select the By File Type... option from the View menu.

8. Key the wildcard and extension *.WRI in the text box, then click on the OK command button.

9. Scroll the *.EXE directory window until the WRITE.EXE file is in view.

10. Point on the PRINTERS.WRI document file icon in the *.WRI document window and drag it on top of the WRITE.EXE program icon in the *.EXE Document window. The Confirm Mouse Operation message box will appear.

11. Click on Yes. The Write application window will appear with the PRINTERS.WRI file opened.

12. Double-click on the Write window Control-menu box to close the application and file.

13. Double-click on the bottom directory window to close it.

14. Select the Cascade option from the Window menu.

15. Double-click on the File Manager Control-menu box to close the File Manager.

16. Exit Windows.

SUMMARY

In this session you witnessed the power of File Manager to manipulate files and directories. You learned how to copy, move, and delete directories, subdirectories, and individual files. You also learned how to associate files with specific applications, and how to unassociate those files if necessary. Finally, you learned a few more mouse and keyboard tricks to use when working with Windows. This experience will prove very valuable and will enable you to use Windows productively and efficiently!

OBJECTIVES

When you complete this session, you will be able to:

- Explain the purpose and value of using the Windows Accessories that serve as Personal Information Managers (PIMs).

- Create, edit, save, and print a Notepad document.

- Copy and move text using the Clipboard.

- Insert, delete, replace, copy, and move text in a Notepad document.

- Use the Calculator to perform basic arithmetic computations.

- Maintain an appointment calendar, set message reminders, and print daily appointment pages in the Windows Calendar.

- Create, maintain, and utilize Cardfile to retrieve stored information.

● ● ● ● ● ● ● ● ● ● ● ● ● ●

SESSION 6   *ACCESSORIES: WINDOWS PERSONAL INFORMATION MANAGERS*

VIEWS
Notepad
Calculator
Calendar
Cardfile

119

ACCESSORIES: WINDOWS PERSONAL INFORMATION MANAGERS

A major feature of Windows is that it can run several programs simultaneously. For example, Windows comes with a number of helpful desktop accessory applications (sometimes called **applets**) that are designed to be used *while* you are working in a program application—that's why they are called **accessory applications**. Thus, while working in *Word for Windows*, you could use the calculator accessory to add a column of numbers; while in *Excel* for Windows, you could use the Notepad accessory to write a short note or reminder. Equally important, desktop accessories do not use much computer memory.

In this session, you will learn to use the Notepad, the Calculator, the Calendar, the Cardfile, and the Clock. These desktop accessories are sometimes referred to as **Personal Information Managers**, or **PIMs**, because these tools closely resemble the physical objects you might keep on your real desk to help you manage your work, your time, your files, and your notes. In later sessions, you will learn to use Write (a word processing program) and Paintbrush (a graphic illustration program). All of these accessories are located in the Accessories group window.

To start these PIMs, or any other accessory, open the Accessories group window by double-clicking on its icon in the Program Manager and then double-click on the program-item icon for the specific application you want to run. PIMs are loaded into memory while you are working with them, and they remain loaded in memory when you move to other applications. As a result, you can access PIMs easily (with an [Alt] + [Tab]).

VIEW 1
NOTEPAD

PREVIEW

Notepad is a simplistic word processing program that reads and writes ASCII text files (files that contain words and numbers but no formatting information). Notepad has limited formatting and editing capabilities and uses only one font, so it works more quickly on screen than programs that do display text in different fonts, styles, and sizes (for example, Write).

Notepad is generally used to:

• Create files that can be sent to a computer bulletin board or through an electronic mail system.

• Create and modify DOS files (such as the AUTOEXEC.BAT file) or Windows system files (such as the WIN.INI or SYSTEM.INI files).

• Key simple notes, quick reminders, records of phone calls, and daily "to do" lists.

Notepad is *not* used to create long, complex documents. When your documents need formatting or other more complicated features, use Windows Write, a more comprehensive word processing program which is presented in Session 7.

Starting Notepad and Keyboarding Text

To start Notepad, double-click on the Notepad icon in the Accessories group window. You are able to begin keying your text immediately.

As shown in Figure 6.1, at the top of the Notepad window, you see Notepad (Untitled) on the Notepad title bar and under it, the menu bar with its four options:

- File - This option lets you open, save, and print Notepad files.

- Edit - This option includes several editing functions, including Select All, which selects everything that is keyed. The Time/Date option is used to insert the current time and date whenever you open a file, and Word Wrap is used to make the text wrap automatically at the right-hand window border.

- Search - Using the Find and Find Next Options, Notepad lets you quickly locate and move to specific text within a Notepad document.

- Help - This feature lets you access more information on Notepad.

Figure 6.1

When the Notepad window opens, the cursor appears as a thin vertical line immediately below the FIle option.

Cursor

Scroll bars

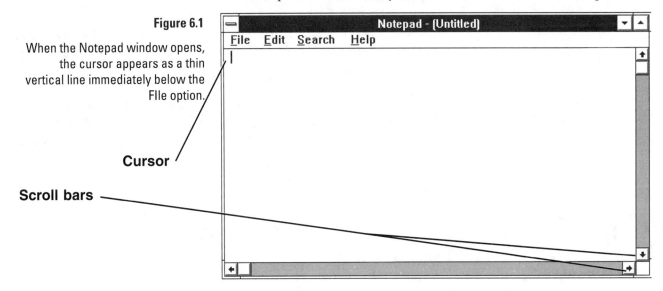

Look just below the word *File* on the Notepad menu bar and you will find the cursor, a thin vertical line that indicates the *insertion point*, the place where text will be entered when you begin keying. On screen, the cursor appears as a blinking line. The insertion point is controlled by the keyboard, but you can change it by using the mouse. When you enter text, each character you key will appear to the *left* of the cursor. Actually, you will find that you have two cursors: the insertion point changes to an I-beam pointer when controlled by the mouse.

You can move around the Notepad window several ways by using the mouse or the keyboard. You cannot move beyond the end of the document.

Moving Around Notepad With the Mouse

Follow these procedures to move around Notepad by using the mouse:

- To scroll up or down the page, click on the arrows at either end of the *vertical* scroll bar. You will note that using the scroll bar does not move the insertion point.

- To move the page to the left or right, click on either end of the *horizontal* scroll bar.

• To move the cursor anywhere on the screen, position the mouse arrow and then click.

Moving Around Notepad With the Keyboard

You can also use the keyboard to move around Notepad.

• Scroll a page by pressing [Pg Up] or [Pg Dn].

• Scroll one line at a time by pressing the up arrow or down arrow.

• Move to the beginning of a line by pressing [Home].

• Move to the end of a line by pressing [End].

• Move to either the beginning or the end of the document by pressing [Ctrl]+[Home] or [Ctrl]+[End].

• Use the [Spacebar] and [Enter] as needed to move the text to the desired location.

Now look at Figure 6.2, which shows all the options on the File, Edit, and Search menus. Note especially the Word Wrap option in the Edit menu. (Other options will be discussed later.) Notepad does not automatically word wrap.

NOTE: **Word wrap** means that the computer determines how much text will fit on a line and automatically moves text to the next line when necessary. This means you only press [Enter] at the end of paragraphs instead of at the end of each line.

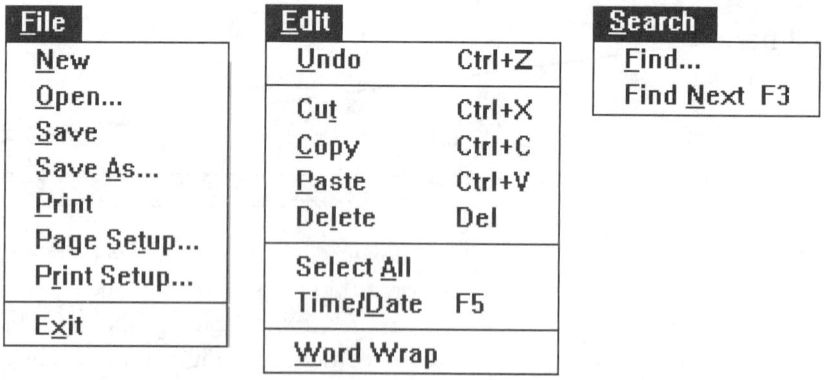

Figure 6.2

Notepad's File, Edit, and Search menus expanded

File	Edit		Search
New	Undo	Ctrl+Z	Find...
Open...			Find Next F3
Save	Cut	Ctrl+X	
Save As...	Copy	Ctrl+C	
Print	Paste	Ctrl+V	
Page Setup...	Delete	Del	
Print Setup...	Select All		
Exit	Time/Date	F5	
	Word Wrap		

With Notepad, you must select the Word Wrap option if you want Notepad to fit the text in the window. In Figure 6.3 the top window shows the text without the Word Wrap option active. The smaller window shows the results of selecting the Word Wrap option. Or if you prefer, you can indicate your own line breaks by pressing [Enter]. Otherwise, Notepad continues text across the screen.

EXERCISE 6 • 1   STARTING NOTEPAD AND KEYING TEXT

1. Start Windows, if it is not currently running.

2. Open Notepad by double-clicking on its program-item icon in the Program Manager's Accessories group.

3. Select the Word Wrap option from the Edit menu.

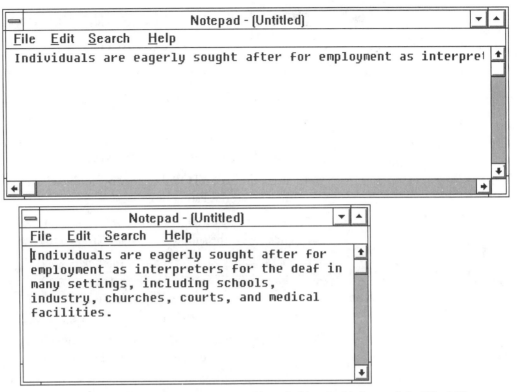

Figure 6.3 Notepad text shown without (top) and with (bottom) the Word Wrap option selected

4. Key text:

   a. Use the [Backspace] or the [Delete] key to correct errors as necessary.

   b. Press [Enter] only at the end of a paragraph, not at the end of each line. Let Notepad word wrap the text for you.

   c. Now key the following text:

Because Notepad creates files, you can open and edit Windows system files and other text files. Text files generally have a .BAT, .INI, or .TXT file extension.

A Notepad document can hold nearly 50,000 characters, about 8 to 10 pages. If you exceed that amount, you will get an error message saying you have insufficient memory. This message will appear regardless of your system's memory capacity.

Saving and Printing a Notepad Document

You can save Notepad documents on disk and print Notepad files (paper printouts are called **hard copy**). To save documents, use the Save or the Save As... option on the File menu. Use Save As... the first time you save a file, because Save As... requires you to name your file. Once you save a file the first time, Windows will know the name of the file; you can save revisions simply by selecting the Save option. (Actually, Windows will not accept your Save command if it doesn't know the name of the file. It will proceed as if you had selected Save As... and will ask you to name your new file.)

Saving a file under a new name is another way of copying a file. To do so, use the File menu's Save As... option. Simply key the new filename in the dialog box and click on the OK command button.

Use the Print option on the File menu to print a document.

EXERCISE 6 . 2   SAVING AND PRINTING A NOTEPAD DOCUMENT

1. Insert your *Win Practice* disk in one of the floppy disk drives.

2. Select the Save As... command from the File Menu.

3. Select the drive that contains your *Win Practice* disk. Click on the down arrow in the Drives listing box. From the drop-down list, click on the icon of the drive that contains your *Win Practice* disk.

4. Select the DESKTOP directory by double-clicking on the directory name in the Directories listing box.

5. Select the STORIES subdirectory in the DESKTOP directory by double-clicking on the subdirectory name in the Directories listing box.

6. Double-click on the *.TXT in the Filename listing box to highlight the text. (Notepad will automatically delete the *.TXT name that appears as the filename when you key your filename.)

7. Key the filename *NOTEPAD* in the File name text box, then click on the OK command button. (Notepad will automatically assign your file a .TXT extension. If you want a different extension, key it along with the filename.)

   Continue with Step 8 only if you have a printer attached to your computer system:

8. Select the Print option from the File menu. Inspect the printed document.

Inserting, Deleting, and Replacing Text

Notepad offers a number of features to help you edit your documents. For example, with Notepad you can:

- *Add* characters by moving the cursor to the desired location, clicking the mouse button, then keying the text.

- *Delete* characters by pressing the [Del] or the [Backspace] key, depending on the position of the cursor.

- *Replace* characters by keying new text over old text. First, select or highlight the undesired text by clicking an insertion point to left of the location where the replacement is to go, then click the mouse button and drag the mouse across the undesired text. The next character keyed will replace the highlighted text (the highlighted text will be deleted).

- *Undo* the changes you have just made by selecting the Undo option on the Edit menu. The Undo command gives you an opportunity to change your mind. Undo will reverse only your most recent edit.

EXERCISE 6 . 3   INSERTING, DELETING, AND REPLACING TEXT

1. Click an insertion point immediately after the letter **s** in the word **creates** in the first line of text.

2. Press [Spacebar] once, then key the word *text*.

3. Click an insertion point immediately following the letter **d** in the word **and** near the end of the first line of text.

4. Press [Backspace] nine times to remove the letters **d**, **n**, **a**, and **space**, then remove the letters **n**, **e**, **p**, and **o** and the space following the letter **o**.

5. Click an insertion point immediately before the letter **n** in the word **nearly** in the first sentence of the second paragraph.

6. Press and hold the mouse button, then drag across the word **nearly** to select it.

7. Key the word *almost*. Notice that the keyed text replaced the original text.

8. Click an insertion point immediately before the comma following the word **characters** in the first sentence of the second paragraph.

9. Press and hold the mouse button, then drag across the text up to the period at the end of the sentence—do not include the period.

10. Press [Delete] to delete the text. **Do not do anything until you have read the next instruction!**

11. Select the Undo option from the Edit menu. Notice the deleted text is placed back into the document in the same place it was before it was cut.

12. Select the Print option from the File menu. Inspect your printed document.

Copying and Moving Text Using the Clipboard

Notepad's Edit menu, shown previously in Figure 6.2, offers a number of additional options for editing text. The two most often used editing features are *copy* and *move*.

• The **copy** feature lets you duplicate text from one area of a document and use it in another. To copy text, use the Copy and Paste options:

   - Highlight the text.

   - Select Copy from the Edit menu.

   - Position the cursor where you want the copy to go.

   - Select Paste from the Edit menu.

   It is that simple!

• The **move** feature allows you to *remove* text from one area of the document and transfer it to another area. To move text, use the Cut and Paste commands in the same way you use Copy and Paste.

In either case, the Copy and the Cut commands place a block of text onto the Windows Clipboard, a temporary storage area. Notepad's Paste command empties the contents of the Clipboard and places the stored block at the cursor position.

EXERCISE 6 • 4   COPYING AND MOVING TEXT USING THE CLIPBOARD

Copying Text

1. Click an insertion point immediately before the letter **A**, the first word in the first line of the second paragraph.

2. Press the mouse button and drag across the sentence up to and including the two spaces following the period to select the sentence.

3. Select the Copy option from the Edit menu. The text is copied to the Clipboard. Notice the text still appears in the document. You will not see anything happening to the text you have copied to the Clipboard.

4. Click an insertion point immediately following the period at the end of the second paragraph.

5. Press [Spacebar] twice.

6. Select the Paste option from the Edit menu. The text is copied from the Clipboard and pasted to your document at the position of the insertion point.

Moving Text

7. Click an insertion point immediately before the first word in the first paragraph ("Because").

8. Drag to select the entire paragraph (up to and including the period after the word "extension").

9. Select the Cut option from the Edit menu. The selected text is cut from the document and placed on the Clipboard.

10. Click an insertion point immediately following the last word in the last paragraph.

11. Press [Enter] twice to create a blank line after the last line of the second paragraph.

12. Select the Paste option from the Edit menu.

13. Select the Print option from the File menu. Inspect your document when it is printed.

Searching a Notepad Document

The Search menu lets you quickly locate words and phrases in a Notepad document. Using the insertion point as the starting position, Notepad searches the document in either a forward or a backward direction.

The Search menu has two options—Find... and Find Next. When you select Find..., the Find dialog box (Figure 6.4) displays. To begin the search, key the text you are searching for (called the **text string**) in the Find What text box. In the Direction box choose Up (if you want to search to the beginning of the document) or Down (if you want to search to the end of the document). (Remember: The starting position is the cursor's present location. Click on the Find Next command button to begin the search.)

Figure 6.4

Find dialog box

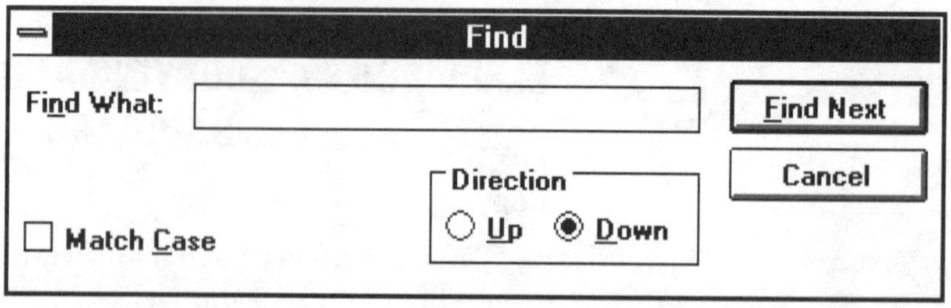

Unless you check the Match Case check box, Find will locate all occurrences of the text string—that is, *any* match, regardless of capitalization. For example, if you enter *And* in the Find What text box and do not check Match Case, Find will consider *AND, and,* even comm*and* to be the same text string. But if you want to limit the search to occurrences of *And* only, then check the Match Case box and Find will disregard *and, AND,* comm*and,* etc. In other words, Find will match the Find What text string <u>exactly</u>. Then, once you've used the Find command, you can use Find Next to search for the next occurrence of the same text string.

EXERCISE 6 • 5   SEARCHING A NOTEPAD DOCUMENT

1. Click an insertion point immediately before the first word in the document.

2. Select the Find... option from the Search menu. The Find dialog box opens.

3. Key *files* in the Find What text box.

4. Click on the Match Case check box to select it.

5. Verify that the Down Direction button is selected, then click on the Find Next command button. When Notepad finds the first occurrence of the word *files*, it stops the search and highlights the word. The Find Dialog box remains displayed in front of the Notepad document. (You may need to move the Find Dialog box to see the highlighted word.)

6. Double-click on the Find Dialog box Control-menu box to close the dialog box.

7. Select the Find Next option on the Search menu. The search will begin again, this time starting at the last occurrence of the word.

8. Select the Find Next option on the Search menu to search the remaining text. Select the Find Next option again. When Notepad finds no more occurrences of the search string, it shows the message box shown in Figure 6.5.

Figure 6.5

A Find message box tells you when it can find no further occurrences of the search string.

Printing in Notepad

Notepad offers only a few printing options—namely, margins, headers, and footers. To see the default settings for these options, select Page Setup on the File Menu. As you see in Figure 6.6, the default settings are:

Left and right margins: .75 inch

Top and bottom margins: 1 inch

Header: &f (which prints the name of your file as the header text)

Footer: Page &p (which prints the word *Page* and the page number as the footer text)

Figure 6.6

Sample of Notepad default page setup settings

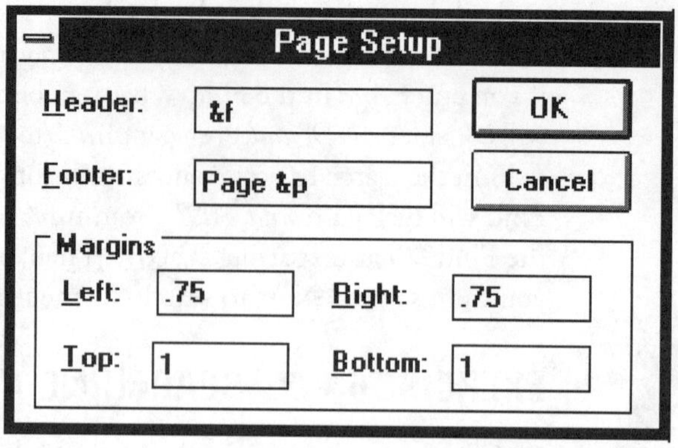

Page Setup

Header: &f

Footer: Page &p

OK

Cancel

Margins

Left: .75   Right: .75

Top: 1   Bottom: 1

To change these defaults, use the text boxes in the Page Setup dialog box. For example, if you wish, you can use the title of your report for the header text or "Draft Copy" (see Figure 6.7 listing of the special header and footer codes recognized by Notepad and their uses).

Figure 6.7

Notepad header and footer codes

Header and Footer Codes	
Used in Windows Accessories Programs	
Key . . .	to get . . .
&d	current date
&t	current time
&f	name of your file
&p	page number
&l	flush left alignment
&r	flush right alignment
&c	center alignment

EXERCISE 6 . 6   PRINTING A NOTEPAD DOCUMENT WITH A HEADER AND FOOTER

1. Select the Page setup option from the File menu.

2. Key the header &r&d. These codes will position the header flush with the right margin (&r) and print the current date (&d).

3. Key the footer &cPage &p. This command will produce a footer that consists of the word *Page* followed by the page number (&p), centered between the right and left margins (&c).

4. Click on the OK command button to accept the changes and close the Page Setup dialog box.

5. Select the Print option from the File menu to print the document. Inspect your document when it is printed.

Closing a Notepad Document

You can close a Notepad document by:

- Opening a new file.

- Closing the Notepad program.

To open a file, select the Open... option from the File menu. To close a document and quit Notepad, select the Exit option from the File menu. Remember to save your file before you exit.

EXERCISE 6 . 7   CLOSING NOTEPAD

1. Select the Save option from the File menu.

2. Select the New option from the File menu. This will close the current file, but Notepad will remain open.

VIEW 2
CALCULATOR

PREVIEW

Calculator is a handy personal information manager that has two operating modes—standard and scientific. On screen, Calculator appears in its own window, and its title bar is labeled Calculator, of course. As shown in Figure 6.8, the standard calculator and the scientific calculator both offer the same three menu options: Edit, View, and Help.

Figure 6.8

The standard calculator window (top) and the scientific calculator window (bottom)

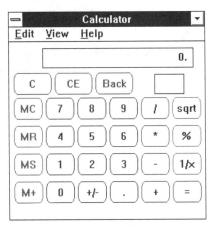

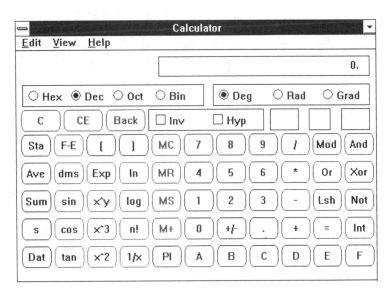

You can minimize the calculator to an icon, but it has no maximize button; the Calculator window cannot be resized. To switch from one mode to the other, use the View menu.

In either Calculator mode, you can use the mouse or the keyboard. The numeric keypad (to the right of your alphabetic keyboard) functions like a standard 10-key calculator. Just turn on [Num Lock] to activate the numeric keypad.

The standard calculator can compute addition, subtraction, multiplication, and division, of course, as well as square roots, percentages, reciprocals, and much more. The scientific calculator is capable of very complex computations. The scientific calculator works the same as the standard calculator but contains 30 or more advanced mathematical features. Both calculators have a memory for storing data.

Opening and Closing Calculator

To open the Calculator, double-click on its icon in the Accessories group. Whether the Calculator opens in the standard or the scientific mode depends on its last setting. To change the mode, select Standard or Scientific on the View menu.

To close the Calculator, click on the Control-menu box and select Close.

EXERCISE 6 • 8   OPENING CALCULATOR AND SELECTING A VIEW

1. Double-click on the Calculator icon to open the Calculator window.

2. Select the Scientific option on the View menu. Notice that the scientific calculator has more buttons than a standard pocket calculator.

3. Select the Standard option from the View menu.

Using the Standard Calculator

To operate the Calculator, press the appropriate buttons, using either the mouse or the numeric keypad to the right of the keyboard. This is one Windows application when the mouse is *not* easier than the keyboard! When using a mouse, select number and function keys on the Calculator by clicking on the appropriate keys. Numbers appear in the display window as you select them or as the Calculator computes them.

When using the numeric keypad, just press the appropriate numbers and arithmetic operators on the numeric keypad. Notice all the basic arithmetic operators are to the right of and below the keypad. To edit the display or perform calculations using the keyboard or a mouse, note these instructions:

To	Using the Keyboard *Press*	Using the Mouse *Click On*
Add	[+]	+
Subtract	[-]	-
Multiply	[*]	*

To	Using the Keyboard *Press*	Using the Mouse *Click On*
Divide	[/]	/
Clear (erase) the memory	[Esc]	C
Clear last function or displayed number	[Delete]	CE
Delete the last number in the displayed value	[Backspace]/ Left Arrow	Back
Clear the Calculation	[Esc]	C
Add displayed number to current value in memory and place result in memory	[Ctrl]+[P]	M+
Clear memory	[Ctrl]+[L]	MC
Recall value from memory	[Ctrl]+[R}	MR
Store current value in memory	[Ctrl]+[M]	MS
Compute square root of displayed number	[@]	sqrt
Treat the current value as a percentage	[%]	%
Change the current value's sign	[F9}	+/-

Note that for division, you press [/] or click on the slash (/) button, and for multiplication, you press [*] or click on the asterisk (*) button. If you make a mistake while making an entry, press [Backspace] or click on the Back button on the calculator to erase the last digit or arithmetic operator from the display. Continue erasing one character at a time until you correct the error.

To clear the last entry in a series of entries, press [Del] or click on the CE (Clear Entry) button. For example, if you are adding a series of numbers and make a mistake on the third entry, simply click on the CE button immediately after entering the incorrect number, and then re-enter the last number. You do not need to start again.

To clear the calculator entirely and return the display to 0, press [Esc] or click on the C button.

The simplest way to learn to use the Calculator is to do a few exercises using the keypad and the keyboard.

EXERCISE 6 • 9   MAKING SIMPLE CALCULATIONS

Use the standard calculator to complete this exercise.

Addition

1. Compute the sum of 4 + 2:

   a. Key *[4]* then *[+]*. The number **4** should appear in the display.

   b. Key *[2]* then *[=]*. The answer **6** should appear in the display.

Subtraction

2. Compute the remainder 100 - 60:

    a. Key *[1][0][0]* then *[-]*. The number **100** will appear in the display.

    b. Key *[6][0]* then *[=]*. The answer **40** will appear in the display.

Multiplication

3. Compute the product of 50 x 3:

    a. Key *[5][0]* then *[*]*. The number **50** will appear in the display.

    b. Key *[3]* then *[=]*. The answer **150** will appear in the display.

Division

4. Compute the quotient of 100 / 25 (100 divided by 25):

    a. Key *[1][0][0]* then *[/]*. The number **100** will appear in the display.

    b. Key *[2][5]* then *[=]*. The answer **4** will appear in the display.

After you click [=], you can repeat the last instruction by clicking [=] again. For example, in problem 4 above, the first time you press [=] you are giving the **instruction** to divide by 25. You get the answer **4**. If you repeat this instruction, then Calculator will divide 4 by 25 (to give 0.16). Each time you press [=], you will divide by 25 again.

EXERCISE 6 • 10 MAKING MORE COMPLEX CALCULATIONS

Calculating Percents

1. Find 28% of 75:

    a. Key *[7][5]* then *[*]*. The number **75** will appear in the display.

    b. Key *[2][8]* then *[%]*. The answer **21** will appear in the display.

    c. Press [Esc] to clear all numbers and functions. You must always clear the calculator display after computing a percentage.

Computing Square Roots

2. Find the square root of 144:

    a. Key *[1][4][4]*.

    b. Press [@]. The answer **12** will appear in the display.

    c. Press [Esc] to clear all numbers and functions.

Using Memory Functions

The memory buttons MC, MR, MS, and M+ on both the standard calculator and the scientific calculator let you save a number in the calculator's memory. When you put a number in memory, an **M** appears in the display box immediately to the right of the Back key, as shown in Figure 6.9

To put a number in memory, select the number in the display, then click on the M+ button. To save the result of a calculated number, click on the MS

Figure 6.9

The **M** displayed in the box to the right of the Back key informs you that a number is stored in memory.

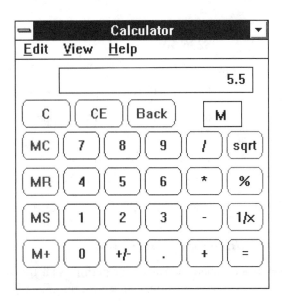

(memory store) button once the result is calculated. To recall a stored number from memory, click on the MR (memory recall) button.

EXERCISE 6 ● 11 USING MEMORY FUNCTIONS

Use the keypad to the right of the keyboard in this exercise.

1. Compute the sum of (15 x 23) + (224 / 16):

    a. Key *[1][5]* then *[*]*; key *[2][3]* then *[=]*. The answer **345** will appear in the display.

    b. Press [Ctrl]+[P]. The letter **M** appears in the display beneath the number **345**.

    c. Key *[2][2][4]* then *[/]*; key *[1][6]* then *[=]*. The answer **14** appears in the display.

    d. Press [Ctrl]+[P]. The **14** remains in the display.

    e. Press [Ctrl]+[R]. The number **359** is shown in the display.

    f. Click on the MC button to clear the memory.

    g. Click on the C button to clear the display.

    The memory function is especially useful when you want to multiply or divide a number of values by the same amount.

2. Compute the earnings at $5.50 an hour for 32.5, 43, and 27 hours:

    a. Key *[5][.][5]*, then press [Ctrl]+[P]. The letter **M** appears in the display window along with the number **5.5**.

    b. Key *[3][2][.][5]* then *[*]*.

    c. Press [Ctrl]+[R]. The memory value **5.5** appears in the display.

    d. Key *[=]*. The result, **178.75**, appears in the display window. The answer is **$178.75**.

    e. Key *[4][3]*, then *[*]*. The value **43** appears in the display window.

    f. Press [Ctrl]+[R]. The memory value **5.5** appears in the display.

g. Key *[=]*. The result **236.5** appears in the display window. The answer is **$236.50**.

h. Key *[2][7]*, then *[*]*. The value **27** appears in the display window.

i. Press [Ctrl]+[R]. The memory value **5.5** appears in the display.

j. Key *[=]*. The result **148.5** appears in the display window. The answer is **$148.50**.

3. Clear the memory and display:

a. Click on the MC button to clear the memory.

b. Click on the C button to clear the display.

Using the Scientific Mode

The scientific calculator performs all the arithmetic functions of the standard calculator plus these advanced functions:

- Exponential and logarithmic operations.

- Trigonometric calculations.

- Arithmetic calculations in the binary, octal, and hexadecimal number systems.

- Statistical calculations such as the average and standard deviation.

You can explore these features on your own.

VIEW 3
CALENDAR

PREVIEW

Windows Calendar is designed to support your appointment book or diary. It also provides an alarm clock, for which you can set a number of alarms (audible or visual) minutes, hours, days, or even years in advance.

To start Calendar, double-click on the Accessories group and then double-click on the Calendar icon. The Calendar window opens, with all the standard window elements (as shown in Figure 6.10):

- A title bar, **Calendar (Untitled)**.

- A menu bar, which shows seven menus: File, Edit, View, Show, Alarm, Options, and Help.

- Then, below the menu bar is the status line, which displays the current time (according to your computer's internal clock) and the calendar date.

- Beneath the status line, an appointment page is displayed in either Day view or Month view. You can switch between the two views by selecting Day or Month on the View menu.

- Finally, at the bottom of the Calendar (below the appointment area) is a box called the *scratch pad.*

Figure 6.10

You can look at your calendar in Day view (top) or Month view (bottom). Only one of these views will be displayed on your screen.

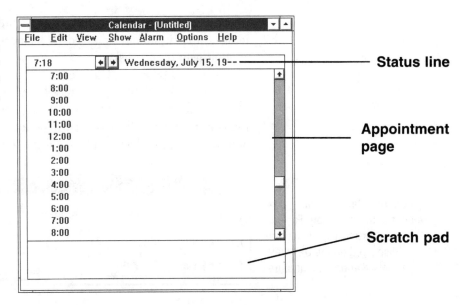

Status line

Appointment page

Scratch pad

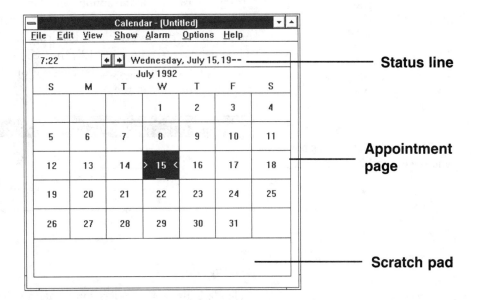

Status line

Appointment page

Scratch pad

EXERCISE 6 • 12 OPENING THE CALENDAR AND CHANGING ITS VIEW

1. Start Windows if it is not currently running.

2. Double-click on the Calendar icon in the Accessories group to open a Calendar window.

3. Select the Month view option from the View menu.

4. Select the Day view option from the View menu.

Making and Tracking Appointments

To record appointments in the time slots on the Day view calendar page, click an insertion point at the correct time and then key the entry on the scratch pad. Each line will hold about 80 characters. Press [Enter] after you key an appointment to indicate that it should be saved in memory. (This action will not save the appointment on the disk.)

Calendar displays the Day view appointment page in 60-minute intervals. If you prefer 15- or 30-minute intervals, select the Day Settings... option on the Options menu. The Day Settings dialog box (Figure 6.11) appears, with three Interval choices, as well as a choice in hour format (that is, a choice between a 12-hour or a 24-hour clock display) and the starting-time hour for the Day view.

Figure 6.11

In the Day Settings dialog box, select the Interval, Hour Format, and Starting Time you want displayed on the Day view appointment page.

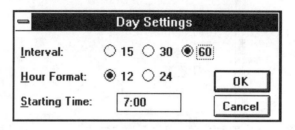

If you wish to make an appointment at a time other than one listed on the page, you can add a new time slot. Select the Special Time... option on the Options menu. When the Special Time dialog box displays, key your choice in the Special Time text box (see Figure 6.12), then click on the Insert command button. A special time can be deleted by clicking on the Delete command button after recording the time in the text box.

Figure 6.12

The Special Time dialog box lets you key in appointments at any time slot.

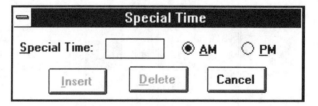

Setting Alarms

Calendar's alarm system lets you set alarms to notify you of appointments. You set an alarm by selecting the day and time, then selecting the Set option from the Alarm menu. A bell symbol indicating that the alarm is set appears to the left of the time.

By default, the alarm activates at the time you set for it. But you can use the Controls... option from the Alarm menu to create an "early warning system." The Alarm Controls dialog box (Figure 6.13) lets you specify the number of minutes prior to the specified time that you want the alarm to sound. Sound is a check box that lets you enable or disable the audible alarm. Of course, for the alarm to be audible, Calendar must be running as either a window or as an icon.

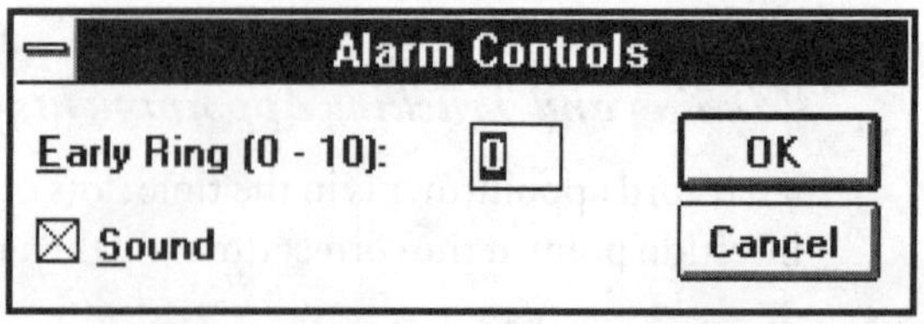

Figure 6.13

In the Alarm Controls dialog box, you can set an "early warning" ring.

Alarm Controls	
Early Ring (0 - 10): [0]	OK
☒ Sound	Cancel

At the scheduled time, Calendar beeps or plays the appropriate sound (if sound is enabled) and then notifies you of the alarm in one of the following ways:

• A reminder dialog box. If Calendar is the active window when the alarm goes off, a Please remember... dialog box follows with the message you keyed in, as shown in Figure 6.14.

Figure 6.14

Whenever an alarm is set, the Please Remember. . . dialog box displays the message you keyed.

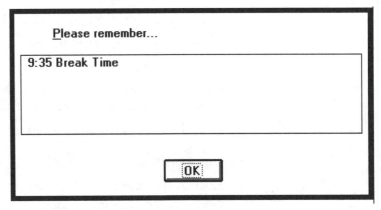

• Blinking Calendar title bar. If Calendar is open but is not the active window, the Calendar title bar flashes and beeps at the alarm time.

• Blinking icon. If calendar has been minimized to an icon, the Calendar icon flashes and beeps at the specified time. When you click on the flashing icon, the Please remember... message is displayed.

As you can see, the alarm works only if Calendar is active and running. If Calendar is not running when it is due to go off, Calendar will not beep, nor will any icon or menu bar flash. Instead, the next time Calendar loads the file that has the alarm, Calendar will post any reminder boxes that were missed.

EXERCISE 6 • 13 MAKING AND TRACKING APPOINTMENTS

Entering Appointments

Calendar should be open and displaying today's date in order to complete this exercise.

1. Enter an 8:00 a.m. appointment with Sandra Collins regarding payroll records:

   a. Click an insertion point to the right of the 8:00 a.m. time slot.

   b. Key the appointment text as shown here:

      Meeting with Sandra Collins - Payroll Records

   c. Press [Enter].

2. Enter a 12:00 noon Budget Committee luncheon meeting:

   a. Click an insertion point to the right of the 12:00 p.m. time slot.

   b. Key the appointment text as shown here:

      Lunch with Budget Committee

   c. Press [Enter].

Displaying a Different Date

3. Enter an appointment for an applicant interview at 2:00 p.m. one week from today:

   a. Click on the right scroll arrow on the status bar until the same day of the week, one week from today, appears displayed on the status line.

   b. Click an insertion point to the right of the 2:00 p.m. time slot.

   c. Key the appointment text as shown here:

      Joyce Findley - Applicant Interview

   d. Press [Enter].

   e. Select the Date... option from the Show menu, then key the current date in the text box. Use the mm/dd/yy format.

   f. Click on the OK command button.

Setting an Alarm

4. Enter an appointment for 9:55 a.m. and set an alarm:

   a. Select the Special Time... option from the Options menu. A Special Time dialog box will display.

   b. Key the time *9:55* in the text box, click on the AM button, and click on the Insert button.

   c. Select the Controls... option from the Alarm menu, verify that the Sound check box is selected, then click on the OK command button.

   d. Key the appointment text as shown here:

      Call New York office

   e. Select the Set option from the Alarm menu.

   f. Press [Enter].

5. Enter an appointment exactly three minutes from the current time:

   a. Select the Special Time... option from the Options menu. A Special Time dialog box will display.

   b. Key the time three minutes from now in the text box, click on the appropriate time button (AM or PM), and then click on the Insert button.

   c. Key the appointment text as shown below.

      Remember to print this page.

   d. Select the Set option from the Alarm menu.

   e. Press [Enter].

      When the alarm goes off, you will hear a faint beeping sound and the appointment text you keyed (Step c above) will be displayed in a window. Do the following when the alarm sounds.

   f. Click on the OK command button in the appointment text window.

6. Record a message in the scratch pad at the bottom of the page:

   a. Click an insertion point on the scratch pad and key the following note:

      (Your Name) created this calendar page.

   b. Press [Enter].

Saving Calendar Files

Calendar stores schedule information in files with the extension .CAL. You can create and save as many Calendar files as you need. For example, you may make a different calendar file for each person using the computer or for each of your projects. Save a Calendar file as you would any other document file.

EXERCISE 6 • 14 SAVING A CALENDAR FILE

You will now save your appointment book on your *Win Practice* disk, so place that disk in the appropriate drive before you begin this exercise.

1. Select the Save as... option from the File menu.

2. Select the appropriate drive.

3. Double-click in the File Name text box to highlight the *.CAL in the text box.

4. Key the name *MY_CAL* (use an underscore between the words) in the File Name text box.

5. Click on the OK command button.

Printing a Calendar File

You can print the appointments in your calendar in Day view format a day at a time. You can print one calendar page or a range of calendar pages. Note that although the calendars will print in Day view, your display can be in Month view when you print the calendars.

EXERCISE 6 • 15 PRINTING A CALENDAR FILE

1. Select the Print... option from the File menu.

2. Key the appointment day for which you have been recording appointments (today's date) in the From text box, if it is not already displayed in the box. (Use the mm/dd/yy format.) Leave the To text box blank. If you want only one date, you do not need to key a date in the To text box.

3. Click on the OK command button.

Purging Appointments

A Calendar file can grow quite large after a while. If your Calendar files take too long to load or need too much disk space, use the Remove option on the Edit menu to delete past appointments. You can remove one or more days of past appointments by completing the From and To dates text boxes in the Remove dialog box (see Figure 6.15).

Figure 6.15

You can remove a day or series of day appointments by completing the From and To dates on the Remove dialog box.

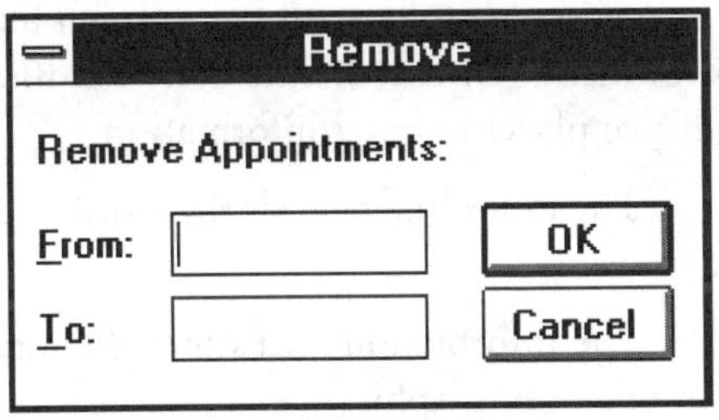

```
┌─────────────────────────────────────┐
│ ▬          Remove                    │
├─────────────────────────────────────┤
│ Remove Appointments:                 │
│                                      │
│ From: │            │    ┌────────┐   │
│       └────────────┘    │   OK   │   │
│                         └────────┘   │
│ To:   │            │    ┌────────┐   │
│       └────────────┘    │ Cancel │   │
│                         └────────┘   │
└─────────────────────────────────────┘
```

EXERCISE 6 • 16 PURGING APPOINTMENTS

1. Select the Day option from the View menu.

2. Remove all the appointments that appear on your calendar for one week from today:

   a. Select the Remove... option from the Edit menu.

   b. Key the date one week from today in the From text box.

   c. Click on the OK command button to remove the appointments.

3. Verify that the appointments are removed:

   a. Click on the right scroll arrow on the status bar until the date one week from today is displayed.

   b. Verify that the appointments are removed.

   c. Select the Today option from the Show menu.

EXERCISE 6 • 17 CLOSING CALENDAR AND THE CALENDAR FILE

1. Select the Save option from the File menu.

2. Double-click on the Control-menu of the Calendar window to close the Calendar.

VIEW 4
CARDFILE

PREVIEW

Windows Cardfile, an electronic stack of three-by-five index cards, was designed to replace the rotary-type file many individuals keep on their real desktop. But Cardfile will do more than the typical rotary-type file.

Cardfile allows you to create index cards on screen, file them, sort them, review their contents, and use the information on the cards in other applications. You can even include pictures as well as text on your cards. For example, you might maintain a cardfile of names and addresses, and you might use them when creating form letters in Write. You can even use Cardfile to dial a telephone number (if you have the proper equipment).

Starting Cardfile and Creating a Cardfile

To open Cardfile, double-click on its program icon—a stack of cards. You will see the familiar window elements, shown in Figure 6.16. By now you must surely appreciate the consistency of these window elements!

A menu bar and a staus bar—much like the ones in Calendar—are beneath the **Cardfile (Untitled)** title bar. Cardfile's workspace displays an empty card with two places to enter information:

• The index line records the word or phrase that Cardfile uses when it sorts the cards.

• The information area stores the information that you key or paste in the form of text or graphics.

Figure 6.16

The opening Cardfile window

Index line

Insertion point

Information area

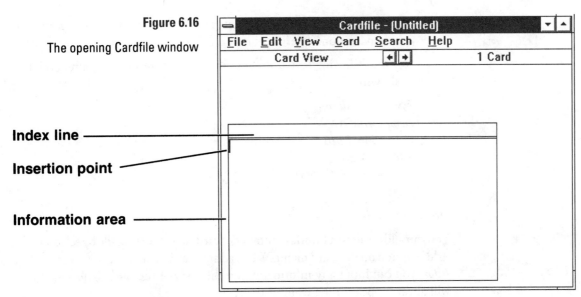

EXERCISE 6 • 18   STARTING CARDFILE

1. Double-click on the Cardfile icon in the Accessories group to open Cardfile.

2. Maximize the Cardfile window.

Cardfile automatically sorts cards alphabetically according to their index lines, so you should use the index line to define the information stored in the information area. Therefore, if you are using Cardfile to store information about people (a mailing list or client list, for example), you would key their full names—last name first—on the index line. You can key up to 40 characters on the index line.

When you open a new Cardfile, you are given one blank card with an insertion point in the information area of the card. You can key information in the information area; however, it is good practice to complete the index line first. You cannot move the cursor to the index line; you must double-click on the index line or select the Add option on the Card menu. Either technique displays an Index dialog box (Figure 6.17) that lets you enter an index line. When you double-click on an existing index line, the Index dialog box will open, permitting you to edit the current line.

The information area of the card can hold up to 10 lines, with 40 characters on each line. You can also include graphics in the information area.

Figure 6.17

The Index dialog box permits you to enter an index line on a new card or to revise an index line on an existing card.

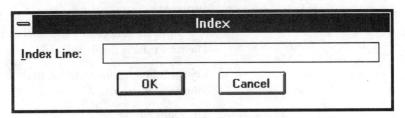

EXERCISE 6 • 19   CREATING A CARDFILE

1. Create a card for James Allison of Acme Printers:

   a. Double-click on the Index line to display the Index dialog box (Figure 6.17).

b. Key the Index line text *Acme Printers* in the text box and click on the OK command button. The index line text is recorded on the index line of the card.

c. Key the following text at the insertion point (press [Enter] after each line as shown):

Mr. James Allison
Acme Printers
(213) 555-1246
146 So. Main
Los Angeles, CA 90001

Adding Cards

You can add an almost limitless number of cards to an existing file by selecting the Add... option on the Card menu. When adding cards, you must key the index line *before* you can input any information on the body of the card. The added card will always appear in the front of the stack.

EXERCISE 6 • 20 ADDING CARDS

1. Add a card for Dorothy McMillan of the Baker Paper Company to the existing cardfile:

a. Select the Add...option from the Card menu. An Add dialog box is displayed.

b. Key the index line *Baker Paper Co.* and click on the OK command button. A new card with the index line you have just entered is displayed at front of the stack.

c. Key the following information in the information area of the card, then click on the OK command button.

Ms. Dorothy McMillan
Baker Paper Co.

(714) 555-2364
1650 So. Broadway
Santa Ana, CA 92674

2. Add a card for Louis Chang of Chang Graphics to the existing cardfile:

a. Select the Add...option from the Card menu. An Add dialog box is displayed.

b. Key the index line *Chang Graphics* and click on the OK command button. The new card is displayed at the front of the stack.

c. Key the following information in the body of the card, then click on the OK command button:

Mr. Louis Chang
President
Chang Graphics

(213) 555-6533
123 Los Angeles St.
Los Angeles, CA 90023

3. Add a card with your name and your school or work address. Include the text *Chapter 6, Exercise 6.20* on the index line.

As shown in Figure 6.18 the card can be displayed in Card view (one card in front of the other, in cascade format) or in List view (only index lines in a listing format). To switch between views, select List or Card on the View menu.

Figure 6.18

The Card view (top) permits you to see the cards in cascade format; the List view (bottom) permits you to see only a listing of the Index lines.

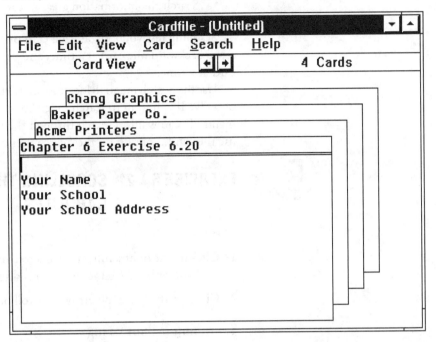

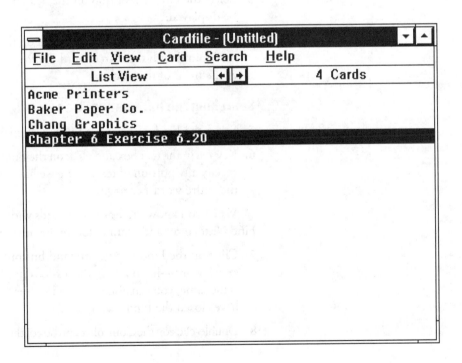

Scrolling Through and Searching Cardfiles

The real value in Cardfile is the speed and the ease with which you can search for and retrieve information. Cardfile offers several ways to search through a stack of cards in order to locate information. Three of the most commonly used methods are to:

- Scroll through the cards one by one.
- Search the index lines of cards to locate a specific word or phrase.
- Search the information areas of cards to locate a specific word or phrase.

Scrolling lets you look at each card one by one. Use Cardfile's left arrow to scroll backward one card at a time, and use the right arrow to scroll forward one card at a time.

Use the Search menu to locate a card with specific information in the index line or body. If you want to search index lines, use the Go To... option on the Search menu. If you want to search through the information in the body of the cards, use the Find... option on the Search menu.

EXERCISE 6 • 21   SCROLLING THROUGH AND SEARCHING CARDFILES

Scrolling

1. Click on the right scroll arrow to scroll forward through the cards until the first card you entered (Acme Printers) is displayed at the front of the stack.

2. Click on the left scroll arrow to scroll backward one card.

Searching by Index Line

3. Select the Go To... option on the Search menu. The Go To dialog box will be displayed.

4. Key *Printers* in the text box and click on the OK command button. The first card found with the search word *Printers* on the index line will be positioned at the front of the stack.

Searching the Information Area

5. Select the Find... option on the Search menu.

6. Key *Los* in the text box and click on the Find Next command button. You can specify any portion of text. Here we have used just the word *Los*, rather than the entire word *Los Angeles*.

When you know there are more cards with the search word, you can issue the Find Next command again to locate the next card that contains the search word.

7. Click on the Find Next command button. You do not have to re-enter the search word—it remains in the text box until changed. Also, if the search word is the same, you can also use the Find Next option on the Search menu if you have closed the Find dialog box.

8. Double-click on the Control-menu box of the Find dialog box to close the window.

Saving, Closing, and Opening a Cardfile

Save cardfiles as you would all other files—with the Save or Save As... option on the File menu. Cardfiles are automatically given the extension .CRD when they are saved. You can create and save as many cardfiles as you wish, but be sure to give each one a unique name (or save files with the same names on different disks).

Close a cardfile by opening a new file or by selecting the Exit option from the File menu. You can open any existing cardfile using the Open... option on the Edit menu.

EXERCISE 6 • 22 SAVING, CLOSING AND OPENING A CARDFILE

You will need your *Win Practice* disk in order to complete the remaining exercises in this session. Before proceeding, insert your *Win Practice* disk in the appropriate disk drive.

1. Select the Save As... option on the File menu.

2. Select the appropriate drive.

3. Double-click in the File Name text box to select *.CRD.

4. Key the filename *MY_FILE* in the text box.

5. Click on the OK command button.

Opening an Existing Cardfile

6. Select the Open... option on the File menu.

7. Select the drive containing your *Win Practice* disk from the Drives list box on the File Open dialog box.

8. Select the file called MY_FILE, then click on the OK command button.

Duplicating, Editing, and Deleting Cards

You can perform all the same editing functions in Cardfile that you can in Notepad.

EXERCISE 6 • 23 DUPLICATING, EDITING, AND DELETING CARDS

Duplicating and Editing

1. Add a card for Michael Jones, who works at Chang Graphics. He and Louis Chang have the same address and phone number.

   a. Select the Go To... option on the Search menu.

   b. Key *Chang Graphics* in the text box and click on the OK command button. Louis Chang's card displays at the front of the stack.

   c. Select the Duplicate option on the Card menu.

   d. Click an insertion point in front of the name Mr. Louis Chang and drag to the end of the word **President**. Key the name *Michael Jones*. The new name should replace the old name and title.

   As shown above, body text on any card can be edited with the usual Windows text-editing procedures. If you want to edit the index line, you must select the Index... option on the Edit menu.

Deleting Cards

2. Delete the card for James Allison at Acme Printers:

   a. Select the Go To... option on the Search menu.

   b. Key *Acme Printers* in the text box and click on the OK command button. James Allison's card displays at the front of the stack.

   c. Select the Delete option on the Card menu. A confirmation box will appear before the card is deleted.

   d. Click on the OK command button to delete the card.

3. Save the changes by selecting the Save command on the File menu.

Printing a Cardfile

When printing cardfiles, you have the option of printing the top card only (Print option) or all the cards (Print All option). The printed cards will be the same size as standard rotary file cards.

EXERCISE 6 ● 24 PRINTING A CARDFILE

1. Arrange the cards so the card with your name on it is on the top.

2. Select the Print All option on the File menu.

EXERCISE 6 ● 25 CLOSING CARDFILE

1. Select the Exit option on the File menu. Respond to the confirmation message, if prompted.

   If you made a change to the cardfile, a message box will appear asking if you want to save changes before closing.

2. If necessary, click on the Save button to save the changes and close the file.

SUMMARY

Windows provides a number of desktop accessories designed to help you while you are working in other programs. In this session, you learned to use Notepad, Calculator, Calendar, and Cardfile.

Notepad lets you create simple notes, quick reminders, records of phone calls, and daily "to do" lists. Notepad's Edit menu provides you with several options for editing text, including copying and moving text using the Clipboard.

The Windows Calculator provides standard calculations, plus the ability to compute square roots, percentages, and more.

The Calendar is designed to support your appointment book or diary. It can even set an indefinite number of alarms (audible or visual) minutes, hours, days, and even years in advance.

Cardfile is like an electronic stack of three-by-five index cards and is designed to replace the rotary-type file many individuals keep on their real desktop. This accessory allows you to create index cards on screen while filing and sorting them. It also allows you to review their contents and use the information on the cards in other applications.

The Accessories programs in Windows are important time-management tools for handling desktop applications that help you manage your appointments, schedules, phone numbers, and many other daily details. The Accessories tools can be minimized on your desktop so that they are available any time you are working in Windows.

OBJECTIVES

When you complete this session, you will be able to:

- Explain the purpose and function of Windows Write.

- Access Write, enter text, and create new document files.

- Save and retrieve documents.

- Edit a document.

- Enhance text copy by using bold, italic, or underlining.

- Format the characters and paragraphs within a document, as well as the document itself.

- Repaginate and print documents (or print selected pages from a document).

SESSION 7 *WRITE*

WRITE

CREATING DOCUMENTS WITH WRITE

PREVIEW

Windows Write is a word processing program that is easy to use. It contains basic features common to nearly all word processing programs, such as the ability to create, save, and retrieve document files; move, copy, enhance, and edit documents; set text margins and align text in various ways; and search for and replace words or phrases throughout the entire document. Although Write lacks a spell checker, a thesaurus, and other more advanced features, Write does let you create all basic documents such as letters, reports, and memos—complete with graphics, if you wish.

Starting Write

Windows Write is an accessory program located in the Accessories program group (unless you have moved it to another group). To start Write, double-click on the Write icon. You will see the opening Write window (shown in Figure 7.1), made up of a title bar, a menu bar, a Control-menu box, scroll bars, minimize and maximize buttons, and a page-status area. The rest of the window is blank (similar to the opening window for Notepad), so that you can input your document.

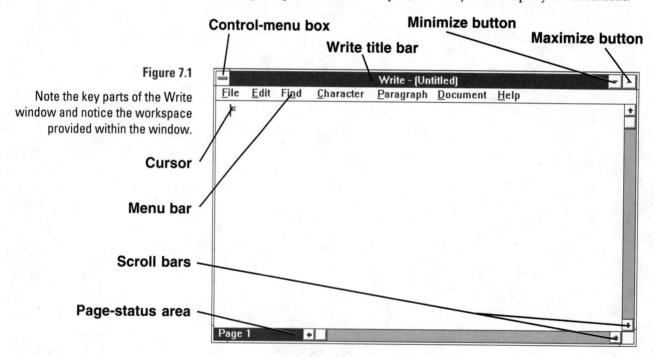

Figure 7.1

Note the key parts of the Write window and notice the workspace provided within the window.

Note that the Write menu bar has seven pull-down menus, which are displayed fully opened in Figure 7.2. Before you begin using the Write program, look at the options in each of these menus. You are already familiar with some of these commands, because they are similar to other Windows menus and commands.

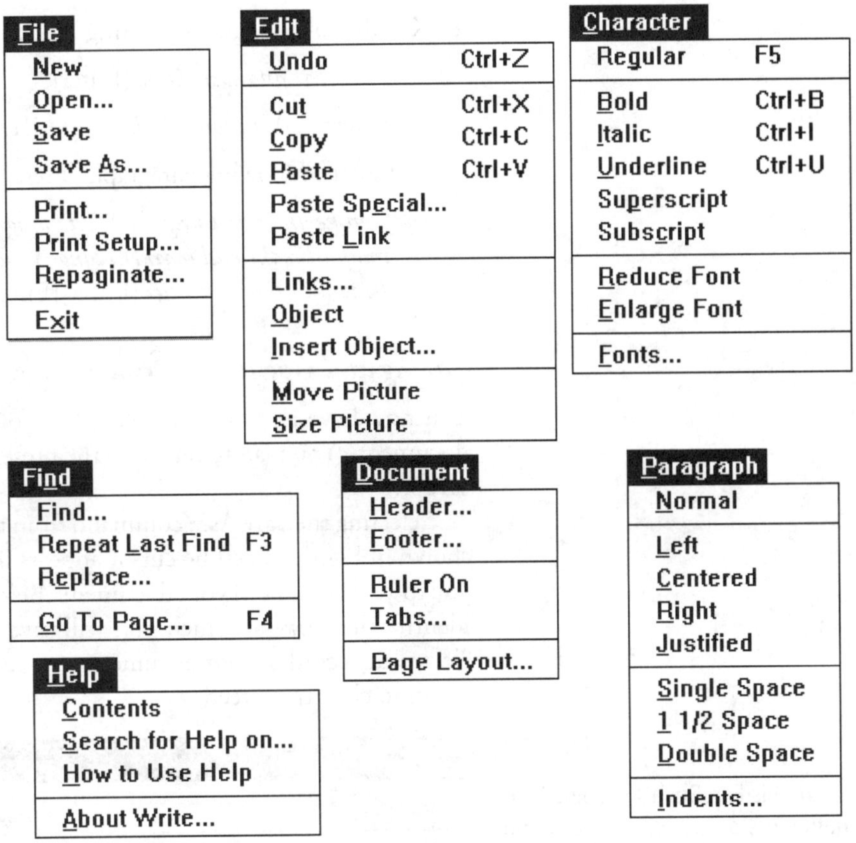

Figure 7.2

Write has seven pull-down menus:
File Edit Find Character
Paragraph Document Help

File
New
Open...
Save
Save As...
Print...
Print Setup...
Repaginate...
Exit

Edit	
Undo	Ctrl+Z
Cut	Ctrl+X
Copy	Ctrl+C
Paste	Ctrl+V
Paste Special...	
Paste Link	
Links...	
Object	
Insert Object...	
Move Picture	
Size Picture	

Character	
Regular	F5
Bold	Ctrl+B
Italic	Ctrl+I
Underline	Ctrl+U
Superscript	
Subscript	
Reduce Font	
Enlarge Font	
Fonts...	

Find	
Find...	
Repeat Last Find	F3
Replace...	
Go To Page...	F4

Document
Header...
Footer...
Ruler On
Tabs...
Page Layout...

Paragraph
Normal
Left
Centered
Right
Justified
Single Space
1 1/2 Space
Double Space
Indents...

Help
Contents
Search for Help on...
How to Use Help
About Write...

Creating Document Files

When you first start using Write, the screen is clear, ready for you to start entering your text. You see **Write (Untitled)** in the title bar because you have not yet named the document you are about to create. You see the **cursor**, a thin vertical line blinking on and off at the start position. Next to the cursor you see the **end marker**, a starlike symbol that identifies the end of the document. When you begin keying text, the cursor will move, of course—and as it moves, it pushes the end marker along. The location of the cursor is referred to as the **insertion point** because this is where the next character you key will be inserted. Now, begin using Write.

EXERCISE 7 • 1   STARTING WRITE AND KEYING TEXT

You will need your *Win Practice* disk in order to complete this assignment.

1. Place your *Win Practice* disk in one of the floppy disk drives.

2. Start Windows if it is not already active.

3. Start the Write program:

   a. Double-click on the Accessories group window to open it if it is not already opened.

   b. Double-click on the Write icon to start the Write program.

   c. Click on the maximize button to maximize the Write window.

4. Key the following text, starting at the cursor:

   a. *Your first and last name* [Enter].

   b. *Session 7, Windows Write* [Enter][Enter].

   c. Key the following paragraph. Press [Enter] only at the end of a paragraph.

      I am keying text using the Write program. As I key the text, the cursor moves and pushes the end marker along. When I reach the end of a line, Write wraps the text to the next line. [Enter][Enter]

Saving and Opening a Document

You now have text on the screen, but you want to begin working on another document. You plan to return to the present document later, but first you must save it.

Selecting the Save As... command from the File menu produces the dialog box shown in Figure 7.3. The cursor appears in the File Name text box, prompting you to key the name of your document. Before you name the document, you must identify the *drive* to which you will save this document. Once you have an electronic record of your document, you can select the New option from the File menu to clear the screen.

Figure 7.3

In this File Save As dialog box, notice the cursor in the File Name text box.

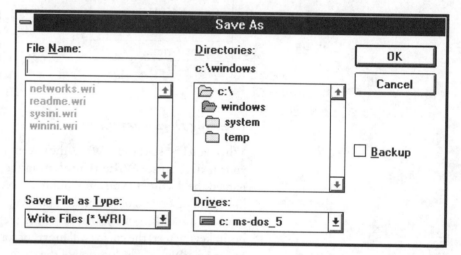

But what if you selected New *before* you had saved the current document? Before Write clears the screen and allows you to begin a new document, it asks you whether you want to save the current document by displaying the message window shown in Figure 7.4.

Figure 7.4

This message window reminds you to save the current document.

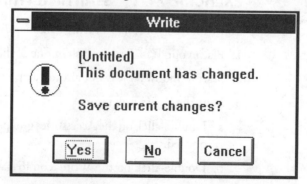

If you select Yes, the File Save As dialog box appears, the same File Save As dialog box shown in Figure 7.3. This is Write's way of protecting you from losing text. In all cases, you use Save As... to save a document *for the first time*—to create an electronic record of your text. For this example, assume you saved your document as PRACTICE.

Once a document is "on record," you can retrieve it by selecting the Open option on the File menu. Then the File Open dialog box shown in Figure 7.5 will list the available files in the current directory, including your PRACTICE file.

Figure 7.5

This File Open dialog box shows PRACTICE.WRI under the correct directory (A:).

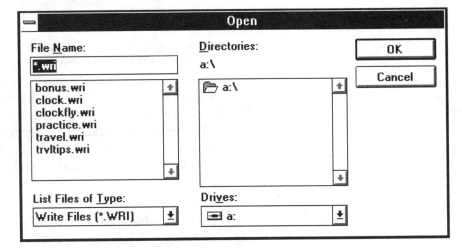

If you open the PRACTICE file and make changes, you will then want to save the *updated* PRACTICE file, the latest version of that document. Because Write already knows the name of this file and has a record of it, you do not need to use the Save As... option. Simply use the Save option.

EXERCISE 7 • 2   SAVING AND OPENING A DOCUMENT

You will need your *Win Practice* disk in order to complete this assignment.

1. Save the sample document you created in Exercise 7.1 on your *Win Practice* disk:

   a. Select the Save As... option from the File menu.

   b. Select the drive that contains your *Win Practice* disk.

   c. Key the filename *PRACTICE* in the text box and click on the OK command button.

2. Create a new document for practice using the text shown in Figure 7.6:

   a. Select the New option from the File menu.

   b. Key the text in Figure 7.6 *exactly* as it appears. As you enter copy, correct any errors by pressing [Backspace] or [Delete]. Do not use any Edit menu commands yet. For right now, align all text at the left margin (do not use [Tab] or spaces to indent the first line of each paragraph). And be sure to use an extra [Enter] for the extra space before and after the headings and between paragraphs. Since you are using the Word Wrap feature, the line endings in your document may not match those in Figure 7.6.

TRAVEL REMINDERS AND NOTES

As we enter the busiest part of our business year, the Travel Department wishes to remind all employees of our general procedures and at the same time to share some helpful travel hints.

Airline Tickets and Car Rentals

Airline reservations and car rentals must be made through the corporate Travel Department whenever possible. We suggest that you make your airline reservations as soon as you can do so; not only will you get less expensive fares, but you will also help guarantee a seat on the flight you want.

When you cannot make car rentals through corporate travel, we remind you that the company gets a discount from certain car rental agencies. Please see your Corporate Travel Directory for details.

Reimbursements

Except for sales representatives, all employees must use the standard Travel & Entertainment Expense Form (Form No. A22). Your monthly form must be completed, signed by your immediate supervisor, and submitted to Accounting no later than the 10th of each month for the preceding month's expenses.

Please be sure to attach receipts for all expenses over $10. This rule allows us to comply with IRS regulations.

Also, please be sure to indicate on each expense reimbursement form (1) your department code number, (2) your personal employee ID number, and (3) your balance from the preceding month's expense report.

For reimbursement of meals with clients or potential clients, always include not only the name of each client but also his or her company affiliation and the nature of the business discussion. All entertainment expenses must be documented.

Flyers and Brochures Available

The Travel Department has a number of useful flyers and brochures for employees, including several that address safety, family vacations, and employee discounts. If you would like any of these materials or a copy of the latest Corporate Travel Directory, please call Mariam Rodriguez, Travel Department Supervisor, Extension 4445.

Figure 7.6 A sample document named TRVLTIPS.WRI

3. Save the document using the Save As... option:

    a. Select the Save As... option from the File menu.

    b. Verify that the drive containing your *Win Practice* disk is selected.

    c. Key the filename *TRVLTIPS* in the Filename text box.

    d. Click on the Backup check box to make a *backup* (that is, an *extra*) copy of this file.

    e. Click on the OK command button.

Your document is now saved on your *Win Practice* disk. You can quit Write or begin a new document.

VIEW 2
EDITING AND FORMATTING DOCUMENTS

PREVIEW

Editing means changing the *words* in the text. Write makes it easy for you to retrieve a file that you have saved and to edit (change) the text as necessary. By using Write's Edit menu (see Figure 7.2), you can easily update a report, correct sales figures, delete sentences or paragraphs, or otherwise *edit* documents.

    Formatting means changing the *look* or the *arrangement* of text—either of individual characters, words, or sentences, or of the entire document. The Write menu bar offers three pull-down menus for formatting text: Character, Paragraph, and Document. Before you continue, look at the options under all three menus in Figure 7.2.

Selecting Text

You will often want to cut a block of text, move a few words, copy a sentence, italicize a phrase, underline a key statement, or otherwise change your copy. How you make each change is really Step **2** of the process. Step **1** is *identifying* the block of copy you wish to change! Whether the process is called **selecting**, **highlighting**, or **blocking**, in all cases you must first identify the text.

    In all Windows documents, you can select text by (1) clicking an insertion point at the beginning of the text you want to select, (2) dragging the mouse to the end of the text, and then (3) releasing the mouse button. In addition, Write offers ways to quickly select:

- **The current line:** Click once to select the current line.

- **The current paragraph:** Double-click to select the entire paragraph.

- **Multiple paragraphs:** Double-click to select the paragraph, hold [Shift], point on the next paragraph, and click once to select both paragraphs. (You can also drag the mouse to the end of the text you wish to highlight.)

- **The entire document:** Hold [Ctrl] and click once to select the entire document.

    For each procedure, you must first position the mouse pointer in the margin to the left of the first line in the paragraph. The mouse pointer will change from an I-beam to a pointing arrow.

Using the Edit Menu to Edit Text

Once you have highlighted or selected text, you may delete it, move it, or copy it:

- **Delete.** To delete highlighted text, use the Cut option on the Edit menu.

- **Move.** To highlight text, first Cut, then Paste: (a) Use Cut to delete the highlighted copy, (b) position the cursor where you want to move the copy, and then (c) select Paste. The highlighted copy will now be moved to its new position.

- **Copy.** To copy text, use Copy and Paste: (a) Copy the highlighted text, (b) position the cursor where you want the duplicated text to go, and (c) select Paste. The new copy will be inserted, and the original text will not be moved.

Note that the Undo Editing command is a safety feature; it allows you to cancel your last editing command. Now practice editing text using the Edit menu.

EXERCISE 7 • 3   ADDING, MOVING, AND CUTTING TEXT

This exercise and the following exercises use the TRVLTIPS document you created in Exercise 7.2. If the document is not currently displayed on your screen, open the document—it has been saved on your *Win Practice* disk.

1. Change the side heading "Reimbursements" to "Expense Reimbursements":

   a. Click an insertion point immediately before the letter **R** in the word **Reimbursements**. (It may take some practice to click an insertion point.)

   b. Key the text *Expense* and space once.

2. Cut item **(1)** from the third paragraph in the "Expense Reimbursements" section and renumber the remaining items:

   a. Click an insertion point immediately before the word **your** in item 1. Do not move the mouse.

   b. Press the mouse button and drag up through the number **(2)** (do not include the space following the right parenthesis).

   c. Select the Cut option from the Edit menu. (You are deleting, not moving, the highlighted text.)

   d. Click an insertion point between the number **3** and the parenthesis that follows it.

   e. Press [Backspace] once to delete the number **3**.

   f. Key the number *2*.

3. Move the second sentence in the paragraph—immediately before the "Flyers and Brochures Available" heading—to the beginning of that paragraph:

   a. Click an insertion point immediately before the letter **A** in the word **All**.

   b. Press the mouse button and drag up to and including the period at the end of the sentence. Do not include the paragraph return at the end of the line.

   c. Select the Cut option from the Edit menu.

   d. Click an insertion point immediately before the letter **F** in the word **For** at the beginning of the paragraph.

e. Select the Paste option from the Edit menu.

f. Press [Spacebar] twice.

Using the Character Menu to Edit or Enhance Text

After you highlight text, you can use the Character menu to change character attributes—that is, to change the *look* of or otherwise *enhance* text copy by selecting **bold**, *italic*, or <u>underlining</u>. (Select Normal to undo these selections.) Occasionally, you may need to use the Character menu to create subscripts and superscripts.

To change more than one character attribute (for example, both the font and the font style), it is easier to use the Fonts... menu option. When you select Fonts... from the Character menu, you will see the Font dialog box shown in Figure 7.7. The Font dialog box permits you to change every attribute of the characters in your document. To change the font, select a new font from the Font list box. A sample of that new font will be displayed in the Sample box. To change the font style, select a new style from the Font Style list box. Again, the Sample box displays your new selection. To change the font size, select the desired size from the Size list box. The Sample box changes once again.

Figure 7.7

Font Dialog box

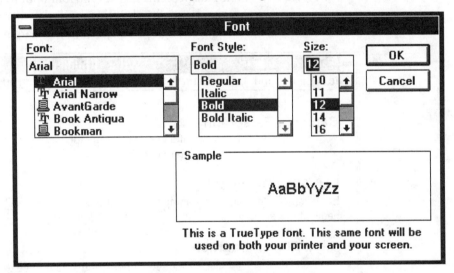

EXERCISE 7 • 4   ENHANCING TEXT

1. Italicize the first word, **All**, in the paragraph above the "Flyers and Brochures Available" heading:

    a. Position the cursor directly over the word **All** and double-click. (Double-clicking on a word is like dragging across it.)

    b. Select the Italic option from the Character menu.

2. Change the title and all document side headings to Arial, bold, 14 point:

    a. Move to the top of the document.

    b. Position the cursor in the left margin opposite the letter **T** in the word **TRAVEL**. The cursor should change to an arrow pointer. If it does not, move the cursor slightly to the left until it changes to a pointer.

    c. Click the mouse button. The entire line will be highlighted.

   d. Select the Fonts... option from the Character menu.

   e. Make the following selections, then click on the OK command button:

      Font: Arial
      Font Style: Bold
      Size: 14 point

   f. Change the three side headings to Arial, bold, 14 point.

3. Enlarge the font size of the title:

   a. Position the cursor in the left margin opposite the letter **T** in the word **TRAVEL**. The cursor should change to an arrow pointer. If it does not, move the cursor slightly to the left until it changes to a pointer.

   b. Click the mouse button.

   c. Select the Enlarge Font option from the Character menu. The font will be enlarged to the next available size (16 or 18 points).

Using the Paragraph Menu to Edit Text

The Paragraph menu gives you four options for formatting paragraphs. You can: center paragraphs, align them at the left margin (Normal), align them at the right margin, or align paragraphs at both margins (Justified) (see Figure 7.8).

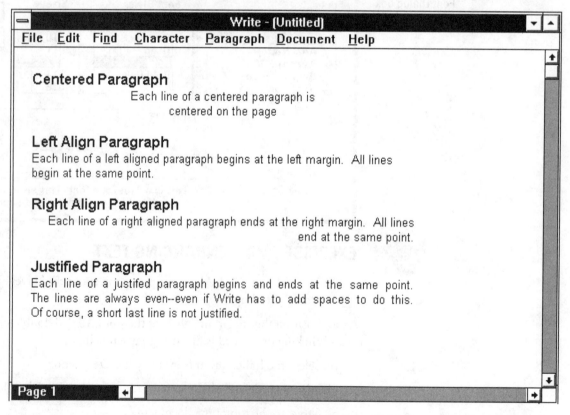

Figure 7.8 Using the Paragraph menu, you can align text at the left or right margin, or you can center or justify text.

The Paragraph menu gives you three options for line spacing: Single Space, 1 1/2 Space, and Double Space (see Figure 7.9).

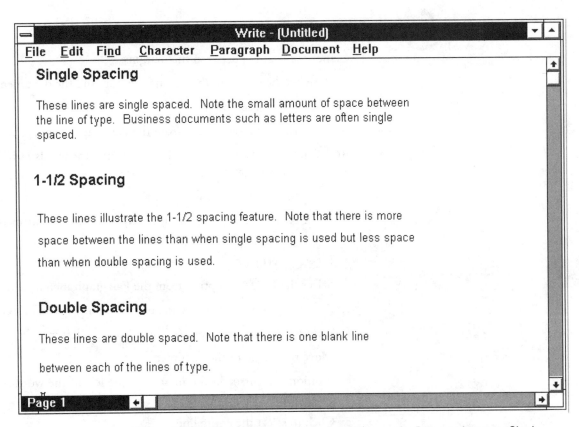

Figure 7.9 Three spacing options are available on the Paragraph menu: Single Space, 1 1/2 Space, and Double Space.

Selecting the Indents... option on the Paragraph menu displays the Indents dialog box shown in Figure 7.10. There, you will find three kinds of paragraph indents—and a fourth variety can be created by combining two of these:

Figure 7.10

Using the Indents dialog box, you can set paragraphs with a left indent, a right indent, a first line indent, or a hanging indent.

Left indent. A left indent is an indent from the left margin that applies to all lines in a paragraph.

First line indent. A first line indent is an indent from the left margin that applies only to the first line in a paragraph.

Right indent. A right indent is an indent from the right margin that applies to all lines in a paragraph.

Hanging indent. A hanging indent is a left-margin indent of all lines except the first line of a paragraph. To set up a hanging indent, specify a positive left indent and a negative first-line indent.

NOTE: This list of four items is set in hanging-indent style.

EXERCISE 7 • 5   FORMATTING PARAGRAPHS

1. Center the heading between the margins:

   a. Position the cursor in the left margin opposite the document title.

   b. Click the mouse button.

   c. Select the Centered option from the Paragraph menu.

2. At the end of the last paragraph, key and center the words *HAPPY TRAVEL-ING!* two lines below the last line of text.

   a. Scroll to the end of the document.

   b. Click an insertion point immediately after the period in the extension number **4445**.

   c. Press [Enter] twice.

   d. Select the Centered option from the Paragraph menu.

   e. Press [Caps Lock], then key the text HAPPY TRAVELING!

3. Indent each of the paragraphs 0.5 inch from the left margin:

   a. Move to the top of the document.

   b. Position the cursor in the margin to the left of the word **As** in the first paragraph.

   c. Click to select the entire line.

   d. Select the Indents... option from the Paragraph menu.

   e. Press [Tab] to highlight the First Line text box.

   f. Key *0.5* in the First Line text box and click on the OK command button.

   g. Position the cursor in the left margin opposite the word **Airline** in the first paragraph under the side heading "Airline Tickets and Car Rentals." Do *not* include the side heading.

   h. Press the mouse button and drag the mouse down to the end of the section (up to, but not including the next side heading). Notice that all paragraphs are highlighted.

   i. Select the Indents... option from the Paragraph menu.

   j. Press [Tab] to highlight the First line text box.

   k. Key *0.5* in the First Line text box and click on the OK command button.

   l. Indent the four paragraphs in the next section and the one paragraph in the last section.

4. Save your document. It is a good idea to save your document periodically.

Using the Document Menu to Edit and Format a Document

You will use the Document menu to create headers and footers, and set tab stops and margins.

A **header** is an identifying title that usually appears at the top (the "head") of the second and all subsequent pages of a document. A **footer** performs the same job but appears at the bottom of each page—again, usually beginning with the second page.

When you select Header... from the Document menu, you will notice that:

- The text screen clears.

- A Header document window displays.

- Within that window, the Page Header dialog box (see Figure 7.11) appears. The dialog box will be inactive.

Figure 7.11

The Page Header dialog box displays within the Header window.

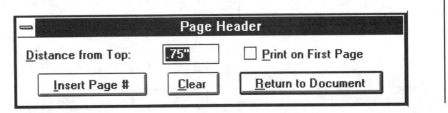

The cursor is positioned at the upper-left corner of the screen. Key the heading text at the cursor position, then click on the appropriate buttons. Once you have made all your selections, click on the Return to Document command button. The Header window clears, and you return to your text screen.

The process is the same when you select Footer; the dialog box labels change to Footer and Page Footer.

The Document menu also shows a Ruler On option. When you select this option, you will see a ruler just below the Write menu bar, as shown in Figure 7.12. (Once the Ruler On option has been selected, the Document menu option immediately changes to Ruler Off.)

Figure 7.12

Selecting Ruler On from the Document menu presents options for tab alignment, line spacing, and paragraph alignment.

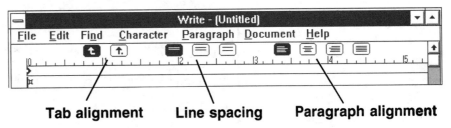

The ruler offers several features besides numbers. Above the ruler are three sets of symbols:

Figure 7.13

Tab alignment icons

Tab Alignment. The first set, the two small arrows, allows you to change normal tab alignment (Write's default, which is highlighted) to decimal tab alignment (used to align periods in decimal numbers—a great convenience when entering dollar amounts). Decimal tabs will be discussed later.

Figure 7.14

Line spacing icons

Line Spacing. The next set shows three miniature screens with lines representing Single Space (Write's default), 1 1/2 Space, and Double Space.

Figure 7.15

Paragraph alignment icons

Paragraph Alignment. The third set shows four miniature screens representing left alignment, centered alignment, right alignment, and *justification* (that is, full alignment at both left and right margins.

The Document menu also lets you set tab stops. Write has preset tabs every half inch along a text line. To change tab settings, select Tabs... and you will see the Tabs dialog box, shown in Figure 7.16. Enter numbers in the Positions boxes to set new tab stops. To align a column of decimal numbers on the period, select the Decimal option by placing an X in the Decimal box. The OK, Cancel, and Clear All buttons allow you to change or approve your selections.

Figure 7.16

The Tabs dialog box lets you change tab settings by entering new numbers in the Positions boxes.

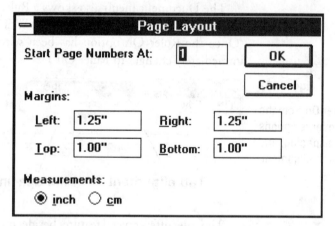

Write has preset left and right margins of 1.25 inches and top and bottom margins of 1.00 inch. To change margins, select Page Layout... on the Document menu and use the Page Layout dialog box, shown in Figure 7.17, to enter the new margin values. Also, if your document does not start with page 1, enter the correct starting page number in the Start Page Numbers At box.

Figure 7.17

This Page Layout dialog box shows Write's default values.

EXERCISE 7 • 6   FORMATTING A DOCUMENT

1. Change the left and right margins to 1 inch on each side:

   a. Select the Page Layout... option from the Document menu.

   b. Press [Tab] to highlight the Left text box.

   c. Key the number *1*.

   d. Press [Tab] to highlight the Right text box.

   e. Key the number *1*.

   f. Click on the OK command button.

2. Add three blank lines above the heading:

   a. Move to the top of the document.

   b. Click an insertion point in front of the letter **T** in the word **TRAVEL** then press [Enter] once.

NOTE: You must position the cursor immediately before the letter T to get the I-beam.

   c. Select the Ruler On option on the Document menu.

   d. Position the pointer in the left margin opposite the blank line you added above the heading.

 NOTE: The cursor should change to a pointer; not an I-beam.

   e. Click to select the blank line and drag down to highlight the heading.

   f. Click on the 1 1/2 Space ruler icon.

3. Change the line spacing below the heading to double spacing:

   a. Position the pointer in the left margin opposite the letter **A** in the word **As** in the first line of text. (The cursor should be a pointer.)

   b. Click to highlight the blank line (only the cursor will be highlighted since there is no text on the line).

   c. Press and hold [Ctrl] and [Shift] then press [End]. The text from the first side heading to the end of the document will be selected (highlighted).

   d. Click on the Double Space ruler icon.

4. Change the line space after each side heading and between each paragraph to single spacing:

   a. Position the cursor in the left margin on the blank line above the first side heading.

   b. Click to select the blank line. Be careful to select only the blank line.

   c. Click on the Single Space ruler icon.

   d. Repeat Steps a, b, and c to remove one blank line beneath each of the side headings and one blank line between each of the paragraphs.

5. Select the Ruler Off option on the Document menu to hide the ruler.

6. Add a Footer--*Travel Tips*--and a page number only for the second page:

   a. Select the Footer... option from the Document menu. Notice the Write menu bar changes to Page Footer menu bar and the cursor is positioned in the upper left corner of the document window.

   b. Key the footer text *Travel Tips - page* and space once.

   c. Click on the Page Footer title bar to select the dialog box.

   d. Key *0.5* in the Distance from Bottom text box. Do not check the Print on First Page box because you do not want the footer to print on page 1.

   e. Select the Right option from the Paragraph menu.

   f. Click on the Insert Page # command button in the Page Footer dialog box.

   g. Click on the Return to Document command button.

Using Search Options

Flipping through pages of even a short document in an effort to find a word or phrase can be time consuming and frustrating. Write simplifies such searches. With Write, you can easily find the copy and replace it with revised copy.

Before you continue, look again at the Find menu options in Figure 7.2:

• The first option, Find..., helps you locate a word or phrase. A Find dialog box (similar to the Replace dialog box shown in Figure 7.18) prompts you to enter the word or phrase you are searching for in the Find What text box.

• The Repeat Last Find option looks for the next occurrence, if any, of that same word or phrase for which you just searched.

• The Replace... option displays the Replace dialog box (Figure 7.18), which prompts you to enter two key pieces of information: Find What and Replace With. (Look again at the Find dialog box and you will notice that it does not have a Replace With text box.)

Figure 7.18

Replace dialog box

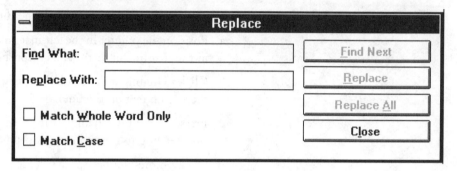

EXERCISE 7•7   SEARCHING AND REPLACING

1. Change the letters **IRS** to **Internal Revenue Service**.

   a. Move to the top of the document.

   b. Select the Replace... option from the Find menu.

   c. Key the letters *IRS* in the Find What text box, then press [Tab].

   d. Key the words *Internal Revenue Service* in the Replace With text box.

   e. Click on the Match Case check box to select it. You want to check this box because you want to find only the uppercase (capital) letters that *match* the search.

   f. Click on the Find Next command button. Write will search the text and will stop at and highlight the search word when it is found. (If you do not see a highlighted word when the search stops, point on the title bar of the Replace dialog box and drag the dialog box aside to display the text beneath it.)

   g. Click on the Replace command button. A message box tells you **Search operation complete**.

   h. Click on the OK command button to close the message box.

   i. Click on the Find Next button. Since no further match is found, this message box appears: **Text not found**.

   j. Click on the OK command button on the message box.

   k. Double-click on the Control-menu box to close the Replace dialog box.

2. Change the word **flyers** to **fliers** (there are two occurrences).

   a. Select the Replace option from the Find menu.

   b. Key the word *flyers* in the Find What text box.

c. Key the word *fliers* in the Replace With text box.

d. Click on the Match Case check box to deselect it.

e. Click on the Find Next command button.

f. When the search word is located in the text, click on the Replace command button. The word will be replaced and the next search will start.

g. Click on the Replace command button when the second occurrence is located in the text. (If you click on Replace again, the **Search operation complete** message will display. Click on the OK command button.)

h. Double-click on the Replace dialog box to close the window.

3. Save your revised TRVLTIPS file once again.

VIEW 3
REPAGINATING AND PRINTING DOCUMENTS

PREVIEW

The purpose of creating documents is almost always to print them. But editing and formatting alone do not ensure that your document will print exactly as you want it to print. Before you print, therefore, Write allows you to view the document page by page *on screen*. If you want to change the page breaks, you can use the Repaginate... option on Write's File menu. Repaginate... and Print... are used hand in hand.

Repaginating Documents

To see page breaks on screen *before* printing, pull down the File menu and select the Repaginate... option. The Repaginate Document dialog box has only one choice: Confirm Page Breaks (see Figure 7.19). When you select this option and click on OK, another dialog box appears, the Repaginate Document dialog box. While this box is on screen, Write will show you how it plans to break pages in your document. You approve each page break by pressing the Confirm button, and you use the Up or the Down button to suggest different page breaks.

Figure 7.19

Repaginate Document dialog box

> **Repaginate Document**
>
> ☐ Confirm Page Breaks
>
> OK
>
> Cancel

Printing Your Document

To print a document, pull down the File menu and select the Print... option. The Print dialog box will appear, as shown in Figure 7.20. After Copies, enter the number of copies of the document you want to print. After Print Range, select All if you want to print the entire document; if not, select Pages and then fill in the range of pages you want to print by entering the appropriate page numbers after From and To.

Figure 7.20

Notice the options under Print
Range in this Print dialog box.

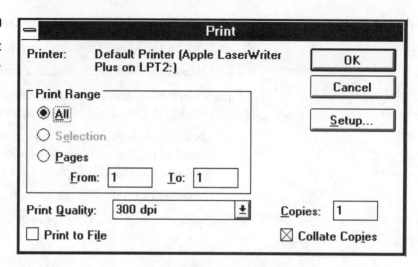

EXERCISE 7 • 8   REPAGINATING AND PRINTING A DOCUMENT

To practice repaginating and printing a document, in this exercise you will use the TRVLTIPS file saved on your *Win Practice* disk. Open this file before you proceed.

1. Check the document's page breaks:

   a. Select the Repaginate option from the File menu.

   b. Click on the Confirm Page Breaks check box to select it, then click on the OK command button. (You want Write to stop at each page break and display it on the screen before proceeding.) A small arrow will appear in the left margin indicating the suggested page break.

   c. Click on the Up command button to move the page break up one line. Notice the line becomes highlighted.

   d. Click on the Down command button to move the page break down one line; then confirm the page break by clicking on the Confirm button.

2. Save your document.

3. Print one copy of the document:

   a. Verify that your printer is available and ready.

   b. Select the Print option from the File menu.

   c. Click on the OK command button.

   Assume you have just learned that Miriam Rodriguez left the company and Shellee Winston is taking her place. You need to retrieve the document, make the name correction, and print a revised copy of TRVLTIPS.

4. Change **Miriam Rodriguez** to **Shellee Winston**:

   a. Select the Replace... option from the Find menu.

   b. Key the name *Miriam Rodriguez* in the Find What text box, then press [Tab].

   c. Key the name *Shellee Winston* in the Replace With text box, then click on the Find Next command button. When the next occurrence is found, click on the Replace button. The Search operation complete message box appears.

    d. Click on the OK command button to close the message box.

    e. Double-click on the Control-menu box to close the Find dialog box.

5. Save your file.

6. Print one copy of the revised document:

    a.   Select the Print option from the File menu.

    b.   Click on the OK command button.

VIEW 4
WORKING WITH TABS

PREVIEW

The Write program has two kinds of tab stops, **left** and **decimal**:

    ● A **left tab stop** aligns the left edge of the text at the position of the tab stop.

    ● A **decimal tab stop** aligns a column of numbers on the decimal point at the tab-stop position, with whole numbers to the left and decimal numbers to the right of the tab stop. If the line does not contain a decimal point, all text is aligned to the right of the decimal tab stop.

Write's default left tab is set every .5 inches. You can change those default tabs by setting your own tabs. To set tabs, fill in a dialog box or use the tab stop icons on the ruler.

Tab stops apply to the entire document; you cannot set different tab stops for each paragraph, as you can with some word processing programs.

Using the Tabs... Option

To set tab stops with the dialog box, select the Tabs... option on the Document menu. A Tabs dialog box (Figure 7.21) displays. Note the wider boxes after Positions and the smaller check boxes after Decimal. Note, too, that *two* lines of each are displayed.

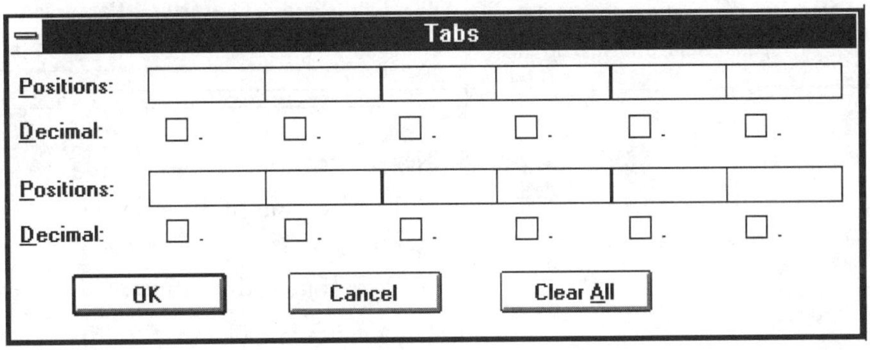

Figure 7.21

The Tabs dialog box makes the setting easy: In the Positions boxes, just key in the distance from the left margin.

In the Positions boxes, you indicate the location of the tab setting by keying the distance from the left margin. Write assumes you are using inches. Use decimals for fractions of an inch (for example, key 1.5 for a tab 1 1/2 inches from the left margin).

To set a decimal tab stop, click on the box below the filled-in Positions box. Write assumes all tab stops are *left* tab stops unless the Decimal check box is checked.

Using the Ruler to Set Tab Stops

To set tab stops with the ruler's tab-stop icons:

- Display the ruler.

- Click on the appropriate tab-stop icon (the bent arrow for a left tab stop, the straight arrow with a decimal point next to it for a decimal tab stop).

- Position the top of the mouse pointer directly below the ruler position where you want the tab stop and click. The appropriate tab marker will appear on the ruler line.

You can adjust the position of any tab stops by dragging the tab marker along the ruler to the desired position. To remove a tab stop, simply drag the tab stop down and off the ruler and release the mouse button.

EXERCISE 7.9   WORKING WITH TABS

You will need your *Win Practice* disk in order to complete this exercise.

1. Open the Write program if it is not already open.

2. Select the New option from the File menu.

3. Make the following document format settings:

   a. Font: Arial, Regular, size 12.

   b. Ruler On

   c. Page Layout: Left and Right margins, 1.5 inches; Top and Bottom margins, 1 inch.

4. Set the tab settings on the ruler as given below (shown in Figure 7.22).

.75 (decimal)	2.50 (left)
1.00 (left)	4.00 (left)
1.75 (left)	4.50 (decimal)

Figure 7.22

Note the tab settings at .75, 1.00, 1.75, 2.50, 4.00, and 4.50 on this ruler.

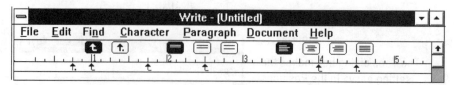

5. Key the heading:

   a. Key the name of the form, *M E M O R A N D U M*, in capital letters with one space between letters as shown.

   b. Press [Enter] three times.

6. Key the heading block:

   a. Key the following line (press [Tab] where indicated, and do not press [Enter] until requested):

   [Tab] *To:*[Tab] *May Fong, Payroll Manager* [Tab]*Date: Current Date* [Enter][Enter]

b. Key the From line as shown below:

[Tab] *From:*[Tab] *Your Name* [Enter][Enter]

c. Key the Subject line as shown below:

[Tab] *Subject:*[Tab] *Bonus Pay*[Enter][Enter][Enter]

7. Key the message:

a. Key the first paragraph as shown below:

The following part-time workers have earned a bonus for their work on the monthly promotion project.[Enter][Enter]

b. Key the table as shown below:

[Tab][Tab]*Miriam Smith*[Tab]*3457*[Tab][Tab]*$350.75*[Enter]

[Tab][Tab]*Charles Lujan*[Tab]*5787*[Tab][Tab]*$254.00*[Enter]

[Tab][Tab]*Susan Charles*[Tab]*7889*[Tab][Tab]*$36.50*[Enter][Enter]

c. Key the final paragraph:

Please mail the checks directly to the employees.[Enter]

8. Format the form title:

a. Position the cursor in the margin to the left of the heading "MEMORANDUM" and click to select the line.

b. Select the Centered option from the Paragraph menu.

c. Select the Fonts... option from the Character menu.

d. Select Bold and Size 18 from the Font dialog box, then click on the OK command button.

9. Change the To:, From:, Date:, and Subject: lines to boldface.

a. Select the word **To:**.

b. Select the Bold option from the Character menu.

c. Boldface each of the three remaining words: Date, From, and Subject.

10. Proofread your document and correct any errors.

11. Save a copy of your document on your *Win Practice* disk with the filename BONUS.

12. Print one copy of your memorandum:

a. Verify that your printer is available and selected.

b. Select the Print option from the File menu.

c. Click on the OK command button.

SUMMARY

In this session, you worked with Write, the word processor included with Windows. You saw how Write, which is located in the Accessories group, allows you to create, save, and retrieve document files; move, copy, enhance, and edit documents; set text margins and align text in various ways; and search for and replace words or phrases throughout the entire document. The more you practice using Write, the more familiar and comfortable you will be using it.

• • • • • • • • • • • •

OBJECTIVES

When you complete this session, you will be able to:

• Explain the purpose and function of Windows Paintbrush.

• Access Paintbrush and use its electronic tools to create, save, retrieve, and print graphic files.

• Import graphic files from other programs into Paintbrush and edit and save the images.

• Color, insert, cut, copy, and move text and drawings.

• Use the modifying tools, text tools, and the fat-bit editor to edit graphic files.

SESSION 8 *PAINTBRUSH*

VIEWS
Working with Paintbrush
Modifying, Saving, and Printing Drawings

PAINTBRUSH

Windows Paintbrush is an accessory designed specifically for **graphics**—drawings and images of all kinds, from simple to complex. Paintbrush provides tools that make the process of drawing images quite simple, and it offers an array of features that make revising and modifying artwork more fun than work (even for people who tremble at the thought of sketching on paper). The finished art can be used as stand-alone images or placed in newsletters, posters, letterheads, advertisements, notices, fliers, and other documents.

In this session, you will use Paintbrush tools to create, save, edit, and print your drawings. You will also learn how to "import" images (that is, transfer an image created in another graphic program and save the image in a Paintbrush file). As you work with Paintbrush, you may sometimes find it a bit puzzling at first, but stick with it. After a while, the results will be rewarding!

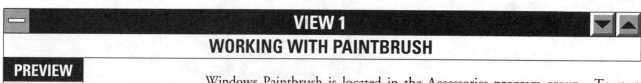

VIEW 1
WORKING WITH PAINTBRUSH

PREVIEW

Windows Paintbrush is located in the Accessories program group. To start Paintbrush, double-click on the Paintbrush icon, which resembles a painter's palette (see Figure 8.1). When Paintbrush opens, you see a window like others you have seen, complete with a Control-menu box, a title bar, minimize and maximize buttons, scroll bars, a work area (for drawing), and of course a menu bar (see Figure 8.2). But the Paintbrush window also has three unique tool areas: a Toolbox, a Linesize box, and a color and shades Palette. Before these tool areas are discussed, electronic painting and drawing is explained, as well as how the Paintbrush program works.

Figure 8.1

Paintbrush icon

Figure 8.2

The Paintbrush window has a Toolbox, a Linesize box, and a Palette.

Toolbox

Color and shades palette

Linesize box

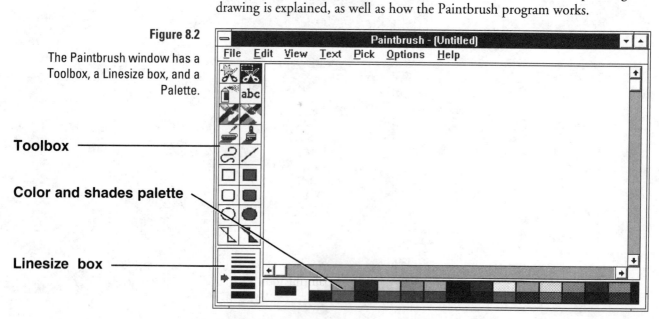

The Paintbrush Tools

The drawing area of the Paintbrush window is where all the action takes place. The tools you need are to the left of and beneath the drawing area, as shown in

172

Figure 8.2. To draw or paint, you must first select (that is, click on) a tool from the Toolbox (see Figure 8.3), then move the pointer to the drawing area. When you move the pointer to the drawing area, the pointer becomes an icon of the tool you selected.

Figure 8.3

When you select (click on) a tool from Paintbrush Toolbox, the pointer becomes an icon of the tool you selected.

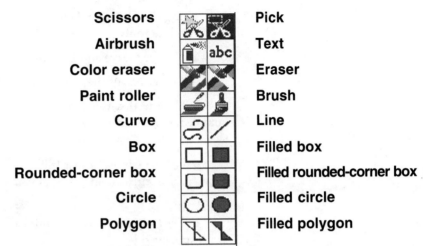

Scissors		**Pick**
Airbrush		**Text**
Color eraser		**Eraser**
Paint roller		**Brush**
Curve		**Line**
Box		**Filled box**
Rounded-corner box		**Filled rounded-corner box**
Circle		**Filled circle**
Polygon		**Filled polygon**

The tools in the Paintbrush Toolbox (Figure 8.3) can be classified into four groups: *drawing tools, painting tools, modifying tools,* and a *text tool:*

• **Drawing tools** are used to draw lines, boxes, circles, or any other shapes. These tools include Curve and Line and four pairs of shape (or geometric) tools known as Box, Rounded-corner Box, Circle, and Polygon. Each shape tool is available in both *open* and *filled.*

• **Painting tools** are used to paint or "color" objects. These include Airbrush, Paint Roller, and Brush.

• **Modifying tools** allow you to edit drawings and painting. These tools include Scissors, Pick, Color Eraser, and Eraser.

• **Text tool** is used to add text to your graphic. Only one Text tool exists.

The procedures for using each tool differ slightly. You will master each as you practice using Paintbrush. In the meantime, look at some basic Paintbrush techniques:

• Before you begin to draw, determine the line thickness you want by selecting from the Linesize box. Similarly, if you have closed objects in your drawing, determine color, shade, or pattern from the Palette.

• When using the drawing tools, position the tool's icon where you wish to begin the drawing, click on the mouse, drag the tool's icon to where you want to end the drawing, then release the mouse. The shape you drew (line, box, circle, etc.) appears in the size and location you indicated.

• When using a painting tool, position the tool's icon *inside* the area you wish to paint. Be sure the area is a *closed* area or the paint will "leak" outside the "cracks" in the borders.

• Use the Text tool to insert text in a graphic as you would using a word processing program. Select the Text tool, click an insertion point, then key the text. The text can be moved around the screen easily—it can even be placed inside a graphic.

Many tools and menu options are available to enhance your drawing. For example, you can color and shade objects; insert, cut, copy, and move text; and change the type attributes. You can even tilt, flip, stretch, or shrink all or portions of your drawing!

Using the Drawing Tools. Paintbrush has ten drawing tools. Two **line tools** for curved and straight lines:

- Use the **Curve** and **Line** tools to draw lines.

And four *pairs* of **shape** (or **geometric**) **tools** for drawing objects:

- Use the **Box** (filled and unfilled) and **Rounded-corner Box** (filled and unfilled) tools to draw boxes and rectangles with square or rounded corners. If you want a perfectly square box, hold [Shift] as you draw the box.

- Use the **Circle/Ellipse** (filled and unfilled) tools to draw circles and ovals. For a perfect circle, hold [Shift] as you draw the circle; otherwise you may get an oval.

- The **Polygon** (filled and unfilled) tools are used to draw multisided objects with straight sides.

Before you use the line tools or the shape tools, determine the width of the border by selecting from the Linesize box. In addition, before you use the shape tools, determine the shade, pattern, or color of a filled shape by making a selection from the Palette (Figure 8.4).

Figure 8.4

Using Paintbrush, shapes such as these are easy to draw (and to fill with a color or pattern).

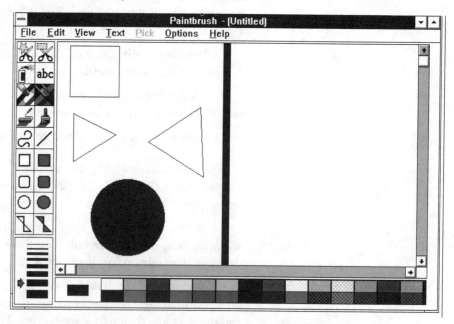

EXERCISE 8 . 1   USING THE DRAWING TOOLS

You will now use the drawing tools to create simple drawings, including some illustrated in Figure 8.4. Don't worry about "artistic ability"! Your graphic may differ slightly from the illustrations in the Paintbrush exercises—just do your best and have fun!

1. Start Windows if it is not already active.

2. Start the Paintbrush program:

    a. Double-click on the Paintbrush icon in the Accessories group to start the Paintbrush program.

    b. Click on the maximize button to maximize the Paintbrush window.

3. Draw a thick vertical line down the center of the screen, as shown in Figure 8.4):

    a. Select the Line tool from the Toolbox.

    b. Select the thickest (the last) line from the Linesize box.

    c. Position the Line icon approximately in the center of the drawing area— *not on the Menu bar* (refer to Figure 8.4).

    d. Press and hold [Shift], press and hold the mouse button, then drag to the bottom of the drawing area. Release the mouse, then release [Shift] when you reach the bottom of the screen. (You hold [Shift] to make sure you have an absolutely straight line. You release the mouse **before** you release [Shift] to insure that the line remains straight.)

    (Hint: If you make an error or if you click or release the mouse button before you intend to, select the Undo option on the Edit menu. Undo cancels all the work you have done since you selected the tool you are currently using.)

4. In the upper half of the left side of the page, draw a perfect square box with a thin border, as shown in Figure 8.4:

    a. Select the unfilled Box tool.

    b. Select the thinnest (the topmost) line from the Linesize box.

    c. Position the Box icon in the upper portion of the drawing area (*not on the menu bar*) approximately between the Edit and View menu names (see Figure 8.4).

    d. Press and hold [Shift], press and hold the mouse button, then drag down and to the right until you have a box similar to the one in Figure 8.4. Release the mouse, then release [Shift] when you have the desired box size.

5. Draw a perfect filled circle in the lower half of the left side of the page (see Figure 8.4):

    a. Select the filled Circle/Ellipse tool.

    b. Select the color of your choice (if you have a color monitor) or the pattern of your choice (if you have a monochrome monitor) from the Palette. The color or pattern will fill in your completed circle.

    c. Position the filled Circle/Ellipse draw icon in the lower portion of the drawing area (*not on the menu bar*) so that the circle lines up between the Text and the Pick menu names.

    d. Press and hold [Shift], press and hold the mouse button, then drag down and to the right until you have a circle similar to the one in Figure 8.4. Release the mouse, then release [Shift] when you have the desired box size.

6. Experiment with the other graphic tools by drawing one or two filled or unfilled objects on the left side of the drawing area. Do not draw anything on the right side.

Using the Painting Tools. Unlike the drawing tools, the painting tools have no constraints. You can use the painting tools to draw freeform objects and fill graphic objects:

• Like a can of spray paint, the **Airbrush** tool sprays a light circular pattern of colored dots, instead of painting a solid color. Click once on the mouse button to get one "spirt" of color; hold the mouse button and drag to get a trail of spray color.

• The **Paint Roller** tool fills a shape with color or shading. The shape must be completely enclosed (like a box or a circle); any opening will cause the paint to spill out of the shape. The Paint Roller icon looks like a paint roller spreading paint.

• The **Brush** tool paints a solid stroke of color the width of the line selected in the Linesize box. The shape of the brush can be changed, as you will see later.

In order to use these painting tools properly, you must understand the purpose and function of the Paintbrush Palette.

The Palette

The Palette offers two choices: a **foreground color** and a **background color**.

• The foreground color is the color that is applied by the drawing tools or painted with one of the painting tools. The foreground color is also the fill color that goes inside filled shapes (boxes, circles, and so on).

• The background color is the color of the border around the edges of filled shapes, as well as the background color of your screen whenever you start a new Paintbrush file.

Palette colors and patterns can be changed easily. To change the foreground color or pattern, point on the desired color or pattern and click the *left* mouse button. To change the background color or pattern, point on the desired color or pattern and click the *right* mouse button. Now practice using these painting tools on the right side of the drawing area, as illustrated in the samples in Figure 8.5.

Figure 8.5

Paintbrush's drawing tools were used to create the drawings on the left; Paintbrush painting tools were used to create the figures on the right.

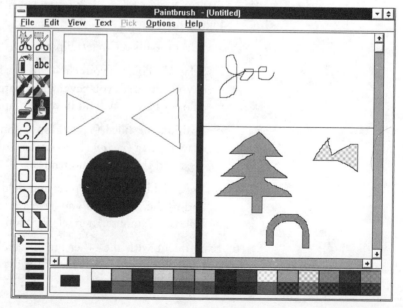

EXERCISE 8 • 2 USING THE PAINTING TOOLS

1. Draw a thin horizontal line across the center of the right-hand side of the screen (see Figure 8.5):

   a. Select the Line tool from the Toolbox.

   b. Select a thin line from the Linesize box.

   c. Position the Line icon about halfway down the right-hand side of the drawing area, press and hold [Shift], then drag a line across the page.

2. With the Brush tool, write your first name in the upper portion of the right side of the drawing area (see Figure 8.5):

   a. Select the Brush tool.

   b. Select a foreground (fill) color (or pattern) of your choice by pointing on your selection on the Palette and clicking the left mouse button.

   c. Select the thinnest (the topmost) line from the Linesize box.

   d. Position the Brush tool icon (small square) at the starting point, click the mouse button, and "write" your name.

3. With the Brush tool, draw three different closed shapes in the lower portion of the right side of the drawing area (see Figure 8.5):

   a. Select the Brush tool, if it is not already selected.

   b. Select a background color (or pattern) of your choice by pointing on your selection on the Palette and clicking the right mouse button.

   c. Draw the shape. Be sure you make a closed shape.

   d. Repeat Steps *a* through *c* above to create two additional objects. Remember, you can select the Undo option on File menu to delete unwanted objects; Undo will delete everything that you did since selecting the current tool.

4. Use the Paint Roller to fill the interior with a different color or pattern of two of the objects you created in Step 3:

   a. Select the Paint Roller tool from the Toolbox.

   b. Select the foreground color or pattern from the Palette by clicking on the color or pattern of your choice with the left mouse button.

   c. Position the pointed tip of the Paint Roller tool icon inside the object you want to fill.

   d. Click the left mouse button.

   e. Repeat Steps *b* through *d* above to fill one more object only.

5. Use the Airbrush tool to fill the interior of the last of your three objects with a different color or pattern:

   a. Select the Airbrush tool from the Toolbox.

   b. Select the foreground color or pattern from the Palette by clicking on the color or pattern of your choice with the left mouse button.

   c. Position the Airbrush tool icon inside the object where you want the airbrush stroke, press and hold the mouse button, and "spray" the interior of the object.

6. Exit the Paintbrush program. (Since this was a learning exercise, you will not save and print your graphic.)

    a. Select the Exit option from the File menu. A warning dialog box will display indicating that you have not saved the current document.

    b. Click on the No command button to clear the screen and exit the Paintbrush program.

Importing Graphic Files into Paintbrush

Now that you can use Paintbrush's tools, you can create your own graphics. But you are not limited to *your own* graphics. You can also **import** graphic files into Paintbrush!

Import means to bring into Paintbrush a graphic file that was created outside of Paintbrush. You can import graphic files that were created with another paint program or with another draw program. You can also convert a paper drawing or photograph to an electronic file format with a device called a **scanner**. Once converted to a graphic file, that drawing or photograph can also be imported. Thus, importing a file into Paintbrush is as easy as using the Open command on the File menu.

While Paintbrush offers you many, many options for developing graphics, it does have some limitations:

• You can open (import) graphic files only if they have BMP, MSP, or PCX formats:

    - BMP is the original format for Bitmap (thus the extension .BMP).

    - MSP is the format for <u>M</u>icro<u>s</u>oft <u>P</u>aint files (from earlier versions of Windows).

    - PCX is the graphic-file format developed by ZSoft Corporation and is used in its PC Paintbrush application. PCX is a well-known standard for graphic files.

• Another limitation is your monitor and the circuit board that connects it to the computer (video adapter).

    - Some monitors and video adapters are capable of displaying only black and white (monochrome); others can display from 16 to 256 colors. If your monitor and video adapter are capable of displaying only 16 colors and you import a 256-color image, Paintbrush adjusts the colors to its 16-color limitation. As a result, the imported graphic will lose some of the original's color.

    - A monochrome monitor, of course, cannot display color; a monochrome video adapter will convert color images to shades and patterns of black and white.

If a 256-color image is loaded into Windows with the right driver and adapter combination, the image appears with all its original color detail. You can then edit and resave it, and the colors are saved properly.

To import a file into Paintbrush, use the Open command on the File menu.

EXERCISE 8 • 3   IMPORTING A FILE

1. Start Paintbrush if it is not already running.

2. Open the WINLOGO.BMP file in your WINDOWS subdirectory:

a. Select the Open option from the File menu.

b. Verify that Bitmap files (*.BMP) are displayed in the List Files of Type listing box.

c. Switch to the WINDOWS subdirectory, if it is not already active.

d. Select the WINLOGO.BMP file displayed in the directory listing.

e. Click on the OK command button.

You have imported a file into Paintbrush! Once the drawing is in the working area, it is a Paintbrush file. You can modify it, save it, and print it.

Figure 8.6

Sample screen showing completed Exercise 8.3

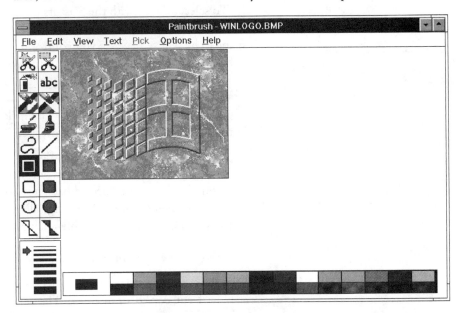

VIEW 2

MODIFYING, SAVING, AND PRINTING DRAWINGS

PREVIEW

Even if you have steady hands and a good imagination, you may need to or want to modify your work. To do so, Paintbrush provides a number of modifying tools and menu options. And while a picture will often be all you need to express your thought, feeling, or mood, you will sometimes want to include text in your graphics. Paintbrush offers you a great variety of type fonts and sizes. Finally, of course, you will want to print your work. Again, Paintbrush offers great flexibility; you may print all or only part of a drawing, as you wish.

Modifying a Drawing

You can use several techniques to modify drawings. You have already learned one of the easiest—the Undo command. But that command will only erase work in progress (work completed since you last selected a tool). Also, the Undo command is not selective; that is, it forces you to erase everything you have completed.

To overcome these problems, Paintbrush has four modifying tools—Scissors, Pick, Eraser, and Color Eraser. Look at how to use each one.

Scissors and Pick Tools. The Scissors and the Pick tools resemble one another. Their icons hint at the subtle difference in their functions. Because the

Scissors tool is used to select irregularly shaped portions of a drawing, its icon shows a pair of scissors cutting an irregular shape. Because the Pick tool is used to select rectangular areas, its icon shows a pair of scissors cutting a rectangular shape.

To select a shape with the Pick tool, position the cursor just above and to the left of the object to be selected. At this position, press the left mouse button and drag the cursor down and to the right until the dotted line completely encloses the desired selection, then click the right button. Be sure that the entire object is within the dotted rectangle that is displayed. Only the area within the dotted rectangle can be modified.

To select a shape with the Scissors tool, position the cursor near the object to be selected, press the left mouse button, and drag an irregular line around the shape to be selected. Since you control the form the line takes, you can enclose as much or as little as needed within the dotted rectangle.

Once you have selected an area, you can move the selection or use the options on the Edit and Pick menus to modify the area in several ways. The Edit menu options are Cut, Copy, and Paste. The Pick menu options are Flip Horizontal, Flip Vertical, Inverse, Shrink + Grow, and Tilt.

Erasers. Paintbrush has two erasers—Eraser, which erases anything in its path, and Color Eraser, which erases only a selected color. To change the selected foreground color to the selected background color over a selected area, drag the Color Eraser over the area. To change all of the selected foreground colors to the selected background color, double-click on the Color Eraser.

Moving and Copying a Selected Cutout

When an area is selected with either the Pick tool or the Scissors tool, the selection can be moved, cut, copied, or modified. The portion of a drawing that is cut or copied is called a **cutout**. To move a cutout, point on the cutout and drag it to a new location. To copy a cutout, hold [Ctrl] while dragging the cutout to its new location.

You can move or copy a cutout in one of two ways: *transparently* or *opaquely.*

• When you move a cutout **transparently**, any part of the cutout that is in the background color assumes the underlying color of the location to which it is moved.

• When you move a cutout **opaquely**, all parts of the cutout retain their original colors at the new location.

The mouse button you press while dragging the cutout determines whether the move is transparent or opaque. Press and hold the *left* mouse button to move or copy a cutout transparently; drag it with the *right* mouse button to move or copy it opaquely.

EXERCISE 8 • 4   USING THE MODIFYING TOOLS

Now you will use the modifying tools to create an image similar to the one illustrated in Figure 8.7.

Figure 8.7

Image modified from CARS.BMP file.

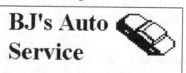

1. Open the CARS.BMP file.

   a. Choose the Open option from the File menu.

   b. Change to the WINDOWS subdirectory.

   c. Select the CARS.BMP file.

   d. Click on the OK command button.

2. Copy the car in the drawing to the Clipboard:

   a. Select the Scissors tool (*not the Pick tool*).

   b. Place the Scissors icon above and to the left of the car.

   c. Press the mouse button and draw a freeform line around the graphic.

   d. Select the Copy option from the Edit menu. The car will be copied to the Clipboard.

3. Select the New option from the File menu to close the CARS.BMP file.

4. Paste the car into the new document:

   a. Select the Paste option from the Edit menu. The cutout car will be pasted onto the drawing area.

5. Save the new file on your *Win Practice* disk:

   a. Select the Save As... option on the File menu.

   b. Select the drive that contains your *Win Practice* disk.

   c. Key the filename *CAR.BMP* in the text box.

   d. Verify that the Save File as Type listing box shows .BMP.

   e. Click on the OK command button. (Be patient after you issue this command because it may take a long time to save a graphic file.)

6. Remove the gray color from around the object:

   a. Select white as the background color (click on white with the right mouse button).

   b. Select gray as the foreground color (click on gray with the left mouse button).

   c. Double-click on the Color Eraser (the one on the left). All of the gray color should be erased.

7. Save the work you have completed so far:

   a. Select the Save command on the File menu.

Using the Pick Menu Options to Create Special Effects

Figure 8.8

Options on the Pick Menu permit you to create special effects with graphics.

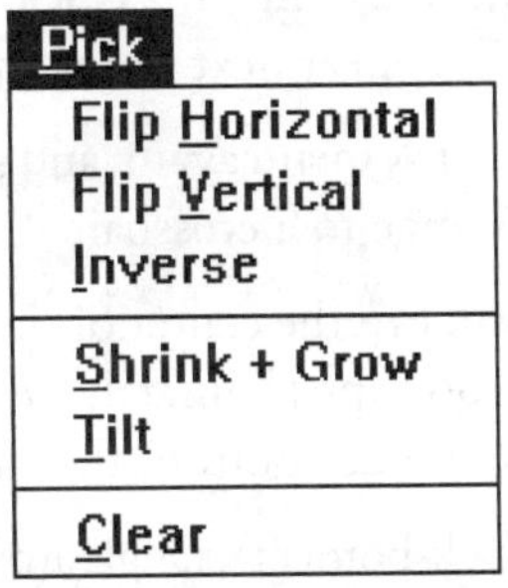

Pick
Flip **H**orizontal
Flip **V**ertical
Inverse
Shrink + Grow
Tilt
Clear

You may have noticed that the Pick menu is often grayed out, which means "not available." When you select an area of the drawing with either the Scissors or the Pick tool, the Pick Menu becomes "available," giving you access to five special-effects options:

- **Flip Horizontal** rotates (turns) the selected object from left to right.

- **Flip Vertical** turns the object upside down.

• **Inverse** changes the color of the selected object to the color opposite its position on the RGB color wheel. For example, black becomes white, and white becomes black.

• **Shrink + Grow** lets you reduce or enlarge the object. After you have highlighted a drawing area and selected the Shrink + Grow option, outline a box to indicate the new size. If you hold [Shift] as you drag the new box, the graphic will not become distorted; instead, it will be reduced or enlarged to scale.

• **Tilt** lets you slant the object.

• **Clear** works only with Shrink + Grow and with Tilt. Clear removes the original object from the drawing after the enlarged, reduced, or tilted object is displayed. When Clear is off, the original object remains in the drawing.

To use these special effects, first select an object with either the Pick tool or the Scissors. The object will be outlined with a dotted line. If you are going to use the Shrink + Grow or the Tilt option and do not want the original object to remain in the drawing, check the Clear option.

Be careful when using the special-effects options on the Pick menu because the Undo command is not available with all options. The Undo command is available only with the Shrink + Grow and the Tilt options.

EXERCISE 8 • 5   USING SPECIAL-EFFECTS OPTIONS

1. Open the CAR.BMP graphic file on your *Win Practice* disk if it is not currently opened.

2. Flip the object vertically:

   a. Select the Pick tool, click above and to the left of the object, drag a dotted line down and to the right, then release the mouse button. Make sure the entire car is enclosed in the box.

   b. Select the Flip Horizontal option from the Pick menu.

3. Move the car to the center of the screen.

   a. The car should still be outlined. If it is not outlined, use the Pick tool to draw a dotted box around the car.

   b. Position the pointer in the center of the object. The pointer will become an arrow.

   c. Press the mouse button, drag the car to the center of the screen and release the mouse button.

4. Enlarge the car.

   a. Pull down the Pick menu. Click on the Clear option to select it (a checkmark will appear next to the option when it is selected).

   b. Pull down the Pick menu again, and select the Shrink + Grow option. The pointer will change to a crosshair.

   c. Move the pointer to the center of the screen, press the mouse button, and draw a dotted box approximately 3/4 inch tall by 1 1/4 inch wide. When you release the mouse button, the car will "grow" to fill the box.

5. Add an unfilled black-border rectangle around the graphic, as shown in Figure 8.9:

Figure 8.9

An unfilled black-border rectangle
has been added around the car.

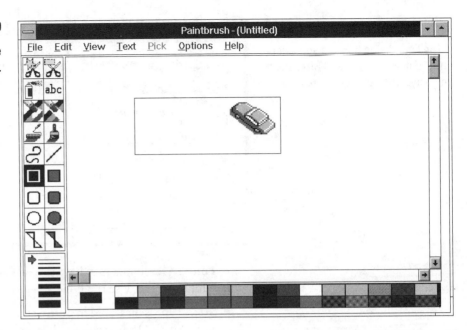

a. Click on the color black on the palette. Next, select the unfilled Box tool. Select a thin line.

b. Drag an unfilled box around the graphic. (Remember: If you misplace the box, select the Undo option from the File menu.)

6. Save your work to this point by selecting the Save option on the File menu.

Adding Text to a Drawing

One tool in the Toolbox, the Text tool, allows you to add text to any drawing. The Text tool icon is **abc** (see Figure 8.3). When the Text tool is selected, the pointer changes to an I-beam (the same cursor shape used by Write and Notepad).

To use the Text tool:

• Select the Text tool on the Toolbox.

• If you want to change the type specifications (discussed below), you *must* do so now, before you complete the next step.

• Click an insertion point where you want the text to begin.

• Key the text.

Changing the Type Specifications

In item 2 above, you have the option of changing the appearance of text you add to a Paintbrush drawing. Here, *appearance* means type specifications—that is, the *font*, *font style*, and *size* of type.

To change type specifications, select Fonts on the Text menu. The Font dialog box, shown in Figure 8.10, appears, giving you these options to select from:

• **Font.** Select the desired font from those available on the Font list. Scroll through the list to see your choices. Think of "font" as a type family—the specific design or look of all the characters from a to z, all the numbers, and all the symbols that make up one family of type. Three common fonts are Courier, Times Roman, and Helvetica.

Figure 8.10

The Font dialog box lets you select the Font, Font Style, and Size, and it displays each choice in the Sample box.

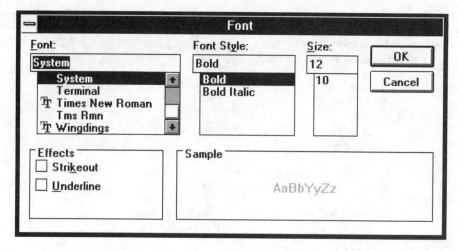

- **Font Style.** Fonts may have several variations or *styles*—bold, italic, and outline, for example. Use the Font Style list to select a desired style.

- **Size**. Type is measured in **points**, the printer's unit of measure. (There are 72 points to 1 inch. To better grasp the concept of points, remember that the type used for textbooks like this one is usually 10- or 12-point size.) Only certain sizes are available for each font or style. As you make selections from the Font and Font Style lists, the sizes available for your selections will display on the Size menu. Again, simply make a selection from the choices available.

- **Effects**. Leave the Strikeout and Underline check boxes empty (that is, deselected). You may use Underline occasionally, and Strikeout rarely, if at all.

As you make selections, your choices are reflected in the Sample box display in the lower right corner of the Font dialog box.

EXERCISE 8 • 6   WORKING WITH TEXT

1. Open the CAR.BMP graphic file on your *Win Practice* disk if it is not currently opened.

2. To the left of the graphic, place the text *BJ's Auto Service* in 20-point Times New Roman bold (see Figure 8.7):

   a. Select the Text tool from the Toolbox.

   b. Select Fonts... on the Text menu.

   c. Select Times New Roman on the Font System menu. (Note: Bold type is the default for this font.)

   d. Select 20 on the Size menu.

   e. Click on the OK command button to return to the drawing screen.

   f. Click an insertion point where you wish the text to begin, and key *BJ's Auto* and press [Enter] to start a new line. Then key the remainder of the text, *Service*.

      (Hint: It is a good idea to key the text outside of the box you created. You can move the text into place after it has been keyed.)

3. Adjust the position of the text, if necessary:

   a. Select the Pick tool from the Tool menu.

b. Draw a dotted box around the text.

c. Point inside the box of text, then press and hold the mouse button while dragging the text to the desired spot.

4. Place a background of gray (color monitor) or a simple pattern (monochrome monitor) inside the box:

a. Select the Roller tool from the Toolbox.

b. Select the lightest gray (or pattern).

c. Point inside the rectangle, but not directly on any of the lines or objects, then click the mouse button.

d. Point inside the enclosed portion of the letters with open areas (B, A, and so on) then click the mouse button. Make sure the tip of the roller is completely inside each letter; otherwise, the border of the letter will also be changed to gray.

5. Save your work to this point.

Printing a Drawing

Paintbrush provides several options for printing your drawings. You can print (1) the whole drawing or just a portion of it, (2) a final copy or a rough draft, (3) one copy or multiple copies, and (4) actual, reduced, or enlarged sizes.

To print a drawing, select Print on the File menu. The Print dialog box (shown in Figure 8.11) displays, offering you several options:

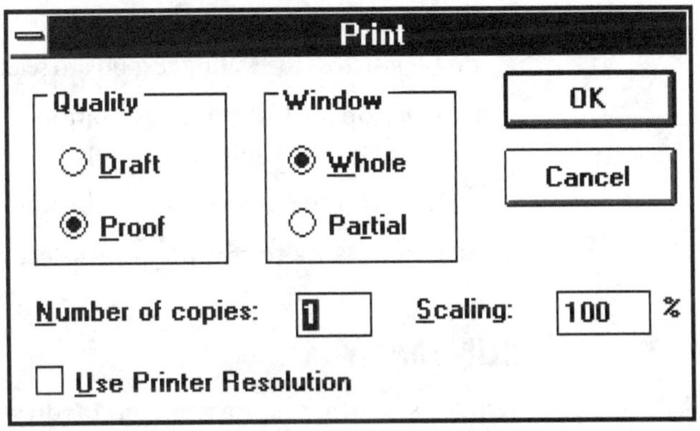

Figure 8.11

The Print dialog box provides several options for printing Paintbrush drawings.

- Under Quality, you can select Draft or Proof. Draft Quality has lighter, less-defined letters and takes less time to print than Proof Quality output.

- Under Window, select Whole if you want to print the entire drawing. Click on the Partial button if you wish to print only a portion of your drawing. First, use the Pick tool to select the part you want to print.

- The Number of copies text box shows 1—its default. If you want to print more than one copy, indicate how many in the box.

- In the Scaling text box, indicate the size of your printed copy. The default is 100%, which means *actual size*. You can print the drawing in the same size, or you can reduce or enlarge its on-screen size:

- To print the copy in the *same size* as it appears on screen, select the default, 100%.

- To *reduce* the printed copy, select a number smaller than 100 (for example, enter 75% to print the image three-quarters of its on-screen actual size).

- To *enlarge* the printed copy, select a number greater than 100 (for example, 125% enlarges the drawing by an *additional* 25% of its on-screen size).

EXERCISE 8 • 7   PRINTING A DRAWING

1. Open the CAR.BMP graphic file on your *Win Practice* disk if it is not currently opened.

2. Print a draft copy of your drawing:

   a. Select the Print... option on the File menu. The Print dialog box (Figure 8.11) displays.

   b. Click on the Draft button.

   c. Verify that the Whole button is selected in the Window box, that Number of copies is 1, and that Scaling is 100%.

   d. Click on the OK command button.

   e. Inspect your printed drawing, then make any adjustments that are needed. (Remember, this is Draft Quality, so the drawing may not be very sharp.)

3. Print a 75% Proof copy of your drawing:

   a. Select the Print option on the File menu.

   b. Click on the Proof button *if it is not already selected.*

   c. Verify that the Whole button is selected in the Windows box and that Number of copies is 1.

   d. Drag across the scaling text box to select the number, then key the number 75.

   e. Click on the Use Printer Resolution check box to select it. This will produce a much better quality output.

   f. Click on the OK command button.

4. Save your work to this point by selecting the Save option on the File menu.

SUMMARY

Windows Paintbrush provides tools for drawing simple to complex graphics. Paintbrush is located in the Accessories group. The drawing area of the Paintbrush window is where all the action takes place. The Paintbrush toolbox provides many tools and menu options to enhance your drawing. Among other things, Paintbrush lets you:

- color and shade lines

- insert, cut, copy, and move text

- flip objects

Paintbrush also supplies you with painting tools to allow for drawing of freeform objects and to fill objects with color or shading. The Palette is another enhancement to the Paintbrush program; it offers choices to place color in the foreground or background of your drawing.

Producing newsletters, reports, letters, and memos with text in varying sizes and typefaces is nice, but it is not enough today—not when you have the tools available to you like those provided in Windows Paintbrush. Paintbrush is the answer to livening up documents to capture the attention of your reader.

APPENDIX

WINDOWS 3.1 COMMAND REFERENCES

COMMAND REFERENCES

CALCULATOR

To--	Select		Then--
	Menu	Option	
Copy a Value to Clipboard	Edit	Copy	[Ctrl]+[C]
Exit Calculator	Control-menu box	Close	[Alt]+[F4]
Paste into Calculator	Edit	Paste	[Ctrl]+[V]
Use Advanced Statistical Functions	View	Scientific	
Use the Standard Calculator	View	Standard	
Use the Scientific Calculator's Statistical Functions			STA button

CALENDAR

To--	Select		Then--
	Menu	Option	
Add Text to the Calendar Scratch Pad			[Tab] toggles insert point between calendar and scratch pad
Add and Remove Special Times	Options	Special Time...	[F7]
Change Printers and Printer Options	File	Printer Setup...	
Change the Day Settings	Options	Day Settings...	
Copy Information	Edit	Copy	[Ctrl]+[C]
Create a New Calendar	File	New	
Cut Information	Edit	Cut	[Ctrl]+[X]
Exit Calendar	File	Close	
Mark Dates in a Month	Options	Mark...	[F6]
Move Around in Month View			[PgUp] next month [PgDn] previous month
Move to a Specific Date	Show	Date...	[F4]
Move to Today's Date	Show	Today	
Open a Calendar File	File	Open...	
Print a Day or a Range of Days	File	Print...	
Page Headers and Footers	File	Page Setup...	
Remove Alarm	Alarm	Set	[F5]
Remove Entries from Appointment Days	Edit	Remove...	
Save a Calendar File	File	Save... or Save As...	
Set an Alarm for Appointment Times	Alarm	Set	[F5]
Set Margins	File	Page Setup...	
Set the Alarm for an Early Ring	Alarm	Controls... (Ring Early)	
Switch Between the Day and Month View	View	Day or Month	[F8] Day [F9] Month
Turn On/Off Alarm Sound	Alarm	Controls... (Sound)	

CARDFILE

To--	Select		Then--
	Menu	Option	
Add a Card	Card	Add	[F7]
Change Printers and Printer Options	File	Printer Setup...	
Close Cardfile	File	Exit	
Continue Search in Card Text	Search	Find Next	[F3]
Copy Information	Edit	Copy	[Ctrl]+[C]
Create a New File	File	New	
Cut Information	Edit	Cut	[Ctrl]+[X]
Delete a Card	Card	Delete	
Dial Automatically	Card	Autodial...	[F5]
Duplicate a Card	Card	Duplicate	
Enter or Edit Text in the Index Line	Edit	Index...	[F6]
Find Text in a Card	Search	Find...	
Find Text in an Index	Search	Go To...	[F4]
Merge Files	File	Merge...	
Move Through a Cardfile			[PgUp] Previous [PgDn] Next
Open an Existing Cardfile	File	Open...	
Paste Cut or Copied Information	Edit	Paste	[Ctrl]+[V]
Print All Cards	File	Print All	
Print the Top Card	File	Print	
Print Headers and Footers	File	Page Setup...	
Restore Cards to a Previous Text	Edit	Restore	
Save a Cardfile	File	Save or Save As...	
Switch Between Card and List View	View	List Card	
Undo Edits	Edit	Undo	[Alt]+[Z]

CLIPBOARD VIEWER

To--	Select		Then--
	Menu	Option	
Clear the Clipboard	Edit	Delete	[Del]
Close Clipboard Viewer	File	Exit	
Open a Clipboard File	File	Open...	
Save a Clipboard File	File	Save As...	
Select Display Format	Display	(Select Format)	

CONTROL PANEL

To--	Select		Option--
	Icon	Select or Press	
Add a Font	Fonts	Add...	
Add a Printer Driver	Printers	Add >>	
Adjust the Keyboard Speed	Keyboard	Repeat Rate	

| To-- | Select | | Option-- |
	Icon	Select or Press	
Change the Border Width	Desktop	Sizing Grid	Border Width
Change the Cursor Blink Rate	Desktop	Cursor Blink Rate	
Change the Date	Date & Time	Date	
Change the Date Format	International	Date Format	Change...
Change the Existing Color Scheme	Color	Color Schemes	
Change the Existing Desktop Pattern	Desktop	Pattern	
Change the Grid	Desktop	Sizing Grid	Granularity or Border Width
Change the List Separator	International	List Separator	
Change the Mouse Settings	Mouse		
Change the Spacing Between Icons	Desktop	Icon	Spacing or Title Wrap
Change the Time	Date & Time	Time	
Change the Time Format	International	Time Format	
Choose the Active Printer for a Port	Printers	Connect...	Port
Choose the Default Printer	Printers	Installed Printers	Set as Default Printer
Configure Communications Ports	Ports	Settings...	
Connect to and Disconnect from Network	Network	Connect	
Create a Custom Color	Color	Color Palette >>	
Display a Custom Wallpaper	Desktop	Wallpaper	
Install a New Printer	Printers	Add...	
Print Manager (On/Off)	Printers	Use Print Manager	
Select a Country Setting	International	Country	
Select a Language	International	Language	
Warning Beep (On/Off)	Sound	Enable System Sounds	

FILE MANAGER

| To-- | Select | | Then-- |
	Menu	Option	
Add a Volume Label to Disk or Hard Drive	Disk	Disk Label	
Associate Documents with an Application	File	Associate...	
Cascade Active Windows	Window	Cascade	[Shift]+[F5]
Choose the Display Order of Files and Directories	View	Sort by Name Sort by Type Sort by Size Sort by Date	
Choose Which Files to Display	View	By File Type...	
Close Windows	File	Exit Windows	[Alt]+[F4]
Collapse Directory Levels	Tree	Collapse	
Copy a Disk	Disk	Copy Disk...	
Copy a File or Directory	File	Copy...	[F8]
Create a New Directory	File	Create Directory...	

| To-- | Select | | Then-- |
	Menu	Options	
Delete a File or a Directory	File	Delete...	[Del]
Expand a Directory All Levels	Tree	Expand All	[Ctrl]+[*]
Expand Directory Branch	Tree	Expand Branch	[*]
Expand Directory One Level	Tree	Expand One Level	[+]
Format a Disk	Disk	Format Disk...	
Make a System Disk	Disk	Make System Disk...	
Move File or Directory	File	Move...	[F7]
Open a Document	File	Open...	[Enter]
Print a File	File	Print...	
Rename a File or a Directory	File	Rename...	
Search for Files or Directories	File	Search...	
Select All Files in a Directory Window	File	Select Files...	[Ctrl]+[/]
Set File Attributes	File	Properties...	[Alt]+[Enter]
Start an Application	File	Run...	
Tile Active Windows	Window	Tile	[Shift]+[F4]

NOTEPAD

| To-- | Select | | Then-- |
	Menu	Options	
Add the Time and Date to a Document	Edit	Time/Date	[F5]
Change Printer and Printer Options	File	Print Setup...	
Continue a Search	Search	Find Next	[F3]
Copy Information	Edit	Copy	[Ctrl]+[C]
Cut Information	Edit	Cut	[Ctrl]+[X]
Delete Selected Text	Edit	Delete	[Del]
Find Text	Search	Find...	
Open an Existing Text File	File	Open...	
Paste Copied or Cut Information	Edit	Paste	[Ctrl]+[V]
Print a Document	File	Print	
Print a Header or Footer	File	Page Setup...	
Save a Document	File	Save or Save As...	
Select All the Text in a Document	Edit	Select All	
Set Margins	File	Page Setup...	
Undo Edits	Edit	Undo	[Ctrl]+[Z]
Wrap Text (On/Off)	Edit	Word Wrap	

PAINTBRUSH

| To-- | Select | | Then-- |
	Menu	Options	
Bold Text (On/Off)	Text	Bold	[Ctrl]+[B]
Change Default Settings for New Drawings	Options	Image Attributes...	
Change Printer and Printer Options	File	Printer Setup...	

To--	Select Menu	Option	Then--
Choose a Font	Text	Fonts...	
Copy Information	Edit	Copy	[Ctrl]+[C]
Cut Information	Edit	Cut	[Ctrl]+[X]
Display All of a Drawing	View	View Picture	[Ctrl]+[P]
Select Font Size	Text	Fonts...	
Invert Colors in Selection	Pick	Inverse	
Italic Text (On/Off)	Text	Italic	[Ctrl]+[I]
Move a Selection		(Drag with Mouse)	
Outline Text	Text	Outline	
Paste Cut or Copied Information	Edit	Paste	[Ctrl]+[V]
Print a Drawing	File	Print...	
Print a Header or Footer	File	Page Setup...	
Print Part of a Drawing	File	Print...	
Retrieve Custom Color Files	Options	Get Colors...	
Retrieve a Selection	Edit	Paste From...	
Save a Custom Color File	Options	Save Colors...	
Save a File	File	Save... or Save As...	[Ctrl]+[S]
Save a Selection	Edit	Copy To...	
Select a Tool		(Click on icons or tool palette)	
Select Background and Foreground Colors		(Click on color palette)	
Set Margins	File	Page Setup...	
Shadow Text	Text	Shadow	
Shrink or Enlarge a Selection	Pick	Shrink+Grow	
Start a New Drawing	File	New	
Tilt a Selection	Pick	Tilt	
Underlined Text (On/Off)	Text	Underline	[Ctrl]+[U]
Undo Edits	Edit	Undo	[Ctrl]+[Z]
Use Microsoft Paint Files	File	Open... (MSP)	
Use the Cursor Position Option	View	Cursor Position	
Use ZSoft Files	File	Open... (PCX)	
View or Modify a Drawing Width	Options	Image Attributes...	
Zoom In	View	Zoom In	[Ctrl]+[N]
Zoom Out	View	Zoom Out	[Ctrl]+[O]

PROGRAM MANAGER

To--	Select Menu	Option	Then--
Add an Item to a Group	File	New... (Item)	
Arrange Application Windows and Icons	Window	Arrange Icons	
Arrange Icons When Changing Window Size	Options	Auto Arrange	
Automatically Minimize Program Manager	Options	Minimize on Use	
Cascade Active Windows	Window	Cascade	[Shift]+[F5]
Change Group Properties	File	Properties...	

| To-- | Select | | Then-- |
	Menu	Option	
Change Item Properties	File	Properties...	
Copy an Item	File	Copy...	[F8]
Create a New Group	File	New... (Program Group)	
Create a New Program Item	File	New... (Program Item)	
Delete a Group			[Del]
Delete an Item from a Group	File	Delete	[Del]
Move an Item	File	Move...	[F7]
Run a Program Without an Icon	File	Run...	
Select a Window by Name	Window	(Number)	
Tile Active Windows	Window	Tile	[Shift]+[F4]

WINDOWS

| To-- | Select | | Then-- |
	Menu	Option	
Access Control Menu Commands	Control-menu box		[Alt]+[Spacebar]
Access Help System	Help		[F1]
Arrange Application Windows and Icons	Window	Arrange Icons	
Cancel Menus			[Esc]
Change a Window's Size	Control-menubox	Size	Drag corner or border
Close an Active Window	Control-menubox	Close	[Alt]+[F4] applications [Ctrl]+[F4] documents
Close a Dialog Box			Select OK or cancel
Copy Information	Edit	Copy	[Ctrl]+[C]
Correct Keyed Text			[Del] or [Backspace]
Cut Information	Edit	Cut	[Ctrl]+[C]
Enlarge a Window to Full Size	Control-menubox	Maximize	
Open a Document or a File	File	Open...	
Open the Control Menu	Control-menubox		
Paste Copied or Cut Information	Edit	Paste	[Ctrl]+[V]
Quit an Application	File	Exit	[Alt]+[F4]
Restore a Window to Its Previous Size	Control-menubox	Restore	
Save a Document or a File	File	Save	
Shrink a Window to an Icon	Control-menubox	Minimize	
Start an Application	File	Run	
Switch Among Application Windows	Control-menubox	Switch To...	[Ctrl]+[Esc] (Task List) or [Alt]+[Tab]
Undo Last Command	Edit	Undo	[Alt]+[Backspace]

WRITE

To--	Select		Then--
	Menu	Option	
Add a Footer	Document	Footer...	
Add a Header	Document	Header...	
Bold Text (On/Off)	Character	Bold	[Ctrl]+[B]
Center a Paragraph	Paragraph	Centered	
Change a Font	Character	Fonts...	
Change Picture Size	Edit	Size Picture	
Copy Information	Edit	Copy	[Ctrl]+[C]
Create a Hanging Indent	Paragraph	Indents...	
Create a New Document	Edit	New	
Cut Information	Edit	Cut	[Ctrl]+[X]
Decrease the Font One Size	Character	Reduce Font	
Display or Hide Formatting Ruler	Document	Ruler On/Off	
Double Space Text	Paragraph	Double Space	
Find Text	Find	Find...	
Go to a Specific Page	Find	Go To Page...	[F4]
Increase Font One Size	Character	Enlarge Font	
Indent a Paragraph	Paragraph	Indents...	
Insert an Object	Edit	Insert Object...	
Italic Text (On/Off)	Character	Italic	[Ctrl]+[I]
Justify a Paragraph	Paragraph	Justified	
Left Align a Paragraph	Paragraph	Left	
Move a Picture Horizontally	Edit	Move Picture	
One and One-half Space Text	Paragraph	1 1/2 Space	
Open an Existing Document	File	Open...	
Paste Cut or Copied Information	Edit	Paste	[Ctrl]+[V]
Print a Document	File	Print...	
Repaginate a Document	File	Repaginate...	
Replace Text	Edit	Replace...	
Right Align a Paragraph	Paragraph	Right	
Save a Document	File	Save or Save As...	
Set or Change Margins	Document	Page Layout	
Set or Change Tabs	Document	Tabs...	
Single Space Text	Paragraph	Single Space	
Select Starting Page Number	Document	Page Layout...	
Subscript Text (On/Off)	Character	Subscript	
Superscript Text (On/Off)	Character	Superscript	
Underline Text (On/Off)	Character	Underline	[Ctrl]+[U]
Undo Last Action	Edit	Undo	[Ctrl]+[Z]

INDEX